Collect What You Produce

Collect What You Produce

2nd Edition

Cathy Jameson

PennWell Corporation
1421 South Sheridan Road
Tulsa, Oklahoma 74112-6600 USA

800.752.9764
+1.918.831.9421
sales@pennwell.com
www.pennwellbooks.com
www.pennwell.com

Managing Editor: Marla Patterson
Production/Operations Manager: Traci Huntsman
Production Manager: Robin Remaley
Assistant Editor: Amethyst Hensley
Production Editor: Sue Rhodes Dodd
Cover Designer: Shanon Moore
Book Designer: Clark Bell
Cover Photo: John Trammel
Cover Photo Hair & Makeup: Scott Bond & George Wilman

Library of Congress Cataloging-in-Publication Data
Jameson, Cathy.
Collect what you produce / by Cathy Jameson.-- 2nd ed.
p. cm.
Includes bibliographical references and index.
ISBN 1-59370-049-0
1. Dental fees. 2. Collecting of accounts. I. Title.
RK58.J35 2005
617.6'0068'1--dc22

2005013259

Printed in the United States of America

1 2 3 4 5 09 08 07 06 05

As always,
to the many mentors, teachers, and friends
who have guided, directed, coached, and taught me
along my path of learning.
Thanks for
the information, the knowledge, the wisdom, and the encouragement.

To John,
my husband, best friend, soul mate,
companion, sounding board,
and my favorite dentist!

Contents

Introduction

Professional success depends on excellent business skills and people skills. Financial arrangements are business skills that are focused on taking care of people's financial issues. There is no greater place where business and people skills need to intersect. Making proper financial arrangements with the patient before treatment is rendered serves both the patient and the dentist. Carefully and caringly informing patients about their financial responsibilities offsets many potential problems and misunderstandings.

In addition, cost is the major barrier to treatment acceptance, according to the most recent surveys by the American Dental Association (ADA). People may want or need the dental care that you are recommending but feel they cannot afford it. Therefore, finding solutions to the financial issues of your patients is critical if your practice is to thrive. You want and need to provide the treatment. And, you need to have options available that will work for the vast majority of your patients. Thus this book. It is my intention to give you solid advice, thorough instruction, and necessary armamentarium to make and carry out successful financial arrangements with your patients.

I hope the business administrators (BA) and financial coordinators (FC) of the practice will find the information in this book helpful on a daily basis. However, this book isn't written just for these vital team members. The book is written for everyone, including the doctor—the owner of the business. Doctors, do not be aloof in the area of financing. This is the lifeblood of your business. You need to be actively involved in deciding what you do and how you do it. Improving on the system of financing can make or break your success. Please read and study this book, along with your team. Take a leadership role. That is, perhaps, your most important role in the business.

A successful business is built upon carefully established and effectively administered systems. A dental practice is a business and, therefore, is dependent upon the quality of its systems. The financial aspect of your practice is a system—or actually, a sequence of systems. The goal of these systems is to accomplish the following:

- Make the financing of your patient's dental care comfortable so that the vast majority of patients will be able to *go ahead* with necessary and desired treatment.

- *Collect what you produce* to ensure a healthy cash flow in your practice.

- Increase patient flow and gain a higher case acceptance.

- Reduce the amount of time your team members spend on statements and collection so that they can spend time on practice-building and patient service.

- Reduce or eliminate private pay accounts receivable. Make sure that your accounts receivable is no more than one-half of your average monthly production. (Only if you are accepting assignment of benefits from insurance.)

There are 25 different management systems that make up a dental practice. The financing system seems to present more challenges for the practice and for the members of the team than any of the other systems. Why? There are several reasons.

1. No clear definition of protocol is in place, and the people administering the practice have no guidelines.

2. Sometimes dental team members are uncomfortable with their own fees—or with discussion of fees; therefore, patients become uncomfortable.

3. Excellent training in the area of financing is not provided for the team members, and the people who are expected to carry out financial responsibilities do so without the necessary expertise.

4. Some dentists feel that they should *give away* their services.

5. Team members get *gun shy* when patients protest fees and think that they must compromise fees or become extremely lenient in financial arrangements so that people will accept treatment recommendations.

6. Communication skills that define a patient's financial concerns and clarify arrangements have not been taught.

Why This Book?

As a management consultant team, we have rarely gone into a practice where a clear and effective financial system is in place. Thus, financial stress becomes a challenge for the practice and for the practitioner. My work at the master's and doctoral level has been focused on "Controlling Stress in the Dental Environment."

Why?

My dentist husband, Dr. John Jameson, and I have experienced just about every kind of problem and every kind of stress known to dental man and woman. Stress can be good. That's what gets you up in the morning. Positive stress gives you the ambition to study and become better at what you do. However, when stress becomes negative—when it leads to psychological or physiological discomfort and illness—it becomes distress. Distress can lead to emotional and physical illness.

Can a book on financing serve this purpose—to control stress? Yes. John and I have known all stresses, but we both feel that nothing has been more difficult than financial stress. Financial stress takes away from the joy of dentistry, it can hinder associations with patients, and it can have a negative effect on personal relationships—particularly marriages.

Goals

Over the last two decades I have spent much time studying financing in order to deal with negative factors that impact a practice's financial security. My goal in writing this book is to give you the armamentarium to establish a quality financial system that will make the financing of your services comfortable for your patients and for you. I plan to give you not only the instruction necessary to develop this system but also the management tools and the communication skills to gain success in this area of your practice.

The following goals will be pursued:

- Establish a clear financial protocol that will produce a *win-win* situation for the patients and the practice.
- Define payment options that are workable.
- Motivate you to get involved with a healthcare financing program and then have the ability to market and build the practice by using the program.
- Teach the communication skills necessary to positively present the financial options.

- Establish a protocol for identifying and overcoming the objections that are related to the fee for dental services.
- Give you the skills necessary to become insurance *aware* but not insurance *driven.*
- Get control of your collection system so that you *collect what you produce.*
- Help you become comfortable with the financial aspect of your practice so that all members of the team feel good about the system and are confident with the proper administration of that system.

You Are Worth It!

As healthcare providers, you are offering a significant service to your patients—a service that establishes health and beauty. What you do for patients enhances their life, their health, and their self-esteem. When patients perceive the quality of care they are receiving in your practice and when they see their dental care as a significant benefit, they will be more than happy to pay for the services. You will have fewer complaints about money, and you will not have people asking you to compromise your treatment plans or your fees.

It is impossible to write a book about financing or to discuss this *system* in a consultation or lecture without establishing the point that when patients perceive quality and benefit of care, they will feel that the exchange of value—money for service—is equitable. Didn't Dr. Pankey teach us that some time ago? It remains true, now and always.

Step One: Attitude

If I could ask you for one thing as you begin reading this book and initiating your study and implementation of the system, it would be the following: Please open your mind.

A mind is like a parachute, it only works when it is open.

— Kevin Murphy in *Effective Listening*

This quotation says it all, doesn't it? I may reinforce and repeat things that you already know and are doing. If so, pat yourself on the back and keep on doing those things. Don't just think, "Oh, we already do that. We don't need to study that." Not so. Repetition is the key to learning. If I talk about things that you are already doing, be proud. But also look for the little things that you can do to refine what you are already doing. It's the little things that can make the big difference. Become a committed student. Always be in the business of self-improvement.

On the other hand, I may ask you to step out of your comfort zone. I will introduce you to things that you may not have heard before. I will be teaching you some communication skills that you may not have used before. Know that these communication skills are *tried and true.* Study the new skills. Practice with commitment. Constantly refine and improve your skills.

Most of all, just like anything, you will get out of the book exactly what you put into it. Know that if you use a part of the skills, you will get partial success. If you implement all of the skills, you will gain incredible success.

Dental professionals would never implement a *portion* of a clinical system and expect success. You do the whole thing—step by step—consistently. Not once, but every time. Thus, the law of averages is in your favor and you gain success most every time you perform a procedure.

However, people do not transfer that same commitment to their management systems. They think they can take one idea out of a presentation or a book and that they will gain great success. Not so! A management system—such as a financial system—takes the same commitment to consistency; consistency in administration of the system, all of it, every time. Then, the law of averages takes your side and success will be yours.

Read. Study. Have team meetings about each chapter. Use this book as a textbook on financing. It is just that. Make a commitment to implement all the strategies. The results will be the following:

- increased cash flow
- less time and money spent on collection, thus reducing overhead
- greater treatment acceptance, therefore higher productivity
- reduced stress
- fun

I hope that the study of this material and the implementation of the system will increase the joy that you receive in the practice of dentistry. Enjoy!

• CHAPTER •

1

The Psychology of Money

A healthy attitude toward money will set you free.

— **Jonathon Robinson**

Psychology is the science of human behavior. A behavior is something that one can *see, hear,* or *feel*. In your practice, money is (1) seen physically—and it is *seen* emotionally in the mind's eye of both you and the patient. Money is talked about, so these discussions can be (2) *heard*, and the impact of money does (3) touch everyone involved—both the person paying and the person being paid. So it is *felt*. Therefore, the psychology of money—its impact on human behavior—is an important and integral part of your practice. It is with this understanding and belief that I start this book—the second edition of *Collect What You Produce!*—with a chapter on the psychology of money.

Since the writing of the first edition of this book, I have completed a PhD in psychology. I based my research and the writing of my dissertation on stress control as it applies to the dental profession. I focused my study on how the development and improvement of communication skills can be a statistically significant factor in controlling stress. There is no question that stress, money, and the communication about money are related. Learning to communicate about money—in its multitude of situations—can support the control of stress.

Jameson Management, Inc. (JMI) is now 15 years old. We have consulted in and coached more than 2,000 practices throughout the country and the world on the management systems that lead to a smooth-running, productive, profitable, and stress-controlled organization. It has been here—in the dental trenches—that my team of consultants and I have seen the total impact of money on the everyday operation of the departments within a practice. There is not one fiber of the practice that is not influenced by money in one way, shape, or form. Practices that are financially healthy are—usually—happier. Practices that are constantly under financial constraints are—usually—stressed. This stress, when left unbridled, can harm the interpersonal relationships of people on the team. It can negatively affect feelings toward patients. It can affect treatment planning—and, thus, every system down the line. When one system begins to falter, there is a domino effect—all other systems will falter, as well.

There are numerous aspects of money that are relevant to this subject of the psychology of money. Many people in the practice are impacted by the various situations that are interfaced with money. Think about it.

1. Money was paid for dental school, hygiene school, assisting schools and certifications for business administrators, such as the Business Management Certification Course developed by JMI.

2. Money was involved with the purchase or the building of the practice and/or facility.

3. Money was paid for the equipment and supplies.

4. Money pays salaries, taxes, and benefits. People cannot work without being paid—and that includes the dentist.

5. Patients pay for and you receive compensation for services provided.

6. Team members have feelings about money—feelings about the worth of the services being provided; feelings related to conversations about money with patients; feelings about how much they are paid, about asking for a raise, and about their financial worth to the practice.

7. Money is the medium that people exchange for a value that they are receiving.

8. Sometimes money isn't collected expediently and collection efforts are put forth. This can, for some people, be difficult and/or avoided.

9. With a well-managed practice, financial goals can be set and accomplished, and appropriate rewards for work well done can be distributed.

10. Money is a measure—a way to monitor many aspects of the health and well-being of your practice. When goals are accomplished, celebrations and acknowledgements can be made and appreciation can be expressed.

11. Some people think that their worth is in direct proportion to the amount of money they make. Other people think that they are not worthy of being paid for the services they provide—or don't think they deserve to be paid well.

12. Money is one part of security and freedom.

13. Money is an important part of providing for one's family.

14. Money is a vehicle.

15. Money is not the reason you are a healthcare provider. However, without money and a financially sound business, you cannot provide the care and treatment you believe are beneficial to your patients. If you are not financially sound, everyone loses—you, your team, your patients, and your community.

16. Money isn't bad. You can and deserve to *Collect What You Produce!*

Money: Your Relationship to It

A person's relationship with money is both complex and important. In the world of business—and you are in business—your dynamic with money can be positive and healthy or it can be negative and stress-filled. If your practice—your business—is financially sound and you and your team are secure and happy, you will attract people who are the same. What you put out there will come back to you. Put up a mirror in front of the face of your practice and know that the patients and the relationships you have with your patients will be a direct reflection of what you are putting out into the world. If you are stressed about money, driven by money, don't have enough money to pay the bills, or you don't feel equitably compensated for your work, those negative feelings will be projected, and you will attract people who are negative, demanding, and dominating or who don't have enough money of their own! The mirror effect.

Have you ever thought about your relationship to money? Think about it for a few minutes. Your attitude toward and relationship with money can have a positive or negative effect on other team members and patients.

If, for example, you are discussing money with a patient but you don't feel comfortable doing so, the patient will pick up on your discomfort. No matter how great the verbal skills, that discomfort may have an adverse impact on the patient and may affect whether or not a patient accepts financial responsibility or the treatment itself.

Can you develop a healthy relationship to money? Yes. Might it take some work? Perhaps. Remember that money is a vehicle. It's not money that you want or need. It's what money will do for you. It is a vehicle. Therefore, take some time to consider what is important to your life and to your ultimate happiness.

For example, if you say, "I want to increase our production. We need to see more patients or do more treatment."

Peel the layer of that onion and look deeper. Why do you want to produce more? Is it the increased revenue that will bring you pleasure? What will you gain from the increase? Will you get to do the following:

- Do more of the procedures that you love to do?
- See more patients accept treatment and get healthier?
- Pay the bills on time?
- Stay in business?
- Have more take-home money for your family needs?
- Take more time off to spend with family or on personal interests?
- Pay your team in a more equitable manner?

- Hire the right people?
- Fund a retirement program?
- Buy that boat that you have yearned for so that you can fish more often—or whatever?
- Or a combination of the previous questions?

In this list of possible reasons for wanting to increase production, it isn't the money that is the *goal*. The money—the increased production—is the means to the end—the vehicle. The ultimate goal could be health, family, quality time, or stress relief. It could be any or all of these things or others. It isn't the money that is the goal here—it's the intangibles that matter—the important things in life such as health, physical well-being, family, communion with nature, peace. These are examples of motivators that are substantial and relevant to life. Motivators are different for each individual.

Getting yourself into a financial bind by spending more than you make or buying something without evaluating the end results you are seeking can cause your relationship to money to become harmful and truly unrewarding. This, in turn, can have a negative impact on the other people in your life. Getting yourself into a financial bind can come from not realizing the things that make the biggest difference for you—the things that will bring you the most satisfaction. Your money may be spent on *things*, and you may miss the joy and peace of a fulfilled life. Be careful. Respect the values that you hold essential and let your relationship to money support those values.

The entire structure of your practice—all of the systems that you put into place and administer on a daily basis need to be grounded in the values that are the core of your being. When decisions are to be made, ask yourself this question, "If we do this, buy this, implement this strategy, hire this person, etc., will this uphold our values and help us to fulfill our ultimate mission?"

If the answer is "no," then step back and revisit your decision. Make sure that the structure of your practice supports your ultimate vision of the ideal practice. Otherwise, you risk spending a career totally unfulfilled. A tragic loss.

Values

Write down the values you deem essential to your personal and professional life.

For example, integrity, honesty, compassion, etc.

____
____
____
____

Write down the long-term goals that you want to accomplish. Include goals in the following three areas:

1. Spiritual, family, and personal

____
____
____
____

2. Business and career

____
____
____
____

3. Self-improvement

____
____
____
____

Each time you make a purchase or invest money, ask yourself if this purchase or investment upholds your values and if it fits with your short-term or long-term goals. (Of course, there will be times when you buy something just for the fun of it.) But at the end of the month, look at your checkbook or analyze your credit card bill—or bills—and ask yourself the following questions:

- Did I make purchases this month that made sense for the most part?
- Do my purchases support my values and goals?

If the answer continues to be "no" (be honest with yourself), then consider making some alterations to your purchasing patterns and decisions.

Your Practice Vision

All of this relates to the vision of your practice. Clearly define what you consider to be your ideal practice. There is no reason for you not to have your ideal practice. The only thing that would keep you from accomplishing the goal of developing and enjoying your ideal practice is you. If you don't clearly have the vision of your ideal defined or if your team doesn't know what that ideal practice looks like or if you don't carefully plan and carry out the strategies to make that happen, it won't. No one can make anything happen for you. You must make things happen. And—the happening starts with clarifying in your mind what the ideal practice looks like.

Consider the following questions. Write out your thoughts. Then, begin developing strategies to make sure that your vision of the ideal practice becomes a reality.

1. What kind of treatment will we provide?

   ____
   ____
   ____
   ____

2. What kinds of procedures will be the major focus of our treatment mix?

   ____
   ____
   ____
   ____

3. In what manner will we provide that treatment?

4. What will our appointments with our patients be like?

5. What do we consider the ideal patient experience in our practice?

6. How can we make that happen every time?

7. What will the team be like?

   A. Attitude?

   B. Work ethic?

C. Talent?

D. Ambition?

E. Energy?

F. Communication?

G. Team spirit?

8. How will the business department function?

9. How will the clinical department function?

10. What will the hygiene department be like? What types of services will we provide?

11. What will the facility be like?

    A. Aesthetics?

    B. Equipment?

    C. Technology?

    D. Patient flow?

    E. Patient comfort?

F. Team comfort?

12. What kind of customer service will be a trademark for our practice?

13. What are the financial goals of the practice?

A. Production?

B. Collection?

C. Overhead percentage?

D. Accounts receivable?

E. Retirement plan?

F. Savings for emergencies?

14. How many days per month will we work?

A. How many hours per week?

B. How many days/weeks of vacation?

C. How many days of continuing education?

15. What will our reputation in the community be?

16. For what kind of treatment do we want to be known?

____
____
____
____

17. What will it take to be recognized as the practice that offers the treatment and service we have described previously?

____
____
____
____

There are many other considerations as you are developing this view of your ideal practice. Take the time now to determine what is important to you.

Know this. Whatever you consider *ideal* for you, is just that—ideal. One of the wonderful things about being a small business owner is that you get to choose that ideal. What you want doesn't have to be what anyone else wants. What the doctor down the street deems ideal may not be ideal to you at all. That's OK. What needs to happen is for you to look inside yourself and see clearly the vision of what you consider ideal and then be about the business of making that happen.

Certainly money is a part of this ideal practice. Having a healthy relationship to money in the practice is as critical as having a healthy relationship to money in your personal life. You will want to carefully determine your values and goals and constantly ask yourself the questions, "Will this purchase honor our values? Will it support our goals?" If not, then you may need to reconsider.

Ultimately, you want your investments to support your vision and to provide long-term satisfaction. Remember to *peel the layers of the onion* when you are making a financial decision in order to determine the core factor behind the purchase. Is it a short-term or a long-term satisfaction that will be fulfilled? In being a wise businessperson, you know that you have to spend money to make money. Certainly there are many short-term purchases that will be made. However, in most cases, if you look carefully and make your decisions wisely, a long-term goal will be accomplished through a series of carefully made short-term purchases. Be cautious about short-term purchases that don't support your values and goals.

Are You Worthy?

Now that you have reflected on and recorded your values and goals—your ideal practice vision—let's turn our attention to other psychological ramifications related to money. My experiences with thousands of dental professionals have given me clear insights into some of the emotional trials related to money—both from the perspective of the professional or from the perspective of the paying patient who is the *customer* of the dental practice. One prevailing issue is the issue of worthiness.

From the dentist or from dental team members, we often hear the following comments/statements:

> "Our fees are too high."
>
> "We haven't raised our fees for a long time, but our fees are high enough."
>
> "Our fees are already above usual and customary. We can't take the fees any higher."
>
> "We work in a low-income area. We can't charge much for our services. No one would come to us."
>
> "The dentist already makes enough money. His wife/her husband just wants more and more and that means we have to work harder and harder to keep her/him happy."
>
> "Our patients are spoiled. The last dentist—the guy I bought the practice from—just filed their insurance and let them pay when they found out exactly how much they owed."
>
> "Our patients belong to the '*one crown a year club*' and that's all they will do." "They won't do anything that the insurance won't cover."
>
> "I can't talk about money to him/her. He/she's the doctor's best friend, and the doctor told me not to talk about money to his friends."
>
> "Oh, we don't talk about money before we do the treatment. If we talk about the money, people will think all we care about is the almighty dollar."

"Our patients won't accept outside financing. They just want to pay us—any way they want. They think of us as their friends—and friends don't talk about money."

"My staff thinks I make so much money. They don't have any idea how much it takes to run a practice. They think I should give them more money even though I am the one who has to pay all the bills."

And so on. Every day we hear these kinds of comments from participants in lectures, private conversations with doctors or team members, and in our in-office consultations. Each and every one of these statements is based on incorrect information—or a lack of information. Each and every one of these comments reflects a lack of self-esteem in terms of being worthy of being paid for services rendered.

There may never be a more vital conversation to be had by a dental team than a conversation related to the value of services provided by each and every one of you. Have a team meeting. Discuss the following questions:

1. What services do we provide our patients both clinically and otherwise?
2. How do our services benefit the patient—physically, mentally, emotionally, and socially?
3. What would be the down side of a person not having a healthy oral cavity—decayed and/or lost teeth, periodontal disease, or an unsightly smile?
4. What would be the up side if the following factors were taken care of by our team: healthy teeth and gums, disease free, and an attractive smile?
5. What do we do in terms of customer service that makes the patient's time with us comfortable, stress-controlled, and pleasant?
6. How do we *go the extra mile* to make sure that our patients receive all that they expect and a little more each and every time they interact with us?
7. What kinds of business and educational services do we offer that enhance our patient's experiences with us?
8. What makes our practice a good choice when a person is selecting a dental home?

Once you have answered these questions, you may discover one or two things. You may discover that you are, indeed, worthy of being paid well for the services that you provide and that when patients perceive the value of your services, they will pay and will pay willingly. Or, you may discover—as you answer these questions—that there are places that need work in your practice and that in order to feel worthy of your fees, an enhancement of your practice protocols and systems would be beneficial. An investment in time and money for the purpose of elevating your practice to the next level will come back to you multifold.

I, for one, do not know anyone who provides a better, more meaningful service to people than dental professionals. I have never worked with people who care more, try harder, provide better service, and enhance people's lives any more than dental professionals. You do not need to apologize for your fees. You do not need to compromise your fees or feel badly for charging people for the treatment they receive from you.

You are a healthcare professional, and you feel a need to provide for mankind in a humanitarian way. That, I hope, will always be a part of your life. However, determine how, when, and where you will provide your missionary work and provide that by the following choices: people within your community who need help; indigent children, nursing home patients without families, missionary trips to poverty-stricken areas within the United States or other countries, etc. Please, always be willing to do some *just because* dentistry—dental care you provide—*just because*. This *love gift* will come back to you in ways that far exceed any monetary reward. However, you cannot run your practice on a missionary basis (unless you are, truly, just that). You are running a business and unless you run that business well, you won't stay in business and you won't be able to provide care to anyone. That is definitely a losing proposition for everyone.

Money as an Exchange of Value

Money is an exchange of value. Your patients are receiving the value of health, well-being, improved appearance, keeping their teeth for a lifetime, comfort, and function. Life enhancing benefits. You are receiving money as the patient's part of the exchange. Money is a moveable entity that flows from one person to another or from one business to another.

Alla Sheptun says in his article entitled, "Philosophy of Money," published in *Philosophy of Economics* magazine, that

> Money is a thing which, irrespective of its material or symbolical form, has its own mode of moving from one person to another and this particular mode of moving makes money into a means of social interaction, into a medium of communication. This is the source of the immense value of money for society.

Money's value to you and to your patients lies in the fact that it serves as a means and an end of exchange of immeasurable value for life enhancement. Both you and your patients benefit from an equitable exchange of value, which occurs when you feel good about the money you receive for services rendered and your patients feel good about the investment they have made in you and in your care.

Now that we have laid a psychological background for a full discussion of money, let's learn how to *collect what you produce!*

• CHAPTER •

2

Establishing a Financial System: A Protocol

When you have disciplined people, you don't need hierarchy.

When you have disciplined thought, you don't need bureaucracy.

When you have disciplined action, you don't need excessive controls.

– **Jim Collins**
Good to Great

Sound Finances

The success of your practice is in direct proportion to the success of your systems. A business is made up of a series of *systems* that direct the various aspects of that business. Your practice has approximately 25 management systems functioning every day. The cohesive functioning and integration of these systems is what makes a practice successful.

The following four attributes impact the success of a business:

1. the right team
2. clear direction
3. effective systems
4. sound finances

And sound finances. There you have it. You cannot have a healthy practice unless the finances are sound. The financial systems of your practice are critical to the soundness and to the success of your practice. These systems are intricate, difficult, and intimate. It is not easy to establish financial systems and even less easy to administer those systems.

As you begin to analyze your financial systems, be aware that there are many primary and secondary systems that are interrelated. We will be looking at these interrelated systems throughout this book. It is my goal in this book to give you a textbook description of how to establish, administer, monitor, and communicate about each financial system or subsystem.

In order for the financial systems of your practice to be clear and comfortable, a written protocol outlining your financial options needs to be established and put into place. I am choosing to use the word *protocol*, for the most part, here and throughout the book instead of the usual and customary word—*policy*. Policy has taken on such a negative connotation in the world of business that I prefer to use it sparingly. Synonyms for the word protocol are procedure, etiquette, code of behavior, set of rules, practice, and modus operandi. That's exactly what I am talking about.

We rarely go into a practice where a written financial protocol is in place—or for that matter, any financial protocol at all. Many practices figure out how they are going to handle the financial aspect of a patient's treatment as they go. The financial system in the practice is a *guess and by golly* system that changes as moods change.

Therefore, establishing a *firm yet flexible* system of financial options—or establishing a financial protocol—is one of the first and most critical steps in developing a well-managed dental practice. No one wins when there is a lack of clarity in this sensitive area—financing.

The oral cavity is an intimate zone of a person's body. So is the pocketbook. That's why it is so important that a person's financial responsibility be clearly defined and mutually agreed upon. Without a set protocol, this would be next to impossible. Trying to figure out what you are going to do with a patient's financial responsibility without any guidelines leads to confusion. A confused person cannot make a decision. Therefore, without clarity in the area of financing, you run the risk of a patient not accepting treatment, putting treatment off, or having to "think about it." Neither you nor the patient wins. You do not get to provide the treatment, and the patient does not receive the necessary or desired care.

Establishment of a Financial System

The following are 12 steps that need to be taken to establish and implement a financial system.

1. **Establish a written financial protocol.** A written financial protocol is essential. Making arbitrary, random decisions about who's going to pay and how they will pay will lead to financial chaos for your practice. Loss of control of accounts receivable can result. Problems and misunderstandings from patients in regard to their financial responsibility can arise.

Historically, many dentists have feared setting a firm financial protocol because they thought that patients would leave the practice if they weren't *lenient* with the financial aspect of treatment. A good financial protocol will allow for desired flexibility but also will provide necessary firmness for a solid practice and solid relationships.

2. **Decide, as a team, what financial options you are going to make available.** In his book, *Making Meetings Work*, Michael Doyle says that "all the people who must ultimately approve, accept, or implement a decision should be involved from the beginning in the process of making the decision." Abiding by this proven management principle, you will see that if the entire team understands the financial options and decides—together—which options are applicable and appropriate to your practice, they will be more likely to support these options. They will be confident that these options serve both the practice and the patients and will not hesitate to discuss these with patients.

If a team member questions the financial protocol and/or the options you make available, that lack of confidence will come through loud and clear to patients. Their insecurity will lead to patient insecurity.

3. **Make sure you are offering a variety of financial options.** Because there is such a variance in your patient's financial situations, you need to offer a variety of options that are good for the practice and good for the patients. Remember the following: you must always be interested in the financial soundness of the organization—the practice. You will be introduced to multiple financial options in this book. These options are proven and are sound. Consider these—as a team—when you are deciding upon your written financial protocol.

4. **Make sure that all monies are collected before—or by the time—treatment has been completed.** Did you know that most lawsuits arise when there is a balance owed to the practice? More than 80% of all dental lawsuits occur when money is owed to the practice. Your relationship to your patients can be put into jeopardy when services are not paid for by the time treatment is complete. People who owe you money forget what they felt like before treatment or they forget what their teeth looked like prior to the smile makeover.

5. **Stay out of the banking business.** As we work steadily through this study of collecting all that you produce, you will learn ways to finance your patients' care without carrying any accounts on your own books. I will say this now, and you will note the repetition of this throughout the book—stay out of the banking business. You are a dental practice—not a bank. Do the things that only a dental practice can do and delegate everything else.

6. **Financial arrangements must be made before any treatment is provided.** Patients have made it clear that they don't like not knowing how much the treatment will cost before it's done.

We must listen to our consumers/patients and respond positively to what they are requesting. They are saying, "Let me know, in advance, what my financial responsibility will be." Mutual respect will result.

Establishing clarity in regard to a patient's financial responsibility before treatment is rendered will reduce post-treatment misunderstandings and quarrels about the fee for the service and about payment responsibilities. Most of the time when a patient leaves the practice unhappy, the cause is a misunderstanding about money.

Some dental professionals think that if they talk about the financial responsibility before treatment is rendered, the patient will think that all they care about is money. Not so! Listen carefully. Surveys of patient satisfaction indicate that the thing they like least about the dentist—or the dental experience—is not knowing how much a procedure will cost before it is performed. Therefore, spending quality time with a patient explaining the fee for the service; discussing the options available for payment; and coming to terms with an agreed-upon payment arrangement is exactly what the patients are asking you to do. They will not resent this. They will appreciate this.

7. **Designate a specific person or persons on the team to administer financial arrangements.** Establish who, when, where, and how this person will make the financial arrangements.

This person, probably the business administrator (BA) or financial coordinator (FC) or the treatment coordinator (TC), needs to work with the patient to make sure there are no clinical questions that have not been answered. She will then define the fees, analyze expected insurance, (if applicable), and work with a patient to determine the financial option that is acceptable.

A financial agreement needs to be written so that neither party forgets or becomes confused about the agreement. It has been said that "most people never remember that they ever agreed to anything." So, practice what I call *preventive management*. Prevent a misunderstanding before it ever has a chance to rear its ugly head. Come to an agreement about the fee and the method of payment, write it down, give the patient a copy and keep a copy for your records.

• KEY POINT •

If a person is given the responsibility to implement and carry out a financial protocol, then she must have the support of the dentist and the entire team. Nothing is more debilitating, embarrassing, and frustrating than to be very clear and very good at making a financial arrangement only to be undermined by the dentist or other team members. This is why the entire team needs to decide what financial options will be made available. This will give everyone the confidence that the arrangement will be good for the patient and for the practice. This support is absolutely necessary if this is going to work.

The dentist may quote the fee, but it is usually more effective for a BA to make the financial arrangements. A qualified BA can give necessary third-party reinforcement to the dentist's recommendations, making sure that there are no clinical questions that have been left unanswered. Patients may be more comfortable discussing financial concerns with the BA rather than the dentist. In addition, the person who has been given the responsibility of handling the financial aspect of the practice will be less likely to make alterations to the financial protocol.

For example, if your dentist is like my husband, John, his heart is so big that it doesn't fit into his body—and we wouldn't want him to be any other way. However, that also means that when sweet Ms. Jones—who was his second grade teacher and now lives on a fixed income—asks is she can pay him out at $2 per month for the rest of her life—and his—he has a difficult time saying, "no." So, we never put him in a place of discomfort. When a patient asks him about the fee—or about a payment methodology—he confidently tells the patient that Jan, his BA, handles all discussions of fees and financial arrangements while he handles all the dentistry. That's good for everyone.

With any system, program, or protocol, you need to be consistent in the administration of the system. Nevertheless, you also need to know when to flex. Determine situations that warrant flexing. However, do not make flexing the rule, make it the exception.

Note

In our own practice, our BA joins the dentist and the patient for the consultation appointment on our larger cases. The dentist asks the patient for permission. He says,

> Ms. Jones, I've asked Jan, my Business Administrator, to join us today for our consultation. Jan handles the financial arrangements for our patients and she schedules the appointments. Therefore, I feel it is important for her to hear the recommendations that I'm making for you. Are you comfortable with that?
>
> (No one has ever said, "no.")

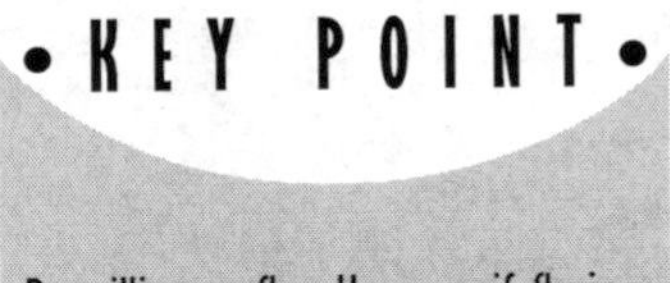

Be willing to flex. However, if flexing becomes the norm, you no longer have a system.

The dentist presents his recommendations, answers treatment questions, asks for the commitment to go ahead with treatment, then—when there are no other questions except financing—he excuses himself. Jan takes over. She reconfirms the treatment, answers any clinical questions where confusion may exist, defines the total investment, and the financial options available for payment. Together, she and the patient clarify all financial responsibilities. She writes this down on our written financial agreement. Then she schedules the first appointment.

8. Do your best to create a time and a place for private consultation—both clinical and financial. As I said earlier, the oral cavity is an intimate zone of the body. So is the pocketbook. To discuss treatment recommendations or financing in public might be uncomfortable and awkward. This could become a hindrance to a person accepting and going ahead with treatment. Plus, privacy mandates require that we make every possible effort to assure confidentiality. So, be cognizant of the need for privacy. Find the place. Create the appropriate environment. It doesn't have to be fancy. It just has to work. Schedule the time for this consultation. This financial consultation is as critical as any phase of your treatment. Don't think that it isn't time-efficient to schedule time for the financial discussion. It is! In fact, the following are two phases of every consultation: the clinical presentation and the financial presentation. A case is not *closed* until the financial arrangement has been agreed upon by both parties. So, is this a valuable use of time? I think so. The responsibility of the BA is to work with the patient to find a financial solution—and that may take some time. If that means a person goes ahead with treatment, I would suggest that this is time well invested.

For privacy, you may use a consultation room, a private area in the business office, the doctor's office or, in some cases the treatment area. If the treatment recommendation is simple and doesn't warrant a full consultation or if the treatment is emergency in nature, stop your inclination to put your hand on that handpiece and prep that tooth. Set the patient up, tell him/her that you will have your BA come back to the clinical area to discuss the financial responsibility and the options you have available for payment. Tell patients that you want to assure their comfort—both physically and financially—so you want to make sure that they are both clear and comfortable with the financial aspect of treatment before you begin.

An attendee of one of my lectures at a national convention said that he first numbs the patient, then has the business person come in to make the financial arrangement. That is assumptive and disrespectful, in my opinion. Do not *assume* that you will be able to find a payment option that is comfortable for this person, and do not spend anyone's money without their permission. So, to administer anesthesia—put the person through this—and not know if they are going to be able to proceed with treatment is inappropriate. The other side of that coin, of course, is that—if a financial agreement has not been obtained—you might go ahead with the treatment, but you may never be paid. That, too, is unacceptable—or can be the choice you make.

Patients want to know what their financial responsibility is before treatment is provided. Respect them and do just that. And you deserve to know that you will be compensated for services rendered. You are providing a great service and deserve to be paid for it.

9. Make sure that the flow of your office makes it easy for patients to pay. Whatever the design of your office, spend some time determining how to begin and end your appointments so that if patients need to have financial discussions, they can have them in private. Or, if a patient needs to sit down to negotiate a settlement of an account, make sure they are escorted to the appropriate person. Make sure that a patient cannot and does not *escape* without spending time with the BA. The BA will need to collect the fee for the day if one is due. At the same time, she will reinforce the fee for the next appointment and the agreed-upon method of payment.

10. Study communication skills for making a financial arrangement and for handling objections. The bottom line to your success in any of your systems is the way you communicate. Whether you are answering the telephone, presenting the treatment plan, scheduling appointments, or determining the financial arrangement, the way you communicate will make all the difference in the world.

Paul Harvey says, "It's not what you say, it's how you say it." Don't you agree? You can present the financial options in one way and get a negative response from the patient; but present these options in another way and get a positive response. Clear communication is necessary if a mutually respectful relationship is to evolve, and treatment acceptance is to result.

As a part of your communication development, you will want to study how to educate your patient not only about the benefits of recommended treatment but also about your financial options—how they work and the benefits these options bring to the patient.

11. Analyze your fees at least every six months. Notice that I didn't say raise your fees every six months, although you might choose to do just that. But I did say analyze your fees every six months. You will probably need to raise your fees at least once per year due to your increased cost of operation. If the costs related to a particular procedure go up due to higher costs of materials or lab fees, etc., then you must increase the fee for that procedure.

You must be willing and able to pass your increased costs of operation on to your consumers—the patients—or otherwise you may become productive without becoming profitable. A full discussion of fees will take place in an upcoming chapter. The important point here is to make sure that your fees are equitable for the services you are providing—and vice versa.

12. Make sure that you have a predetermined protocol for every conceivable situation. As a team, think about every unique situation that may arise where finances are involved. Determine how you are going to handle these situations. Get together on this so that everyone is prepared to handle whatever comes up. Make a list of all the possible situations—even the weird ones—and decide what will work best for you. Practice any communication skills that may be necessary in these situations.

What you don't want to happen is to have a situation arise, go back to the clinical area, interrupt the doctor, and place her in a situation requiring a last-minute, rash decision.

Summary

Just as you would do in the building of any structure—or system—lay the foundation carefully so that when you place one structure or system on top of another, the whole configuration will remain solid. This is what I have outlined in this chapter—the foundational protocols that need to be in place as you move forward in building the financial structure of your practice. I want you to have such a firm foundation that the systems function succinctly, efficiently, and effectively. This foundation is the basis for making sure that you *collect what you produce!*

• CHAPTER •

3

Workable Financial Options

Make the financing of dentistry comfortable for your patients and for you.

— **Dr. John Jameson**

The following is a financial protocol—a series of financial options—that will work for any practice, large or small, new or established, urban or rural, solo or group and any specialty. The options that I am recommending do, indeed, offer flexibility as well as firmness. These options will meet the needs of most of your patients. In addition, consistently following this program will get you out of the banking business and will let you concentrate on what you do best: practice dentistry.

Other benefits of this protocol are as follows:

- lower cost of operation in the area of financial management
- less time spent on statements and collection by your team members
- greater cash flow
- greater treatment acceptance
- enhanced scheduling

You will be able to see fewer patients per day, do more dentistry per patient—when and where appropriate—and see each patient for fewer visits. Everyone wins and your costs of operation are reduced significantly.

Option #1.
A 5% Accounting or Fee Reduction for Payment in Full—Before Treatment is Rendered

For those patients who have healthy savings or checking accounts, this option gives them an incentive to pay in advance. Anyone who has ever been responsible for scheduling will also agree that if patients pay for the treatment in advance, they will show up for those appointments.

Offer this option for cases of a certain amount or more. The amount where this option begins is up to you. Have a discussion with your business team. Ask them where most people begin having trouble writing a check. They will know. Perhaps that would be a good place to begin this option. In our practice, we offer this option for cases of $1,000 or more. We practice in a small rural area where our wonderful patients are *salt of the earth people* who live on budgets. So, for most of our patients, an investment of $1,000 or more is significant. But this can be different for every practice. You decide. However, wherever you decide to begin offering this option—offer it to everyone.

I was discussing this option during a lecture and a doctor came up to me and said that he offered this option—but only to certain people. He said that if he knew that a person had money, he didn't offer this option to them. I must admit that I found this offensive. If you choose to offer this option, offer it to everyone.

How do you present this option?

BA: Ms. Jones, many of our patients have chosen to have their fee reduced. Would that be of interest to you?

Or, more simply,

BA: Ms. Jones, we do offer a payment option that would reduce your fee. Would you be interested in hearing about this?

Or, even more simply,

BA: Ms. Jones, would you be interested in having your fee reduced?

Ms. Jones: Of course. How do I do that?

BA: If you pay for your treatment before the doctor begins, we will reduce your fee by 5%. If we aren't involved with the bookkeeping, that saves us both time and money, and we would like to pass those savings on to you.

Be totally prepared before you make a financial arrangement. Know the total fee for the complete treatment plan and be prepared to present the entire plan and entire fee. Be prepared to offer all of the options because your goal is to find the option that works best for the patient—one that you have already determined works for you. So, know how much the 5% fee reduction (or you may choose to say cash courtesy) would be for the patient and present this in a positive manner. Be sure to always stress how something benefits the patients. That's what they are interested in—how something will benefit them.

Example

Let's say that the patient has a $3,000 treatment plan.

BA: Ms. Jones, we would be more than happy to reduce your fee. If you pay for your treatment in full before the doctor begins, we will reduce your fee by 5%. That would represent a savings of $150. That's a significant savings and I wanted to be sure to offer that to you. Would that work for you?

You will be pleasantly surprised at how many patients are glad to receive an incentive for full payment. If you have done a good job of presenting the dentistry and if you have established a solid, trusting relationship with your patients, they will want the treatment. If they do wish to proceed and you are willing to reduce the fee, many will be thrilled to accept. Many patients take advantage of this option. You are dollars ahead to offer this reduction versus carrying any accounts on your own books.

Option #2.
Half of the Total Fee to Reserve the Appointment and Half of the Total Fee at the Preparation Appointment

Historically, most practices have offered half at the preparation and half at the insertion. There have been some difficulties with the following:

1. Patients have not made a financial commitment but have reserved long appointments only to not show up or cancel at the last minute.

This has made doctors and team members hesitant to schedule long appointments due to fear of large voids in the schedule.

2. Some people do make their payment at the preparation but when they come in for the insertion don't have the agreed upon final payment. You are placed in a predicament of whether or not to insert those crowns now (you don't want to waste that scheduled time!) or to reschedule a time when the final payment can be paid. Be careful with this, however. You are legally required to complete irreversable treatment.

3. At the time of insertion, the patient knows he doesn't have the money for the final payment, so he doesn't show up.

As we all know, when a person cancels at the last minute or just doesn't show up, this is a huge time management problem and is very costly and very stressful to the practice and to all members of the team.

So, I am recommending for your crown and bridge appointments or for any treatments that involve multiple appointments that you ask for an initial investment of half the total fee at the time of the reservation or at the making of the appointment and for the final half to be due at the preparation. Then, at the time of the insertion appointment, the patient's financial responsibility will be complete.

I have been recommending this for quite some time and have found that the practices that have integrated this protocol have been successful and pleased. Patients will respond well when this option is presented well.

> **BA:** Ms. Jones, we will be reserving two hours of Dr. Jameson's time just for you. He and his clinical assistant want to give you their full, undivided attention. In order for us to reserve this much time, we ask for half of the fee to reserve the appointment and then the final half at the day of the preparation. This will let you spread the payments out into two equal payments, we will be able to prepare excellently for you, and we will be able to take care of the laboratory expenses so that they can begin work on your restorations immediately. Will this work for you?

This does let a patient spread the payment out a bit—perhaps more than a couple of pay periods. The point of this option is to get the patient's commitment to show up for the appointment. You are making a commitment to be there for them for an extended period of time, and you are asking for their commitment in return.

There is such an abundance of broken appointments, no shows, and cancellations in the industry that something different must be done. John Maxwell says that "If you keep on doing what you are doing, you will keep on getting what you are getting."

You are running a business. Certainly you want to be gracious and considerate to your patients. However, it is acceptable to ask your patients to realize and respect the importance of a lengthy appointment with you.

Be sure to collect the second half before the patient receives those preps! When you confirm the appointment, reiterate your financial agreement and ask the patient if he is prepared to pay the second half of the fee at his appointment. If he isn't, then reschedule at a time that is more appropriate. I often recommend that you confirm two days in advance (this depends on the practice). If you are doing a *two-day in advance* confirmation, you will have plenty of time to fill any voids left in the schedule. I would rather you be able to fill this void than for you to do the dentistry and not be paid for it.

> **BA:** Ms. Jones, this is Cathy with Dr. Jameson's dental office. Dr. Jameson has asked that I call to tell you that he is looking forward to seeing you Wednesday, June 25th at 8:30 in the morning. As you recall, Dr. Jameson has reserved two hours of his time just for you. He's totally prepared for your appointment.
>
> Ms. Jones, during our consultation appointment two weeks ago, you made an initial investment of half the total fee, or $1,500. The other half of the fee, or the other $1,500, will be due tomorrow. You have chosen to pay with a credit card. So I'll have everything ready for you. In fact, we can take care of that when you arrive and then you can go right back to work when your appointment is finished. Does that sound good?

I am very comfortable with this option. Some people say, "Oh, our patients won't make their full payment until they get the treatment finished and are sure that they like it."

Well, don't you stand behind all your work? Hopefully you do. Hopefully your patients know this about you. Hopefully you are willing to work with patients until they are pleased. So even if there is a problem, you are not going to stop working with the patient. Let them know that you stand behind your work—whether the financial responsibility has been completed or not.

If you want a more lenient option but one that integrates the initial investment—(which offsets no shows and broken appointments), ask for one-third at the reservation, one-third at the preparation, and one-third at the insertion. However, this option still puts you at risk for that insertion appointment, and I am interested in your not being at risk for any payments.

The key to this reservation payment option is to get the financial commitment in order to book the appointment. Being able to rely on patients to show up for their appointments or to not cancel their appointments is becoming an ever-increasing area of concern for many practices. If this is a problem for you, consider this option or preferably Option #1.

Option #3.
Payment by the Appointment

As with all financial discussions, the BA must have a complete treatment plan from the clinical team. It would be impossible to inform a person of his/her financial responsibility per appointment if you are not sure what kind of treatment is going to be provided at the next appointment.

The treatment plan must provide complete information. Just saying that you are going to do some *fillings* doesn't work. How many teeth? How many surfaces? What type of material? All of these details are necessary before proper financial discussions can take place.

Please, always do a comprehensive diagnosis, a complete treatment plan, and a fabulous consultation on all cases for all patients. If you are discussing a full treatment plan that will involve several appointments, and if the person needs to spread his/her payments out over the course of the treatment, do so in the following manner:

1. determine the total fee
2. divide the fee equally into the number of appointments
3. collect those equally calculated payments at each appointment
4. make sure that full payment is accomplished by the end of the treatment

If you calculate—and collect—the specific amount due at each particular appointment based on what procedures you are doing at each appointment, you run the risk of the patients falling out of treatment. They may complete only a part of the treatment and then decide they don't want to spend any more money. By dividing the fee into equal payments spread over the course of treatment, you reduce that possibility. In most cases, the patient would have paid a portion of upcoming treatments in advance and you reduce the risk of the patient falling out of treatment or cancelling appointments.

Example

BA: Ms. Jones, the total investment you will be making for the treatment the doctor has recommended to you is $1,200. Let me tell you about the wonderful payment options we have here in our practice. (Offer Option #1 and/or #2.)

Ms. Jones: No. Those don't work for me. I'd just like to pay as I go.

BA: That will be just fine. We can do that. The way we handle that is like this. The total investment will be $1,200. The doctor will be seeing you for three appointments. So, we can spread the $1,200 out evenly over the three appointments. That would be $400 per appointment. By the time you complete your treatment, your financial responsibility will be complete as well.

Option #4.
Bankcards

The major bankcards are making significant efforts to capture a larger segment of the healthcare market. They are informing the public that using a bankcard for the financing of dental/medical care makes good sense. These companies can afford to market to the consumer in a large way. Every dental office will benefit from their brilliant marketing efforts.

Dr. Charles Blair, of Charlotte, North Carolina, surveyed dental consumers and asked the following questions, "Would you use a bankcard to finance your dental care?" Approximately 75% of the respondents said, "yes."

However, says Dr. Blair, only 6% of the dentistry in the United States is being financed on a bankcard presently. So, he asked the next question of dental consumers, "Most of you say that you would use a bankcard to finance your dental care, but only 6% of you are doing so. Why?"

The answers were, (1) "My dentist doesn't accept bankcards" and (2) "I don't know if my dentist accepts bankcards."

In an interview with VISA®, I was asked, "Cathy, do you recommend that dentists market the use of a bankcard to their patients?"

I answered without hesitation, "yes." Informing your own patient family—and the people within your drawing area—of the fact that bankcards are accepted and encouraged in your practice can make the difference in whether a person or family comes to you or not and in whether a person accepts treatment recommendations or not.

You must ask for these cards. Don't just hang up a sign or put a notice on your front desk and think people will respond. You have to mention and encourage the use of this option. In your patient education newsletters, special mailings, telephone ads, newspaper announcements, on your statements, and during your financial consultations, ask people to use this option. Encourage people. Inform them of the benefits of financing with a bankcard. Do not assume that people know you accept bankcards. Obviously, they don't know! Assumption is the lowest form of communication. Don't assume anything!

Consider developing a form that lets a patient give you a signature on file for use of their bankcard. When asked if this was acceptable, VISA said that not only was this acceptable but this was recommended. They have their own pre-authorization forms but say that it is just fine for dentists to do this themselves.

You can do any of the following things with these authorizations forms:

(1) Place any balance after insurance pays on their credit card up to a certain amount. Or, (2) put the full balance for treatment on the credit card if insurance doesn't pay, for any reason. This is great. If you are accepting insurance on assignment, you do your very best to estimate the amount the insurance program will pay and you collect the co-pay at the time of the service. However, from time to time, the insurance company may not pay what you estimate. Thus, there will be a remaining balance due from the patient. This is tough money to collect. You run the risk of the patient becoming disgruntled at you—not the insurance company! You run the risk of the patient delaying payment—which reduces the bottom-line profit of the treatment. And/or you run the risk of the patient not paying at all—turning the balance due into a source of conflict with you: the fee was too high; the treatment didn't need to be done; another, lower fee service could have been provided; you didn't figure things correctly; and so on. All inaccurate and untrue statements—but not in the mind of the patient.

(3) Place one—or a series—of regular payments on the credit card. Together with the patient, you determine the amount, the date, and the length of time payments will be placed on a credit card. This is a good option for any past-due accounts that you may have lingering as accounts receivable. If the patient needs time to pay, this can be an option.

Don't forget that you can accept a credit card payment over the phone, also. Even if you don't have a pre-authorization, you can call a patient and receive a payment with the patient's verbal authorization. Then, send a copy of the receipt to the patient. This is appropriate for balances after insurance pays and for past-due accounts, if you have any right now.

Soon—once you learn to *collect what you produce*—you won't have any accounts receivable. But if you have accounts receivable right now and if you are sending statements, be sure to choose a billing statement format that will let you include a space for patients to write in their choice of bankcard, the account number, cardholder's name, expiration date, amount of payment (hopefully the entire amount due!), and the signature (Fig. 3–1). Make it easy for people to pay you!

(4) **All visits occurring during a certain period of time can be authorized for the patient's credit card.** This is great for families who may be sending different members of the family to the office at various times or for people with recurring visits, such as orthodontics or periodontal therapy, etc.

Market the option of a bankcard to your patients. Offer all of the major bankcards. Do not be one of those dentists who doesn't accept VISA®, Mastercard®, Discover®, and American Express®.

The service fee for all the programs is about the same. American Express may be a bit higher. (But, don't you want to make sure that you make payment easy for those American Express cardholders!) Depending on how much bankcard usage you do in your practice, you may be able to negotiate lower service fees with your bank. In addition, if you are a member of the ADA, very reasonable rates are accessible.

The minimal amount of service fee you pay for the bankcard usage is far less of a cost than either carrying the account on your own books or losing the case. Don't worry about the service charge. Running your own credit business is financially devastating and inadequate at best. Accept all the major cards (Fig. 3–2).

Do not be one of those dentists who has not informed her patients—on a regular basis—about the advantages of using a bankcard for the financing of dental care.

STATEMENT OF ACCOUNT

CHART NO.	PAGE NO.
HA0003	1

BILLING DATE
09/01/2004

John H. Jameson, DDS
P. O. Box 488
Davis, OK 73030

(580)369-2420

CREDIT CARD #__________ EXP.______

NAME__________
(As it appears on card)

GUARANTOR NAME AND MAILING ADDRESS

Julie Hanson
243 Willis Avenue
Okla. City, OK 73075

SIGNATURE__________

TYPE OF CARD__________

AMOUNT ENCLOSED
$

TO ENSURE PROPER CREDIT, PLEASE DETACH AND RETURN THIS PORTION OF THE STATEMENT WITH YOUR PAYMENT

PLEASE RETAIN THIS PORTION OF THE STATEMENT FOR YOUR RECORDS

DATE	DESCRIPTION	PATIENT'S NAME	CHARGES	CREDITS
08/01/2004	Balance Forward		0.00	
08/31/2004	Periodic oral evaluation	Julie	38.00	
08/31/2004	Prophylaxis-adult	Julie	69.00	

PRIOR BALANCE		CURRENT CREDITS		CURRENT CHARGES		NEW BALANCE
0.00	-	0.00	+	107.00	=	107.00

Insurance Estimates ("Ins. Est.") and "Please Pay" amounts based on insurance estimates are provided as a courtesy. In the event that y insurance carrier pays less than the estimated amount, you are responsible for the unpaid balance.

 DLSTM 5

John H. Jameson, DDS - P. O. Box 488
Davis, OK 73030 (580)369-2420

Fig. 3–1 Dentrix statement of accounts.

[YOUR COMPANY LOGO]

AUTOMATIC CARD BILLING AUTHORIZATION FORM

If you would like to enjoy the convenience of automatic billing to your Visa® card, simply fill out the information below. Upon approval, we will then automatically bill your primary Visa card (or the alternate card if the first one is declined for some reason) for amounts due. Your total charges will appear on your monthly statement. You may cancel this automatic billing authorization at any time by contacting us at [COMPANY ADDRESS].

Name on your [COMPANY NAME] account ____________________

Your [COMPANY NAME] account number ____________________

(   ) Home phone ____________________

(   ) Work phone ____________________

PRIMARY VISA CARD ACCOUNT

Name on Visa card (exactly as printed) ____________________

Billing address for Visa card (Street, Apt.#) ____________________

City, State, Zip ____________________

4 ____________________
Visa card number   Expiration date

Signature   Today's date

ALTERNATE VISA CARD ACCOUNT

Name on Visa card (exactly as printed) ____________________

Billing address for Visa card (Street, Apt.#) ____________________

City, State, Zip ____________________

4 ____________________
Visa card number   Expiration date

Signature   Today's date

I authorize [COMPANY NAME] to automatically bill one of the Visa cards listed above as specified below:

If your bill is for the same amount each [MONTH], check here and fill in transaction amount:
Bill my regular [MONTHLY] charge of $ _________ to my Visa card.

If your bill varies each [MONTH], check here:
Bill all [MONTHLY] charges to my Visa card. Since my payment amount varies each [MONTH], I will receive written notification of the amount and date of the next charge prior to each scheduled transaction date.

Please tell us how long you want us to automatically bill your Visa card.
This authorization is valid for the duration of my contract.
This authorization is valid until I provide you with written cancellation.

[INCLUDE ANY OF YOUR COMPANY'S DISCLAIMERS IN THE SPACE PROVIDED HERE.]

VISA

Fig. 3–2 Pre-authorization form.

Option #5.
Healthcare Financing Programs

These programs have become a tremendous asset to the dental industry by providing convenient financing for comprehensive—or immediate—care.

Use of these programs gets you, the dentist, out of the banking business while still allowing patients the opportunity to spread the payment of treatment out over several months. Monthly payments are small and fit comfortably into the family budget.

Many people need some financial assistance if they are to receive the treatment that is recommended to them. A study performed by the ADA asked the question, "If you needed to make a one-time dental purchase of $500, could you?" About 77% of the American population said, "no," that they could not afford a one time *out-of-pocket* dental purchase of $500 (77% of Americans!) You and I both know that $500 can't even buy a crown, let alone a root canal, post and core, and a crown. Most people live on budgets and care more about what the monthly payments will be than they care about the total investment. If they want the treatment and see the benefit of the treatment, they will want to know if they can make payments and how much they will pay per month.

That is why you must offer a payment option that (1) helps meet the financial needs of the people, (2) helps them to receive quality care, and (3) helps the practice to be financially solid. The answer is to offer a healthcare financing program to those folks who need financial assistance to access the necessary or desired care.

Example

A person comes into your office with some discomfort. You recommend endodontic therapy followed by a crown. We know that 77% of the people probably cannot afford that kind of necessary treatment unless their insurance company is going to pay the vast majority of it or they have some method of *paying it out*. They aren't saying, "I don't want this treatment."They are asking for help—financial help. They are saying, "Help me find a solution to my problem—my money problem." If you have done a good job of presenting the dentistry, and they want the treatment, they may just need a way to pay for it.

However, if you become the bank and if you loan the patient the money for the treatment, you add a costly dimension to your practice—you open a banking business within the practice, and most dental professionals are not financial, business, or banking experts. They are dental professionals and are better off doing what they know best—dentistry—and turning the financing over to professionals in that field.

I often ask the following series of questions in my lectures when I am discussing financing: "If you provide dental treatment for patients, and they do not pay you in full so you begin sending statements, and they begin making monthly payments to you, is that a loan? Are you loaning money to your patients?"

Everyone nods in agreement.

So, I continue by asking the following questions, "So, if you are loaning money to your patients, let me ask you a few questions: How many of you have a person in your office who has professional banking training and experience?" A few hands might go up.

"How many of you have a person in your office who has professional collection training?" A couple of hands usually go up.

"And how about professional training as lending officers?" I've yet to see a hand.

"How many of you do a credit check when you are loaning your patients money?" A few hand might go up.

"How many of you are charging a *carrying charge* or a late payment fee?" A few hands go up.

Then, I make this statement: "So, let me use deductive reasoning here. Most of you are loaning your patients money for services you have provided but you are doing so without a credit check and with no service fee being charged. You have marvelous people on your team who are exceptional in many ways. However, for the most part, these fabulous team members are not professional loan officers, bankers, or collection experts. So, when is the last time you received an interest-free loan, and the issue of whether or not you paid was being managed by someone with no training in this area?"

Think about it. Does that make any sense? This is not a criticism of your team members. Let them focus on what they do best—providing great care and attention to your patients. Let them build relationships and and build your practice. Have them focus on helping patients make a decision to go ahead with treatment rather than have them spend their time running a banking business in your practice.

How many patients come to the business office and say, "I really want this treatment. I know I need this. Can I pay it out or can I make payments to you? The minute the patient says, "Doctor, can I pay this out?" or "Doctor, can you just send me statements for this?" and you say, "yes," then you become a lending institution and you add to the overhead of your practice—significantly. Ultimately, it is not financially wise for you to run a banking business within your practice. However, most people need long-term financing to be able to receive any extensive treatment. Thus, for any long-term or extended payment, offer a healthcare financing program.

A healthcare financing system does the following:

1. **Provides financial assistance for healthcare only.** It is not a service that is in competition with other bankcards. It is not in competition with food, entertainment, clothes, or vacations, etc. This type of program allows families and individuals to establish a line of credit for healthcare.

2. **Offers lower payments.** People can receive needed or desired care, the best available, but make small monthly payments and spread those payments out over a comfortable length of time, dependent upon how much they can afford to pay per month. Thus, the total investment does not become such an enormous barrier. Accessing a comfortable monthly investment becomes the solvable challenge.

3. **Provides convenience.** People do not have to go to a location outside the office to apply for this line of credit. They apply right there in your office. The dentist pays all necessary enrollment fees and there is no annual fee.

4. **Works in conjunction with insurance.** If a patient has dental insurance but cannot afford the co-pay, the patient can place the co-pay on his financing program. He can use the healthcare financing program in conjunction with his dental insurance. This will let him better use the insurance benefits that have already been paid.

5. **Gives you a means for collection.** These financing programs also have pre-authorizations so that patients can give you permission to place any balance after insurance pays on their line of credit, or they can give you permission to place regular monthly payments on their line of credit. Once a person gets involved with one of these financing programs, be sure to get a signed pre-authorization form in the chart to use in either one of these situations.

The following are several kinds of healthcare financing options that I encourage you to have in place:

1. A revolving payment plan. With this option, a person or family establishes a line of credit with the financing company. All members of the family can participate. The person or family is required to pay a minimum payment per month—just like a bankcard. The minimum payment is, usually, about 3% of the outstanding balance. So, for $1,000 worth of dental care, if a patient—or family—can afford $30 per month, they can receive treatment. And, I think we will all agree that most people can afford $30 per month.

The line of credit belongs to the person or family. If they use the credit line, that means that less credit is available. However, as they make monthly payments, that credit is opened up again. If a family maxes out their limit but finds that they need some additional care, you can—or the patient can—request an expanded line of credit. If the family wants to pay the account off early or make higher payments than is required, that is just fine. There is no penalty for prepayment. Again, this option applies to individuals or families.

2. Interest Free Payment Plans. This option has been available for quite some time now and is popular with patients for the obvious reason of the interest free aspect. The various financing companies have different ways of offering this option to your patients. There are some programs that offer 3, 6, or 12 months with no interest, and other programs that offer the interest-free program for up to 18 or 24 months.

Again, depending on the company, there is usually a minimum payment per month required. This is quite small—ranging 2–3% of the outstanding balance. The companies require that the patient pay the account in full by the designated time allotment or the patient will drop back into the revolving payment program and will need to pay all back interest that would have accumulated if the patient had been on the revolving program in the first place.

Tell the patient, "You have a *safety net* and if for any reason you cannot complete payment by the predetermined time frame you can just continue to pay the minimum payment per month. The only requirement would be that you pay all service fees that have, heretofore, been waived."

Another *perk* of this type of payment plan is that if the patient needs further treatment, she can add on these new charges to the existing account without needing to reapply.

3. **Extended Payment Plans.** For more extensive cases, the financing companies have introduced the extended payment plans. These plans cover treatment fees that range from $1,000–$25,000 (although exceptions can be made). Fixed monthly payments are established for the patient. The length of time for the payments depends on how much a patient can pay per month. The companies are offering these extended payment programs of 24–60 months.

These extended payment plans are great for your large comprehensive restorative, implant, and/or cosmetic cases.

You receive fabulous patient educational materials from these companies and support data for your office. The monthly payments and the various lengths of payout are clearly defined for you so that making a financial arrangement and being accurate in providing information for your patients is quite easy.

These programs have made it possible for hundreds of thousands of people to proceed with major treatment that might not have been able to do so otherwise. Again, most people are more interested in how much something costs per month than they are interested in the total amount. If someone wants treatment and the fee fits into their monthly income, the chances of them proceeding are enhanced greatly.

The interest rate is low for your patients. Your service fee—the fee you pay these experts to manage the credit portion of your practice is nothing compared to the cost of you carrying the account on your own books. (See chapter 4.) As with the interest-free payment plan, a patient can place additional treatment fees on her program without needing to reapply.

I will be explaining the healthcare financing programs in more depth in the next chapter. Here, however, I wanted to open the door for conversation about this necessary option. The following key recommendations relate to this option:

1. Study the various companies and get involved with one that you believe will work best for you.

2. Take as much time as is necessary to train on how to administer the program and how to present it.

3. Make sure that you are maximizing your opportunities and the patient's opportunities. Don't get involved and then put the materials in a drawer and never offer this option to your patients. Or, don't offer it to only those patients who can't do anything else. Offer the program

to everyone. People who buy a Mercedes Benz often buy one because they can afford the monthly payments.

Also, don't offer your program a couple of times, have patients turned down for a line of credit, and then never offer it again saying that it doesn't work. The programs work. Most practices don't work the program. (See chapter 5.) Keep offering the program. The law of averages will work in your favor.

There are different types of healthcare financing programs. (See Appendix A for a partial listing of available companies.) The programs listed are nonrecourse, which means that if the patient doesn't pay, you are not responsible for the account. That is the only kind of program with which to get involved—a nonrecourse program.

What if the patient doesn't get accepted? So, you say, "Terrific. But what if the patient doesn't get accepted. Then what?" Some offices have become involved with a healthcare financing program but have become discouraged because they see the benefit of such a financial service, recommend the service, get people to fill out the applications, only to have patients denied. In fact, these offices may get so discouraged with the programs that they are afraid to present this option at all.

There may be several reasons why a program may not have worked well for you in the past. But, please consider looking at these programs with a new light and a new level of encouragement. Without a strong financial program that includes third-party financing, you will stifle your own growth, productivity, and enjoyment.

The key to the success of your financing program is how well you manage the program in your office. The programs work and work well. It doesn't matter what part of the country you live in or how large your city or town may be. We have seen these financing programs make a 4–38% difference in a practice's revenue stream—and it doesn't matter where a practice is located. What matters is how well the practice promotes and administers the program.

Look at the list of companies in the appendix of this book. Contact the companies and gather information of each. Study the variances of the programs carefully. Determine the one that will work best for you. Access their materials and study these intricately. Then, schedule training with the company and get the entire team involved with that training. Once the training has been completed, hold a team meeting where you practice the verbal skills of presenting the program and overcoming objections to it. Study chapter 5 on the "Ways to Maximize a Healthcare Financing Program" and go to work to integrate all these *ways* into your practice.

However, no matter how well you administer the system into your practice, not every patient will get accepted. There will be some people who will not be extended a line of credit. The fact that the company will be doing a very careful credit rating and screening of the patient will help you to make better business decisions about financing your dentistry. If a patient is not granted a line of credit by a professional financing company, ask yourself this question, "Do we want to make a loan to this patient if the professional financial people are unwilling to do so?"

Probably not. Rather, you may need to back off the treatment plan just a bit and provide treatment based on the patient's ability to pay as they go—or *payment by the appointment*. You want to do as much dentistry as possible without financially stressing the patient or you.

If you find that a patient has not received a line of credit, ask him if he could get a family member to cosign with him. I cannot tell you how many of our patients were able to get a line of credit because a family member or a close friend was willing to cosign. Sometimes people are placed in a financial predicament that they didn't create (such as some divorces where one of the party's credit is tarnished and that affects the former spouse). Give people a chance to get healthy and to reestablish a good credit rating. Don't give up too soon.

Another way to deal with the patient who is not granted a line of credit is to do *layaway dentistry*. This means that the patient makes monthly payments to you. You place these payments in an account as a growing *credit*. Then, when he/she has the money saved, you can proceed with the dentistry.

Many times we do *just because* dentistry. John provides care for a person just because. He would rather provide free care as a chosen *love gift* instead of making an unrealistic financial arrangement with a person only to be disappointed or to be placed in a costly situation of having to try to collect an uncollectable account.

In certain situations, we refer patients to the dental school for care by the students. These students will, of course, provide excellent care. This is an excellent service to both the indigent family and to the students.

If a patient doesn't receive a line of credit from your healthcare financing program, address that issue in the following way:

BA: Ms. Jones, our financial partner has let us know that at this time they are not able to extend a line of credit to you. You may, certainly, contact the company to discuss this. We encourage you to do so. Many times there is incorrect information on a credit report and this would give you a chance to update your report. However, for now, let's discuss other financial possibilities so that you don't have to put off this needed care.

Do not use the terms *approved* or *not approved* with your patients. These are demeaning phrases and can cause major embarrassment for your patients. Embarrassment is a primary emotion which—when stimulated—can appear as anger. Be careful with how you handle this issue. People do not like to feel rejected. Great communication is essential here.

Option #6.
Banking and Lending Institutions

Historically, banks and other types of lending instutitions were not generous with their *loans* to dental patients. However, now there is more acceptance of health-oriented loans from these professionals.

Patients that are receiving significant amounts of dental care can go to their bank to access a loan. If a person does this and pays you in full, give her the 5% accounting reduction. This will help her with the interest she will be paying to her bank.

Some people may choose to get a home equity loan to cover the fee for treatment. With this type of equity loan, the interest in deductible and the monthly payments are usually acceptable.

In addition, there are numerous financial or lending institutions other than banks that are making loans for dental care. Working similarly to the healthcare financing programs, the patient receives a diagnosis and a treatment plan, she completes the necessary paperwork in your office or makes a telephone call directly to the company (it depends on the company or organization), and the company will make a loan for the amount requested. Again, depending on the financial institution, there are various methods of repayment: three months same as cash, up to 12–24 months interest free, or a traditional loan where monthly payments are determined by the desired—and accepted—monthly repayments.

These, too, are great programs, and depending on the area of the country and the location within a state, the acceptance rate can be quite high. Each branch handles its dental accounts differently. So schedule an appointment with the branch manager, tell her what you want to do for your patients and see if she would be interested. These companies are not just in the healthcare business but they know that healthcare is big business and can be a boom to their organization. Also, they like *getting in good* with the patients so that when they need money for other kinds of loans they might consider their company. Again, see the appendix for a partial listing of financial institutions that will consider your patient's needs.

Option #7.
Insurance Management

Although this is not truly a financial option, I decided to address insurance briefly here. I will address it more fully in a chapter dedicated to insurance.

It is my hope that you will consider the following:

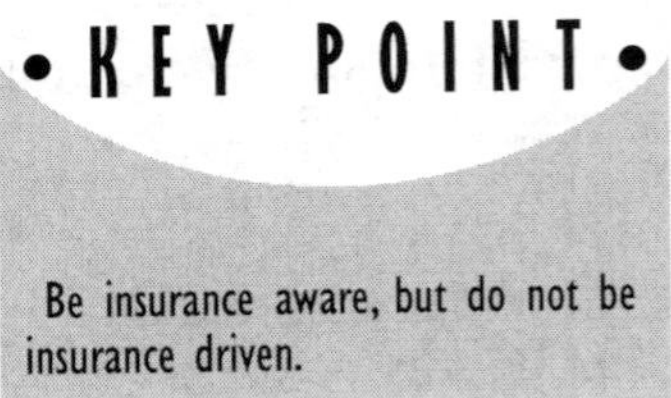

• KEY POINT •
Be insurance aware, but do not be insurance driven.

Certainly, dental insurance has been an asset to the profession and to many people who could not or would not receive dental treatment if they did not have financial support from their insurance plan. However, we all know that insurance is not a pay-all but is a supplement to healthcare.

You are not required to file insurance for a patient. If you do so, this is a service to your patient. That is fine. But be aware—as a team—that you are not required to do so. The contract is between the patient and the insurance company.

Ideally, if a patient has dental insurance, you would collect the entire fee, file the claim for the patient (electronically is preferred), and let the insurance company reimburse the patient directly. The patient can use any of the previously mentioned options for paying for treatment and will receive a reimbursement check quickly—probably more quickly than you would!

If you have chosen to accept assignment of benefits of insurance claims, collect the expected co-pay or estimated patient's portion at the time of service, file the claim, and then, manage the insurance aspect of your practice with care and consistency.

Please see chapter 9 on insurance management for a full directive on this complex subject.

Option #8.
Electronic Funds Transfer

Companies are emerging throughout the country that assist you in accessing regular withdrawals from a patient's checking account. In addition, your bank would, more than likely, work with you to establish this program.

These programs do put a portion of the costs of carrying accounts into the hands of professionals. However, the patients will be more likely to cover these withdrawals from a professional service and their bank than they would be inclined to send you a check following the receipt of your statement. In fact, about 97% of these electronic funds transfer (EFT) payments clear.

The patient completes the necessary paperwork. Together you agree upon the date of the withdrawal as well as the designated amount. The paperwork is given to the appropriate bank. Then, withdrawals begin.

People are familiar with this type of payment option. Many home mortgage, car, and savings plan programs are a withdrawal system. Certainly, specific criteria must be in place. But, for the most part, everyone has a checking account and can place a withdrawal program into effect. If a withdrawal does not clear, the bank will put it through again. Any charges will be filed against the patient.

Another type of bank account withdrawal program establishes a system of pre-authorized checking (PAC). Patients choose the date of payment, the amount of payment, and the appropriate checking account to be accessed. Checks are produced. The dental practice holds the pre-authorized checks in the office until the designated date of deposit. Then the check is sent in. If an emergency does arise, a patient can call the office and ask that the check deposit be delayed for a specific period of time. Certain programs also allow for *over-the-phone* checks to be produced.

While these programs do not put the money into your hands at the beginning of treatment, like the other options, they do eliminate the sending of statements and need for collections. You do not wait for payments, operating costs are reduced, case acceptance will increase because of the elimination of the cost barrier, and your team can focus on practice building. Check into these programs.

What If an Emergency Needs Financial Assistance? If a person comes to your practice in an emergency situation, use the following protocols:

- Determine, on the phone, if the patient is an emergency. Use a patient communication slip to gather necessary information. Then, if the patient does have an emergency situation, see the person that day (Fig. 3–3).
- If this is a new patient, let the patient know that he will be expected to pay the fee for the emergency visit at the time of the service. This is one of the only times to quote a fee over the phone. But the patient does need to know the fee and be expecting to pay the fee that day. Even if he has insurance, collect the fee, give him the necessary paperwork, and let him file his own insurance. Then you can gather necessary data about his insurance plan, do a verification of insurance coverage, and file his insurance at the next appointment if you choose.
- Let the patient know that if the dentist needs to provide treatment, there will be a financial discussion before any treatment is rendered and that the patient will not be put in a position for any financial surprises.
- If the person indicates a concern about finances, inform him of your financial options. If the patient is uncomfortable with cash payments and does not have a bankcard, introduce your healthcare financing program. Ask the patient to come in earlier than the scheduled time to complete an application. Then, while the patient is waiting to be

PATIENT COMMUNICATION SLIP

Date: ______ New Patient _ Patient of Recorder _ Adult _ Child _ Age ______

Name: ______ ______ (Pronounced)

Referred By: ______ Family Member _ Friend _ Parent/Guardian of Child: ______

Address: ______ (Street) (City) (State) (Zip)

Daytime Phone: ______ Home Phone: ______

Work Phone: ______ Email Address: ______

Purpose of Call

Emergency _ How long? ______

Where is the problem located? ______

Swelling? ______

Sensitive to hot/cold? ______

Other: ______

Pre-medication Necessary: ______

Employer: ______

Insurance Carrier: ______

Policy Number: ______

Comments: ______

New Patient Evaluation_ Last time seen by a dentist? ______

Date of FMX: ______ Doctor's Name: ______

Explain scenario of new patient evaluation: ______

1. Hard & soft tissue evaluation: ______
2. Necessary Radiographs: ______
3. No cleaning: ______
4. Statement of philosophy: ______
5. Question & Answer: ______
6. Statement of payment expectations: ______
7. New Patient Packet Sent: ______

Fig. 3–3 Patient communication slip.

seated, or certainly before the dentist renders any treatment beyond the emergency care, process the application. You will know whether or not he has been extended a line of credit and, if so, for how much. (You can process these applications on the Internet).

This is valuable information. You do not know this person. You do not need to make a loan to a stranger! However, you do want to provide the necessary care. By establishing a line of credit with your financing company, both of these needs are fulfilled—they receive needed care, and you receive reimbursement.

- If the patient comes in for the emergency visit and the dentist diagnoses necessary treatment and wants to go ahead with that treatment while the patient is there, the following two things must be in place:

    1. You must have the time to render that treatment without that having a negative effect on your regularly scheduled patients. If you do not have the time, diagnose, prescribe treatment, get the patient comfortable, and reschedule him for the necessary length of time. A trauma case would be an exception. Otherwise, you need to respect the time of your regularly scheduled patients. Palliative treatment only.

    2. Inform the patient of the financial responsibility before treatment is rendered. Patients want to know what is expected of them financially before the fact. In addition, you run the risk of acquiring a bad debt if you do not handle the financial aspect of an emergency visit as carefully as you handle the clinical aspects.

If the patient is in the chair and you diagnose necessary treatment, check to see if you do have time to provide that treatment. If you do, have the BA step back to the clinical area to discuss the fee and the options for payment. If the patient needs financial assistance, get an application for your financial program, help him to complete the application, then, fax, email, use the Internet or call with the information to your particular company. You will know in a matter of minutes whether or not the patient has been extended that line of credit and for how much. Then, let the dentist know that he can go ahead with the treatment or there needs to be a consideration of another alternative.

This procedure only takes a few minutes and can make a big difference in your financial security. If you analyze your accounts receivable carefully, you may find that a significant portion of those accounts may be emergency patients who never had a financial arrangement made and who never paid.

You are there to work with the patient. It's OK for them to be asked to work with you.

How Do You Get Started with a Financial Program?

There are many excellent programs on the market today. Gather the information on the programs listed in the appendix and any others that you may know. Write or call the companies for a packet of material. Study that information. Add this service to your practice. Your challenge is to do enough research to find out which program will fit your practice, your geographic area, and your socioeconomic situation.

There is a service fee for these programs. After you read the next chapter, you will see that the service fee is miniscule compared to how much it costs for you to carry accounts on your own books. There are significant differences in the service fee that each company charges the dentist. The differences are related to the amount of risk or the number of patients that a company is willing and able to approve for credit. The higher the risk, the higher the service fee. You must determine how much of your practice population needs long-term financing in order to receive the dental care and how much you are willing to invest to make that happen.

You will be making an investment in the service fee. However, in the next chapter, I will prove beyond a shadow of a doubt, that the service fee will be less than it is costing you right now to run a banking business in your own practice.

As You Begin to Make This Change

It will be a much easier to inform your new patients of your financial options than it will be to reeducate your existing patient family. In a following chapter, I review several ways to introduce your existing patient population to the financial options—both in writing and in your verbal skills.

However, you may want to inform your existing patient family of the changes in a special mailing before those changes begin. I would recommend that you do this. In a special letter, introduce your patient family to the new financial options, concentrating on how these options will benefit them (Fig. 3–4). Mail this letter 30 days before you make the changes in protocol. This will help your BA make a smooth transition. Then, as patients are flowing through the practice, introduce them to the options.

Dear Patient Friends,

Containing the costs of healthcare has been a subject of great interest to all of us over the last few years. We, too, are interested in containing costs so that you and your family can receive quality, individualized care.

Experts in the field of management have helped us learn new and better ways to serve our patients while remaining constant in our commitment to excellent dental care. After a thorough analysis of our practice, experts made many recommendations. One of those recommendations was to offer a series of financial options to our patients so that the financing of their dental care would be comfortable. Also, we learned that offering these financial options will help us to maintain reasonable fees.

Our costs of operation are soaring. But, we do not want to lower our standards of care and we do not want to go sky high with our fees. Therefore, we are implementing the following financial protocol starting on (insert date here). This protocol will offer numerous ways for you to handle the financial responsibility of your dental care.

We believe that this protocol will prove to be a service to you and to your family.

1. A 5% reduction in your fee if you pay for services in advance of treatment. (This reduction applies to treatment of a certain amount or more.)

2. Payment by the appointment. (This option lets you spread out the payments according to your treatment plan.)

3. Bankcards. (This option will let you budget your payments comfortably.)

4. Insurance on assignment. (We will file your insurance as a service to you and will do our very best to maximize your benefits. We accept assignment of benefits to lower your immediate 'out of pocket' expenditures. We ask that you take care of your estimated co-pay at the time of service.)

5. 3 to 18-month interest-free financing through our financing partner, ABC Financial Company.

6. For any long term or extended payments we offer ABC. (ABC is a financing program for dentistry that lets you make small monthly payments spreading those payments out over a desired period of time.)

These financial options will meet the needs of most families in our practice. We want to be flexible in changing times. We have listened to your concerns and have made great efforts to respond to those concerns. We will do our very best to work out a financial solution for your particular situation. We are here to help you.

Yours for Better Dental Health,

Fig. 3–4 Financial options letter.

Summary

An essential step in gaining control of the financial *system* in your practice is to establish a written financial protocol—one that offers flexibility for your patient's needs and convenience, and one that offers firmness for the financial security of your practice. The previously recommended financial protocol meets the needs of the vast majority of people. People who have healthy savings and checking accounts are offered an incentive to pay in advance. People who want to take care of their payments as treatment proceeds are offered that option. Those who have dental insurance are assisted. Patients who need long-term payments to be able to go ahead with treatment are offered either a bankcard, a healthcare financing program, a loan from a banking or financial institution, or an electronic fund transfer.

Promote bankcards to the fullest degree. Get involved with a healthcare financing program. Use the instruction in the upcoming chapters not only to learn how to present but also how to build your practice with these programs. They are wonderful services for your patients, services that will lead to customer/patient satisfaction, increased new patient flow, and reduced cost of operation.

Work together as a team to determine your financial protocol. Get comfortable with presenting the options. Know that your patients' comfort with your protocol will be a direct reflection of your own comfort.

• CHAPTER •

4

Becoming Involved with a Healthcare Financing Program: Getting out of the Banking Business

There's a way to do it better—find it!

– Thomas A. Edison

Understanding the credit business as it applies to dentistry may be a tedious study. However, clarity in this vital part of your practice will help you to make the following decisions:

- To get out of the banking business and not look back.
- To reduce the amount of money you are spending on the statement and collection portion of your practice.
- To get involved with a healthcare financing program ASAP.
- To be more confident in presenting the program to your patients.
- To build your practice without increasing the overhead in the area of financial management.

Cost of Credit

In the following section, I will outline the cost of carrying accounts on your own books. It costs a great deal to carry accounts on your own books. You are not a bank and, no matter how much you are producing, it costs too much to carrry accounts on your own books or to loan money to your patients.

I will be using generic figures for this illustration. Each practice has its own production figures, so a generalized illustration is imperative. However, the percentages that are included in the calculations are relevant to every practice. Pay close attention to the percentages and apply these to your own practice. The percentages are what make the difference.

Sample Practice

The accompanying illustration represents a practice that is producing $600,000 per year. You will need to get a calculator and do a little math to make these figures appropriate for your own practice.

According to the ADA and Dr. T. Warren Center, the founder and president of The Help Card, the average dental practice receives approximately 50% of its revenue in the form of an insurance check. If a dental practice has a potential gross annual revenue of $600,000, that would mean approximately $300,000 of that practice's revenue would be coming from insurance reimbursement.

About 30% of the income for most dental practices would come from cash, check, or bankcard. For a $600,000 practice that means that about $180,000 of income would come in the form of cash across the counter.

This leaves a remaining 20% that is the credit business, the credit portion of the practice, or the billed charges portion of the business. These are the people with whom you make a financial agreement to make payments directly to the practice. These are the people to whom you begin sending statements and doing your own collections. These monies become your private pay accounts receivable. In our example of the $600,000 practice, this represents approximately $120,000 worth of yearly revenue.

The ADA and *Dental Economics* magazine tell us that the average practice in the United States collects approximately 96%. This means that the average dental practice is writing off about 4% or suffers a 4% loss. You may think that is not too bad—96% collection or a 4% loss—not bad, so you think (Fig. 4–1).

Value Analysis Example	
Annual Gross Revenue	$600,000
Insurance (50%)	$300,000
Cash & major credit cards (30%)	$180,000
Billed Charges (20%)	$120,000
Uncollected Revenue - % of Gross	4%
% of Billed Charges	20%
Statements Per Month	250
Average American Dental Practice Collects	96%

Fig. 4–1 Value analysis example.

Well, let's look at that 4% loss and really look at it with open eyes. It becomes important to identify where the loss is coming from and what that loss really means to the profitability of your practice.

Go back to that average $600,000 practice that is experiencing a 4% write-off. Four percent of $600,000 is $24,000. This dentist would, more than likely, write off $24,000. Now answer these questions. Did the loss come from the $300,000 that was insurance? I doubt it. You may have a little bit of difficulty getting a quick turnaround on insurance. But you do receive payment. Does the 4% loss come from the portion of the practice that is cash across the counter? Probably not. You may have a check bounce every once in a while, but that is not going to have a strong effect on your percentages.

So, if the loss did not come from insurance and it did not come from cash across the counter, there is only one place from which the loss could have come. That is the portion of the practice where you are carrying accounts for patients.

People may not intend to become past-due with their accounts. A patient may say, "I will pay you $100 a month."

Then that becomes difficult for them, and they begin to pay $50 a month. Then something happens and that becomes $20 a month. Then they may miss a month or two and well, you can see that the account that you thought was going to be a 3-month account, is now a 6-, 9-, 12-month account, or you don't collect it at all.

The world of banking lists 36 payables that a family takes care of when they receive their check or checks each month and then outlines the order in which these entities are paid. The first thing a family pays is their house payment or rent. Next, the food and utilities. Then, the car payment—if there is one. The next payment is to the credit card folks—the plastic. The dentist is 35th out of 36. (The veterinarian is last, although this is changing because vets are becoming cash only.) Patients think—"Oh, the dentist is rich and doesn't need my money." Or "They are busy. They won't notice if I miss this payment." Or "They never call or require me to pay anyway, so I'll just ignore this for a while." And the latter is probably true. Most practices do not have a steadfast method of collecting payments that are due or past due and don't make this a priority. I am hoping to change your mind about that.

> **• KEY POINT •**
>
> In the order of being paid, the dentist is 35th out of 36.
>
> Approximately 20% of the credit portion of the average dental practice is being lost as an uncollectible account.

Therefore, we know that if a person or family is having difficulty making ends meet that the dentist may not be a payment priority. I'm not saying that this is good, I'm just saying that this is the way it is. That is why the majority of loss experienced during a year is from the credit portion of your business.

Let's look closer at that loss. More than likely, the entire $24,000 is coming from the $120,000 that is being carried on the practice's books. The $24,000 is 20% of the $120,000 credit business. In essence, this practice is having a 4% total loss of revenue but is having a 20% loss in its credit business.

Direct Cost of Billing and Collecting

Now let's analyze how much it costs to run a credit business within your own practice. If you are sending an average of 250 statements a month, you're going to be investing approximately $1,750/year in materials alone—stamps, envelopes, statements, computer materials, etc.

If you send 250 statements a month and you are paying a person $12 an hour to handle this portion of your practice, and if this person is spending about two minutes on each statement, you are investing approximately $13,500 per year in the labor costs of preparing and sending statements and in time invested in collection management.

If you are carrying accounts and if you are managing the collection of those accounts effectively, you are probably doing some collection calls. Based on a very conservative $40 a month for collection calls (which would be part of the office phone bill), that is $480 per year in telephone expense.

Adding these costs together—labor, materials, and telephone—the cost of billing and collecting for this $600,000 practice is $16,030 (minimally). That's 13% of the credit portion of this practice. No matter what the total gross production for your practice, these percentages remain the same. Again, if you are not taking assignment of benefits, these figures would be altered accordingly (Fig. 4–2).

Direct Cost of Billing and Collecting

Materials & Postage	$1750/year
Labor	$13,800/year
Long Distance Calls/Phone Expense	$480/year
Total	**$16,030**

13% **of Billed Charges**

© *Dr. T. Warren Center*

Fig. 4–2 Direct cost of billing and collecting.

Receivable Management Costs

There is another cost that goes along with managing accounts receivable. In addition to the $24,000 in write-offs or uncollectibles, there is one more cost. The world of banking tells us that for every month that an account sits on your own books doing nothing for you that it loses approximately .83% of its worth—or a 10% loss during the year. This is called *the loss of the dollar.* If you have an average total collection of $120,000 per year in accounts receivable or billed charges, approximately 50% of those total accounts will be sitting on your books at one time, rolling over throughout the months.

So, 50% of the total annual collection of billed charges for our sample practice would be $60,000 sitting on the books each month. If you lose 10% of the worth of that money, that represents a loss of $6,000—10% of $60,000.

If you could have had that money in hand, you could have either invested it or serviced debts. Then your money would have been working for you rather than decreasing in value.

Let's add all of that up. Remember, this practice had a $24,000 loss from the write-off of uncollectibles. Now we see that there is a $6,000 loss of the dollar. That equals $30,000. That's 25% of the credit portion of your practice (Fig. 4–3).

Receivables Management Cost

Accounts Receivable 10% of 60,000	$6000
Uncollected Revenue 20% of $120,000	$24,000
Total Receivable Management Cost for Billed Charges	**$30,000**
	25% of Billed Charges

© *Dr. T. Warren Center*

Fig. 4–3 Receivables management cost.

A $30,000 figure in receivables management plus the $16,030 direct cost of billing and collecting equals $46,030. That is how much it costs a $600,000 practice to run a credit business during a year's period of time. What percentage is $46,030 of the $120,000 credit business? $46,030 is 38% of this practice's credit business (Fig. 4–4)

Total Cost of Billed Charges

Direct Billing and Collecting	$16,030/year
Accounts Receivable Management	$30,000/year
Total	**$46,030/year**
	38% of Billed Revenue

© *Dr. T. Warren Center*

Fig. 4–4 Total cost of billing and collecting.

Let that soak in just a minute—38%. The average general dental practice has an overhead of 65–70%—(or more according to some surveys). If it costs 38% to manage the credit aspect of the practice and the overhead of the practice is 65–70%, guess what? You're breaking even or losing money on the portion of your practice that is credit business. That makes no sense.

The specialists who are managing the healthcare financing programs have the professional ability to collect gently but firmly with the persistence that must be applied to obtain effective collection.

• KEY POINT •

Get out of the banking business. Put the banking aspect or the credit aspect of your business into the hands of professionals—professional people who spend every day working with patients and their accounts.

Again, referring to the ADA, *approximately 30.8% of the people in the United States have not visited the dentist or gone to a dental clinic in the past year.*

According to the ADA's Survey Center's "Public Opinion Surveys," here are the "main reasons that people had for not going to the dentist more often" (Fig. 4–5).

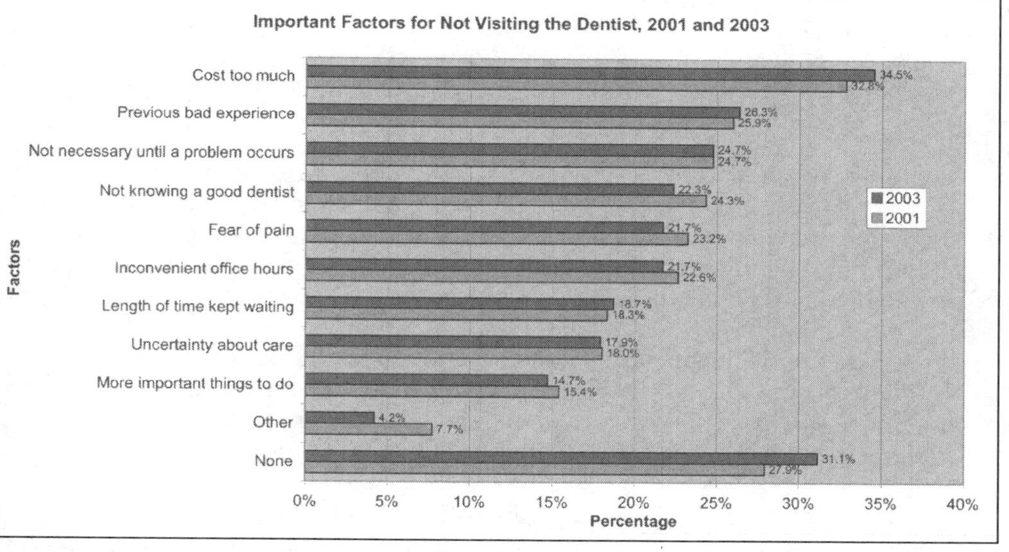

Fig. 4–5 Important factors for not visiting the dentist. *Source: American Dental Association, Survey Center,* Public Opinion Surveys

It costs too much. There is the No. 1 reason for people not seeking dental care. Could we also say that this is the No. 1 reason for not accepting the treatment once it has been presented? Probably.

Therefore, let's use deductive reasoning. This area of the practice—making the financing of dentistry comfortable—becomes all the more imperative.

Offering a healthcare financing program will help both you and your patients deal with the *it-costs-too-much* barrier. Patients will be able to accept treatment that otherwise might be rejected or delayed. You will be able to increase production significantly because of your ability to overcome the barrier of cost. Both parties win.

Also, if you are able to accomplish more dentistry per appointment and see the patient for fewer visits, that helps both parties to deal with the real issue of *time*. The survey also shows that time is a concern to people—convenient hours, not having to wait, having more important things to do. Being able to schedule longer appointments doing more dentistry per appointment when and where appropriate reduces the amount of time and the number of visits a person needs to make.

And, certainly, practicing this way is a very profitable way to practice dentistry. And that's what you want—to practice in not only a productive manner—but also a profitable manner.

How Do These Programs Work?

Think of these companies and the professionals who manage these accounts as your *financial partner.* You are going to pay a salary (in essence) to a professional organization and to qualified people to manage the credit portion of your practice. Spend your time doing what you do best—dentistry. Let the pros handle the money management for your patients.

The available healthcare financing programs are different in protocol, but the vast majority of them are going to have a service charge. That service charge ranges between 4 and 15%. Many practitioners think, "Oh, no, that's terrible. That's too much. I'm not going to pay that much."

However, look at this is a new light. By carrying accounts on your own books, it is costing you approximately 38%. You don't even have to put a pencil to it to realize that if a company will handle or manage the credit aspect of your practice for 4–15%, that you are saving an incredible amount of money in overhead. Instead of 38%, it is going to cost you 4–15%.

This is essential in a dental practice as overhead continues to climb on a regular basis. It doesn't make any sense to try to increase the productivity in the practice without watching the overhead as well. Then, and only then, can you begin to realize profitability. It's not how much you produce that makes the difference, it's how much you collect and keep.

When you have diagnosed necessary or desired treatment and are discussing the financial responsibility, payment options need to be discussed. If a person indicates that she needs to make small payments and spread those payments out over a period of time, you would introduce your financing program.

Example

BA: Ms. Jones, I understand that you feel concerned about the investment you will be making. Many of our patients have felt the same concern until they found out that we do offer long-term financing in our practice. We have a financial partner, ABC Financing Company. You complete an application right here in our practice—you don't have to go anywhere. Once you have completed the application, we can provide the necessasy information to the company to see about establishing a line of credit for you. Once that line of credit is established, we can begin your treatment. You will then be able to make small monthly payments and spread the payments over a long period of time. You will only be required to make a minimum payment each month. Dr. Jameson has paid all necessary fees for you to become involved, and there is no annual fee. Therefore, you only pay for the service when you use it.

Once the patient is extended a line of credit, you will finance her dentistry. In some cases, a charge slip is filled out as service is rendered. In other cases, you submit for the entire treatment plan and are paid in advance. Those slips are then sent to the company for processing or are sent by electronic means directly to the company. Then you will receive payment for the services that you have provided, minus the service fee. Most of the time, the funds are electronically placed into your bank account. Direct deposit is, usually, available.

The patient begins making payments to the financing program. She no longer owes the dentist. If the patient defaults on the account for any reason at all, the dentist is in no way, shape, or form, responsible for the account ever again. The programs are nonrecourse and place the dentist at no risk whatsoever.

Remember, the scenario of the $600,000 practice? Historically, dental practices have been writing off approximately 20% of the credit portion of their revenues. But if you allow a professional financing company to handle that portion of your practice—the credit portion—you will not experience that kind of loss.

Example

Take a $1,000 charge, and let's say the service fee to you is 5%. You would receive a check for $950. That would be the end of that. You would not send statements. You would not handle collection issues. You would receive your money. Think of this service fee as the salary you are paying the company to work for you. They are your financial partner and teammate. These are excellent programs and deserve your careful study and attention.

While working with more than 2,000 dental practices, we at JMI have seen significant increases in productivity when a practice uses a financing program well. We help practices not only get involved with patient financing but also learn how to use the programs effectively. We have seen practice productivity increase 4–38% from the use of patient financing alone.

Why? Because there is a portion of the population that needs this type of financing in order to make a major investment, like that $500 dental treatment. So, not only will you be saving money in cost of operation in the credit aspect of your practice, you will be making it possible for a portion of your patient family to go ahead with treatment that would not otherwise be able to do so.

If I asked you how much dentistry you had sitting in your charts waiting to be done, what would you say? Many dentists say that they have more dentistry sitting in their charts than they have ever provided. Offering this type of program will get some of that dentistry out of the charts and into the mouths of your patients.

The ADA says that for every 10 years that a dentist provides dental care, that he has approximately $1,000,000 worth of dentistry that has been diagnosed but remains undone. Approximately $100,000 per year.

In our own dental practice, we place approximately $100,000 of dental care per year on our financing program. My dentist husband, John, believes that this would be $100,000 worth of dental treatment that he would not otherwise be able to provide were we not able to offer convenient financing. We feel that there are many people who are receiving excellent care who would not have been able to do so if we were not making this option available to them. He is not one of those statistics that says that he has $1,000,000 worth of dentistry sitting in his charts. In the first 10 years that we participated with a healthcare financing program, we placed $1,000,000 on that program.

Benefits

- Increase productivity to make optimum, quality dentistry affordable for the vast majority of your patients.
- Invest less money in running a credit business.
- Maximize time for your staff.
- Focus on practive building and patient care instead of spending lots of time preparing and sending statements and handling collections.

That's how you build a practice. You focus on giving patients all that they expect and a little bit more each and every time.

Summary

Many dentists have understood the benefit of becoming involved with patient financing programs. However, they think that the programs don't work or they can't get people to accept the program or they can't seem to get people accepted or they don't see practice growth as a result of using the program. So they become frustrated.

Your success with one of these programs will be in direct proportion to the (1) the confidence of the team members in the program, (2) how they present the program, and (3) how actively you market the program. I'm not sure that the programs don't work for those practices—I think those practices don't work the programs.

In the next chapter, we will study six ways to maximize a healthcare financing program. These six ways will make a 4–38% positive difference in your practice. These six programs have proven to be effective and powerful in practices throughout America and the world for those who have followed our instructions. You can do the same thing.

CHAPTER 5

Maximizing a Healthcare Financing Program

There is only one boss: the customer. And he can fire everyone in the company from the chairman on down, simply by spending his money somewhere else.

– Sam Walton, Founder, Wal-Mart Stores, Inc.

So, you've become involved with a healthcare financing program, but you're not quite sure what to do with it. You expected to see some practice growth and some financial reward from the program, but that isn't happening yet. You're wondering what you can do to achieve both of these goals; practice growth and financial reward.

In this chapter, I will explain six ways to develop your practice using a healthcare financing program. In addition, I will suggest some verbal skills for explaining the program and for defusing some of the objections your patients may express.

If you will follow these recommendations as outlined, you can increase revenues in your practice 4–38%. Where is your production right now? Would a 4% increase make a difference for you? And what would happen with a 38% increase? The data behind this kind of statement is valid. For most practices, there is more dentistry sitting in the charts waiting to be done than the team has provided to date. Remember, the main reason that people do not come to the dentist at all or why they do not accept recommended treatment is cost.

Determine the value of your average treatment plan. If one more person per week proceeds with treatment because they can afford it, what would that mean to you? Take that average treatment plan fee, multiply that by 4 weeks in the month and that by 12 months in the year, and see what that would mean to the productivity of the practice.

For example, if one person per week goes ahead with $500 worth of treatment, let's see what that looks like for you.

$500 per week

x 4 weeks in the month

$2000 per month

x 12

$48,000 per year

And so on. You do your own math. What would this look like for you?

Or, could it be possible that *one person* a day might be able to proceed with $500 worth of treatment if they had a convenient way to pay?

$500 per day

x 200 days per year (average in the country)

$100,000 per year of additional revenue

This *could* occur if one person per day goes ahead with a minimal amount of treatment because he can spread out the payments and not have to come up with a large amount at one time. (And I am talking about $500—not $5,000!)

This is extremely profitable treatment to provide. You won't be increasing the salaries, but rather you will be maximizing people's talent. You won't add another chair but rather an existing chair will be used by a person who wants or needs something or they wouldn't have come to you in the first place. Your rent is the same. The light bill is the same, etc. You may have a bit more lab fee or a bit more use of disposable product, but for the most part, this becomes extremely profitable treatment.

Perhaps the most gratifying part of this scenario is that someone who wants or needs some care can receive it. They will be healthier or more beautiful—or both. This may be a person who would have walked out the door saying, "Gee, Doc, I'd like to go ahead with this, but I can't afford that right now." Or "Wow. I knew this would be a lot of money, but I didn't know it would be that much. I live on a budget and can't fit that kind of expenditure into my budget."

However, if they truly want or need some care, and you can help them to comfortably finance that care, they may decide to accept your treatment recommendations. Everyone wins.

Give the following ideas a try. They work!

1. Introduce the Program to Your Entire Patient Family

In a special mailing, or in your regularly published patient education newsletter, tell your existing patient family about the financing program. Present the program in an exciting, informative manner—one that stresses the benefits to the patient (Fig. 5–1). There's the key. Point out how the program will benefit the patient and/or the patient's family. Do not stress how much it will benefit you.

In this special mailing include a brochure about the program; some offices include an application. Make it easy for the patient to become involved. Eliminate as many barriers as possible.

Some patients in your practice will not need the program. If they don't need financial assistance, they won't apply. However, some people may not be coming to you on a regular basis or may be putting off needed or desired treatment because of the fear of cost. Others may have completed one phase of treatment but do not want to schedule the next phase of treatment because they owe you money. If this is the case, establishing a line of credit may break the cost barrier. If they owe the financing program instead of you, they may be more willing and able to go ahead with treatment. Plus, the monthly payments will, more than likely, be smaller.

Dear Friends,

It is with great pleasure that I introduce to you a new method of financing for health care that we are offering in our office. The company behind this method of financing is called *(Name of Company)*. I would like to briefly explain what this is, how it works and what benefits it has for you.

(Name of Company) is a company that offers convenient financing for dental care. A person or family applies for the program in our office. It is very easy to apply and the acceptance rate is very high. *(Name of Company)* offers several different options:

- 3, 6, 12, and 18 month interest-free financing
- small monthly payments spread out over a period of time, keeping the monthly payments to a minimum.
- For more extensive treatment, long-term financing is also available

This is definitely a positive and revolutionary addition to the healthcare field and is sweeping the country.

In our office we have found that our patients who are using the program are reaping many benefits, such as the following:

(1) Convenient and regular monthly payments—easily budgeted
(2) Long term pay out, when desired
(3) No large payments due at one time
(4) Balance of your insurance can be financed and then easily budgeted
(5) Necessary treatment does not have to be put off due to financial problems
(6) Hygiene appointments for the family can become more regular—thus insuring proper dental care for ALL members of the family
(7) Emergency treatment does not have to be ignored or "financially fearful."

We feel we offer a quality service to our patients both dentally and personally. Now we feel that we can come full circle in serving you by offering a financial plan that also meets your needs.

Enclosed you will find a brochure that explains the program and an application form. If you are interested, fill out the application in full and mail it or bring it to our office. If you are already a member of *(Name of Company)*, please pass this application and brochure on to a friend or relative.

If you have any questions at all, or if we can help you in any way, please don't hesitate to call the office. We are here to help you.

Yours for better dental health,

John H. Jameson, D.D.S.

Fig. 5–1 Special mailing—new finance program.

Remember the No. 1 reason that people do not come to the dentist is the fear of cost, and no perceived need is No. 3. Introducing a patient to the healthcare financing program via a newsletter addresses both of those issues. This newsletter serves to introduce the new financial options and to educate people about what's going on in dentsitry.

Practices spend a great deal of time nurturing a new patient flow. However, also spending time nurturing the existing patient family makes good sense. Be every bit as interested in gaining a higher level of case acceptance as you are interested in increasing new patient flow. Most practices can double from within by nurturing that which they already have—their own patient family. I'm not saying that you don't want to nurture a new patient flow. Obviously, you do. But I encourage you to maximize your market share by focusing more intently on the patients that you already have in your practice.

• KEY POINT •

Get the information about your financing program into the hands of your consumers—the patients.

Make a concerted effort to nurture your own patient family. Focus on completing the dentistry that has already been prescribed but has not been provided.

Newsletters

Newsletters? Are they effective? Many marketing specialists and I believe that they are. Many practices say that a newsletter takes too much time and money. Please, remember that the lack of dental education is a major reason that people don't receive dentistry—why they either don't come in or they don't say, "yes" to the dentistry that you recommend. And, thus, one of your main commissions as dental professionals is to be educators. One of the very best ways to educate your patient family—next to your in-office one-on-one education—is through the patient newsletter.

Good marketing recommends that you stay in contact with your customer base (your patient family) on a regular basis. The marketing experts recommend contacting your customers/clients/patients every 90 days or once a quarter. At this contact, introduce them to something new and reinforce something that is important to your business. *Repetition is a key to learning* so continuing to address aspects of treatment opportunity, including payment opportunities, is effective.

Let me quickly suggest to you a way of doing a newsletter—one that is both time and cost effective. In our own practice, we have produced a quarterly newsletter for more than 20 years.

This newsletter serves many purposes.

1. Be in the homes of your patient families in a positive way on a regular basis. When they think of the dentist, you want them to think of the dentist in a positive way. When they think of the dentist, you want them to think of you.

2. Inform your patients about what's happening in dentistry. Sometimes it is assumed that patients know about new and improved opportunities in treatment. They don't. It is your commission to educate your patients and your community about the new advances in dentistry.

3. Let your patient family know what you are doing in your practice to stay abreast of the latest and best in health care for their benefit.

4. Express your appreciation for their confidence in you.

5. Invite them to refer their family, colleagues, and friends to you.

Your newsletter needs to be economical and efficient both in time and in money. So the following is a way to do just that.

By a designated day, the dentist and the team members need to have written or gathered data for the newsletter. All the necessary information should be in the hands of a specific person who is going to type or cut and paste the information for the newsletter. You might see an article or just a brief bit of information that is appropriate for your patient family. Cut out that information and utilize it in the newsletter. Many times if we want to reprint an article from the American Cancer Association or American Heart Association or other health-oriented organizations, we will contact them and ask for their permission. They are thrilled. They say, "Our purpose is to educate people, and if you can do that—please do. All we ask is that you send us a copy of your newsletter." So we do.

For our own newsletter, we use a regular size piece of paper printed on both front and back. We take this typed copy with cut and pasted information to a printer. The printer keeps our logo on file. They not only print the newsletter for us, but they return it to us trifolded. On one side of this trifolded piece of paper, they print our return address, our bulk permit number, and *address correction requested* (which keeps the address lists current). The bulk rate mailing permit costs are minimal. With a bulk rate mailing permit, you can mail for approximately half the normal mailing rates. You must mail in volume of 200 or more.

If you mail with a bulk mail permit, you must put your newsletters in zip code order, which is easy to do by running your labels by zip code. You can place your labels onto the newsletters yourself or work with a printing company who will not only make the copies, but will fold, label, and stamp them (Fig. 5–2).

When we became involved with patient financing, we produced one entire issue on the subject to introduce the program. Now in most every issue we reintroduce the fact that we do have financing available, just to keep that fresh in patients' minds.

In January of every year, we remind our patients that a new year has begun and that this new year indicates a new maximum for their insurance. Therefore if they have incomplete treatment, or if they would like to come in for continuous care, or if there are people in their family who have not been able to come in to receive treatment, that this new year offers the opportunity to utilize their new insurance benefits. We encourage them to utilize this wonderful supplement to their health care. If they have dental insurance, they can finance the balance after the insurance pays. If they don't have dental insurance, this is a comfortable and convenient way to take care of the financing of their dentistry.

Also in October of every year, we send a letter to our patients reminding them that if they have not utilized or taken advantage of their yearly maximum of their insurance, now is a good time to do that (Fig. 5–3). If they have existing dentistry that needs to be completed, we encourage them to maximize their insurance benefits. Rather than to wait until the end of the year—a very hectic time for us—we encourage them to call in the fall to schedule an appointment for that dentistry. Again to maximize their insurance, we also tell them that if they have any concerns about the balance after insurance pays, we do have comfortable and convenient financing available for them.

Professionally produced newsletters. There are numerous companies that produce patient education newsletters for practices. These are beautifully and professionally prepared and fulfill all the criteria that I outlined previously. In these professionally produced newsletters, space is reserved for your own name and practice data, your logo, and an article or relevant data pertaining to your practice. This individualizes the newletter for you (Fig. 5–4).

JOHN H. JAMESON D.D.S.

THE PLAQUE WRANGLER

101 JAMESON DR. · P.O. BOX 459

WYNNEWOOD, OK 73098 · (405) 665-2041

FINANCING YOUR DENTAL CARE

In our past two editions of the Plaque Wrangler, we have dealt with two of the most important topics of clinical dentistry facing our practice today. Periodontics and soft tissue management are the first phase of treatment addressed for all patients entering our practice. We covered periodontal therapy in our first issue. The second issue of our newly revised Plaque Wrangler concentrated on cosmetic dentistry.

Both of these areas of treatment became more financially comfortable for many of our patient families when they utilize our extended payment program. This program assists families in budgeting their dental treatments. Dent-A-Med, our healthcare financing program, offers convenient financing for dental care. The acceptance rate into this program is quite high. A person or family can easily apply for the program in our office. Upon being accepted, patients can begin charging their dental treatment and will receive monthly statements from Dent-A-Med. The minimum payment is very small, and the patient is allowed to take many months to pay the bill. A person can conveniently fit this into a budget and know what the monthly payment is going to be. If the bill is paid off early, there is no penalty. This card works very much like a Penneys, Sears or Mastercard. It is a revolving payment plan — every time a payment is made, the next one is smaller. It is definitely a positive and revolutionary addition to the healthcare field and is sweeping the country. The main reason for its success is that it offers such a wonderful service to patients and to families.

In our office we have found that our patients who are involved in the program are reaping many benefits, such as the following:

- Convenient and regular monthly payments - easily budgeted.
- Long term pay out.
- No large payments due at one time.
- The balance of insurance can be placed on Dent-A-Med and then easily budgeted.
- Necessary treatment does not have to be "put off" due to financial concerns.
- Continuous Care/Hygiene appointments can become more regular — thus insuring proper dental care for all members of the family
- Emergency treatment does not have to be ignored or "financially fearful".

> "Make the financing of dentistry comfortable."

The bottom line is that we feel that we offer an excellent service to our patients both dentally and personally — because we care so much for all of you. Now we feel that we can come full circle in serving you by offering a financial plan that also meets your needs.

So, when periodontal therapy, cosmetic treatment or other state of the art dental care is recommended as part of your comprehensive treatment plan, don't allow financing of your care to be an obstacle for you or your family. At your earliest convenience, contact our office for further information about long term financing for the total dental care you desire.

Fig. 5–2 Patient education newsletter.

ATTENTION!!
INSURANCE COVERAGE
ENDING FOR THE YEAR

NOW is the time to plan for the completion of your dental treatment before the end of the year. All insurance plans have a yearly maximum. If you do not use this maximum amount — the remainder is lost forever.

IF you have treatment to be completed, or to be started — take advantage of your benefits this year. We can use the maximum allowed for this year to begin or complete any treatment that needs to be done. If we do not complete all of the treatment then we can start with a new maximum next year.

GOOD planning will allow you to take advantage of the full benefit of your policy. Please do not wait until the last few days of the year when our congested schedule will make it difficult to appoint a convenient time for you.

OUR goal is to provide you with quality dental services. If we can help you maximize your dental insurance coverage in the process, we know you will be very pleased. In addition, we have a financial partner who can help you with any portion of your treatment that insurance does not cover.

Call (405)665-2041 today for an appointment.

Sincerely,

Dr. John H. Jameson and His Dental Team

Fig. 5–3 Insurance/end of year letter.

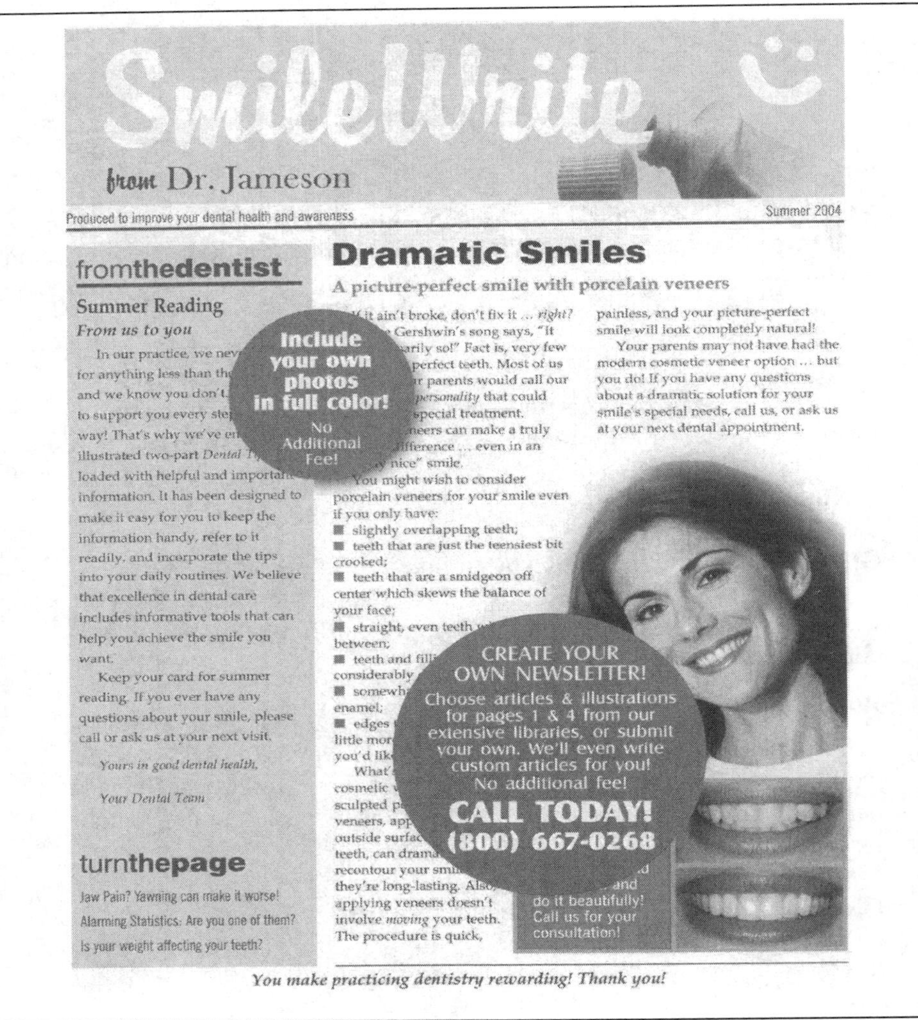

SmileWrite

from Dr. Jameson

Produced to improve your dental health and awareness

Summer 2004

fromthedentist

Summer Reading

From us to you

In our practice, we nev
for anything less than th
and we know you don't.
to support you every ste
way! That's why we've en
illustrated two-part *Dental T*
loaded with helpful and importa
information. It has been designed to make it easy for you to keep the information handy, refer to it readily, and incorporate the tips into your daily routines. We believe that excellence in dental care includes informative tools that can help you achieve the smile you want.

Keep your card for summer reading. If you ever have any questions about your smile, please call or ask us at your next visit.

Yours in good dental health,

Your Dental Team

turnthepage

Jaw Pain? Yawning can make it worse!

Alarming Statistics: Are you one of them?

Is your weight affecting your teeth?

Dramatic Smiles

A picture-perfect smile with porcelain veneers

If it ain't broke, don't fix it ... *right?*
Gershwin's song says, "It
arily so!" Fact is, very few
perfect teeth. Most of us
r parents would call our
personality that could
special treatment.
neers can make a truly
ifference ... even in an
nice" smile.

You might wish to consider porcelain veneers for your smile even if you only have:

- slightly overlapping teeth;
- teeth that are just the teensiest bit crooked;
- teeth that are a smidgeon off center which skews the balance of your face;
- straight, even teeth
between;
- teeth and filli
considerably
- somewh
enamel;
- edges
little mor
you'd lik

What'
cosmetic
sculpted p
veneers, app
outside surfac
teeth, can dram
recontour your smi
they're long-lasting. Also,
applying veneers doesn't involve *moving* your teeth. The procedure is quick, painless, and your picture-perfect smile will look completely natural!

Your parents may not have had the modern cosmetic veneer option ... but you do! If you have any questions about a dramatic solution for your smile's special needs, call us, or ask us at your next dental appointment.

and
do it beautifully!
Call us for your consultation!

You make practicing dentistry rewarding! Thank you!

Fig. 5–4 Professionally produced newsletter.

Some of our clients choose one of these methods for newsletters, some choose the other. I like both methods. There are, obviously, more costs with the professionally produced newletter, but the results of each are beneficial. The point here is that the constant contact with clients is beneficial and needs to be maintained. You select the method that best suits you.

Budget a certain amount of your income for marketing. My definition of good marketing is educating patients. Newsletters are a great place to invest a small portion of your marketing budgtet.

Your new patient flow will increase as patients become involved with a financing program. People will go home and say, "Hey, my dentist has this new program available. You can finance your dentistry and pay it out. The payments are real small." Personal referrals will always be your best source for new patients. However, we have found that many patients are coming to us because they now know that we offer comfortable, convenient, long-term financing.

If you utilize the Yellow Page ads, it is a good idea to let people know that you have comfortable financing available (Fig. 5–5).

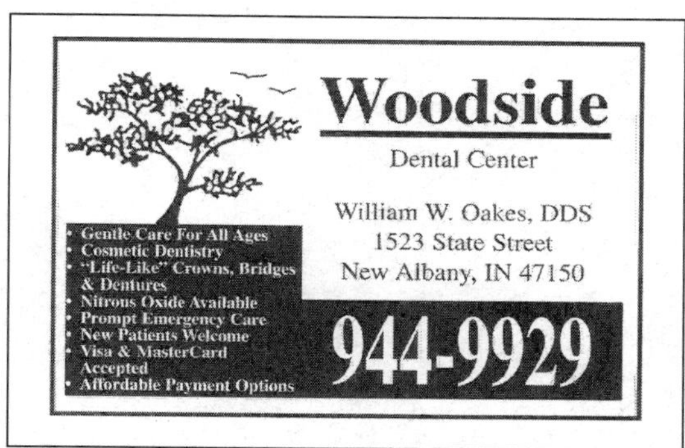

Fig. 5–5 Yellow Pages ad.

In addition to the initial introduction of the program through a special mailing or a patient education newsletter, consider an introduction through a practice brochure (Fig. 5–6).

A practice brochure is a marketing piece that lets people know who you are, where you are, what you do, and what makes you special. It's not a naggy, boring, ugly piece of literature (I use the term loosely) that gets thrown in the trash. Rather, it needs to be attractive, informational, and inviting.

Also, on your patient information sheet, introduce your financial options. We send this information sheet/health history to patients prior to their arrival for their first appointment (Fig. 5–7). We include information about our financing program in our welcome packet (Fig. 5–8).

Our Philosophy is to provide optimum dentistry for our patients in a loving and caring way with emphasis on function, esthetics and prevention.

Welcome to our dental family...

It is our goal to help you feel this way every time you call or come to our practice. Your health, comfort, and individual needs are foremost in our minds.

THE PURPOSE of this brochure is to familiarize you with our office and to make you feel more at home. We hope that any questions you may have will be answered. However, please feel free to contact any member of our team—**we are here for you.**

WE ARE COMMITTED to excellence and to service in all areas of dental care. We are here to help and maintain great oral health for a lifetime.

Professionalism is a must...

- We utilize the latest and best dental techniques and equipment

We work with intra-oral and digital cameras so that our patients can see and better understand their dental needs.

Computerized, digital radiograph techniques are used to make your dental appointment proceed more rapidly. These techniques also decrease radiation exposure by 80–90 percent over traditional systems.

- We practice excellent sterilization and infection control methods for your safety and protection.
- We provide the skills of periodontal therapists/dental hygienists to restore and maintain healthy gum tissue.

BEFORE WE RECOMMEND any type of treatment, we want to LISTEN to and UNDERSTAND your desires, your likes and dislikes, and your concerns about your dental care. Only then are we able to provide you with the excellent care you deserve.

OUR team of professionals is exceptionally qualified to provide expertise in each department within the practice.

Dental Services available in our practice...

RESTORATIVE AND COSMETIC DENTISTRY...
- Bonding
- Porcelain Veneers
- Cosmetic Recontouring
- Crowns and Bridges
- Full and Partial Dentures
- Tooth Whitening

PREVENTIVE DENTISTRY...
- Dental Cleaning
- Comprehensive Oral Health Evaluations
- Radiographs
- Sealants
- Fluoride Treatments

OTHER SERVICES...
- Endodontics (rooot canals)
- Non-Surgical Periodontal (gum disease) Therapy

SELECTED AREAS
- Oral Surgery
- Periodontal Surgery
- TMJ Treatment
- Dental Implants

We treat our patients with special care...

PHYSICALLY...
To make your dental care physically comfortable, we offer nitrous oxide analgesia. As you lay back and relax, your dental appointment will fly by. Many of our patients have found this very comforting.

EMOTIONALLY...
We know that your smile affects all areas of your life. Your smile affects your self confidence and greatly affects your appearance. We can help you achieve the smile you've always wanted.

FINANCIALLY...

To make your dental care financially comfortable, we offer a variety of payment options.

- Cash and personal checks
- 5% fee reduction for advance payment of entire treatment plan
- All major bank cards
- Various healthcare financing partners for long term or regular monthly payments
- We accept assignment of your insurance payment. This means you are responsible for your deductibile and the portion that the insurance company does not cover.

Fig. 5–6 Practice brochure.

PLEASE COMPLETE AND RETURN TO BUSINESS OFFICE

Personal Information

Name Last	First	Middle
Address Street or P. O. Box # City State Zip Code	Phone Number: Home: Work:	
Pager #:	Cell Phone:	Email Address:
Age: Yrs.	Birth Date Mo. Day Year	Birthplace	( ) Married ( ) Unmarried ( ) Separated
Social Security No. (if child, parents)	Driver's License No.	
Occupation	Employer	How long employed?	Address & Phone No.
Person responsible for bill	Age	Address	Relationship	Social Security No. / Driver's License No.
Occupation	Employer	How long employed?
Employer Address & Phone No.		

Insurance Information

Insured Person's Full Name ______ Date of Birth ______

Social Security Number ______ Relationship to Patient ______ Work Phone ______

Insurance Company Name ______ Group or Union Name ______ Group or Local Number ______

Employer's Name ______ Full Address of Employer ______

Getting to Know You

1.Why did you select our practice? ______

2. Whom may we thank for referring you? ______

3. Is another member of your family or relative a patient in our practice? ______

4. Person to contact for emergency: ______
Phone: ______

5. When was your last dental visit? ______

6. When was the last time you had complete dental radiographs taken? ______
Name & Address of last Dentist: ______

7. Have you ever had any teeth removed? ______
How long have these teeth been missing? ______
Have these teeth been replaced? ______
How? ☐ Bridge ☐ Partial ☐ Denture ☐ Implants

Payments Alternatives

Please check appropriate box:

☐ 1. As a special service to you, we offer a cash courtesy if you pay for your entire treatment plan in full, in advance.

☐ 2. Cash and personal checks are accepted as your treatments are provided.

☐ 3. If you have dental insurance, we want you to receive the full benefit of it. Our office team can assist you in completing your insurance forms and verifying the coverage that your particular program provides. We accept assignment of your insurance payment; another service to you. This means that you are responsible for your deductible and the portion the insurance does not cover. Remember, however, that you are responsible for the account if the insurance company, for any reason, does not honor their commitment to you and to us.

☐ 4. Mastercard, Visa, Discover and American Express

☐ 5. For long term or extended payments, we offer a healthcare financing program, which when you are accepted, will allow extended small monthly payments for the treatment received.

FOR ALL PATIENTS

I hereby authorize the doctor to perform any and all forms of treatment, medication, and therapy that may be indicated in connection with the dental care of the patient above and further authorize and consent that the doctor chooses and employs such assistance as he or she deems fit. I also understand that previous to treatment, full explanation of the procedure(s) involved will be given by the doctor and/or team. I agree to pay for all services rendered by this office.

Signature of Responsible Party ______ Relationship ______ Date ______

Fig. 5–7 Health history form.

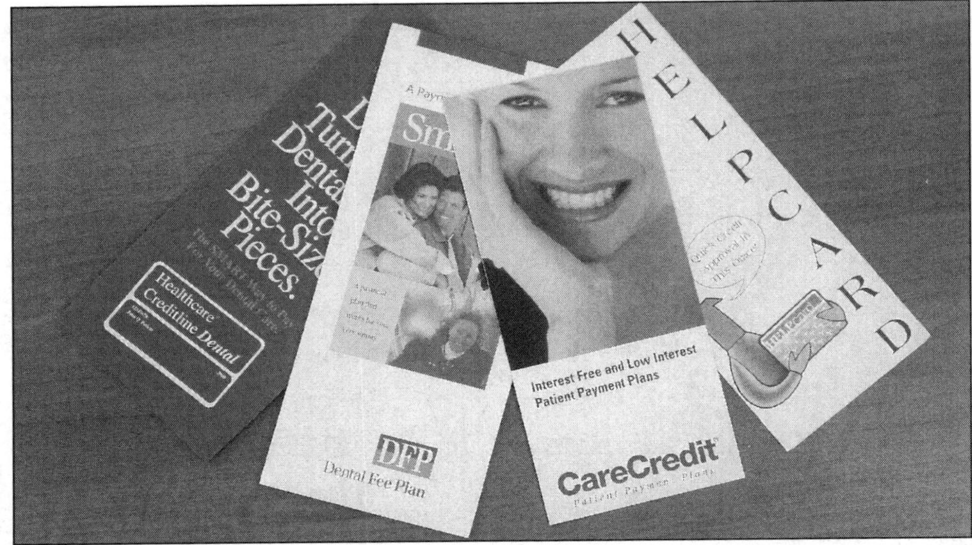

Fig. 5–8 Healthcare financing brochures.

This welcome packet includes the practice brochure, the information sheet/ health history form along with a self-addressed envelope, a card confirming the appointment, a patient education newsletter, and information about our financing program. We send this to a patient as soon as he calls to schedule a new patient evaluation.

You are going out of your way to make your dental treatment affordable—dental treatment that you believe is vital to health and well-being. Let people know that you do have this service available. Defuse the fear of cost in advance of a patient's entrance into your practice.

We introduce the welcome packet to patients in the following manner:

> **BA:** Mr. Jones, I'm going to be sending you some information about our practice before you arrive. I am sending you a card confirming your appointment and a brochure about our practice. We want you to know about us before you get here. Also, I am including your patient information sheet, health history form along with a self-addressed stamped envelope. Please complete this form and send it back to us before your appointment. We have found that our patients are more comfortable filling this out at home where they have all the necessary data and they have plenty of time. In addition, if you send it back to us prior to your appointment, the doctor will be able to review the

information and be better prepared for your appointment. Plus, I will be able to enter all the information into the computer, and we will be able to seat you more quickly. I know your time is valuable.

New patients see our financial options on the brochure and on the information sheet. It is presented in a very positive way. There is no question or confusion. Everything is spelled out before the fact. No confusion. No *after-the-fact* information. Up-front is the best way to deal with any arrangement. Dr. Burt Press, former president of the ADA, has told us for a long time to *inform before you perform*. That applies to the treatment to be rendered and to the financial responsibility. We inform patients of the financial options right from the start. People are glad to know that there are options available for most any financial situation.

Remember that repetition is the key to learning and the key to getting good results from your marketing efforts. Do not introduce your financial policy or your healthcare financing program once and expect it to be readily accepted. It won't be. You must repetitively reintroduce the program to your patients, via newsletters, mailings, telephone ads, newspaper articles, verbal introduction during the financial presentation, and continuous, positive conversations about this option. Remember, you provide your patients a great service when you offer them quality dental care and when you make it affordable.

2. Accounts Receivable Transfer

As was illustrated in the previous chapter, every day that an account sits on your books doing nothing, you lose money because (1) the cost of running a banking business within your practice, (2) the chances of never collecting the account, and (3) the *loss of the dollar* as it sits on your books depreciating in value make the carrying of accounts a difficult business process.

Therefore, if you have existing accounts receivable, consider making an active effort to transfer as many of those accounts as possible to your healthcare financing program. Get the money in the bank and let professionals take over the management of these accounts. Do not think that you are doing your patients a favor by letting them delay payment to you. You are not doing them a favor by letting them get into a negative financial situation with you. You are only supporting behavior that is unacceptable to the world at large. And you are, certainly, not doing anything to support the sound financial status of your own business. People who owe you money usually do not feel good about you or the relationship. Being *square* financially is an asset to relationships while having a financial challenge between you can be detrimental.

Suggested steps for this transfer are the following:

1. Analyze your accounts receivable. Determine the following:

    A. How much is insurance? How much is private pay?

    B. Of the private pay accounts, how much is 30, 60, 90, (or more) days past due?

    C. Those accounts that are extremely past due and have had no activity whatsoever, may need to be turned over for legal action. (Make sure that the dentist approves all accounts to be turned over or written off.) Be certain that you have made concerted effort to collect the account, and that the patient has been unwilling to negotiate a settlement of the account before you turn anything over for collection.

2. For all of the remaining accounts, create a letter introducing the idea of transferring accounts to the healthcare financing program (Fig. 5–9). Expound on the following benefits of the program, such as:

    A. Longer time in which to pay the account.

    B. Smaller monthly payments.

    C. No large payments due at one time.

    D. No initial or yearly fee to become involved with the program.

    E. Available credit for emergencies or for necessary and desired treatment.

    F. If you are charging a service fee that is higher than the financing program, stress the benefit of the lower service fee. (Make sure it is.)

3. Send an application and a brochure with this letter. Send this letter in a separate mailing rather than with statements. Place the letter on your letterhead stationery and place it in one of your letterhead envelopes. This needs to be a special mailing so that it receives special attention from your patients.

    You may wish to offer a 10% cash courtesy if the guarantor comes in and pays his/her balance in full within 30 days of the postmark of the letter. This, in itself, may bring in a great number of payments. (The cost of carrying the account on your own books will be greater than the courtesy given.)

NAME
STREET
CITY, STATE ZIP

Dear *NAME*:

Our office has found that we must constantly keep abreast of the latest dental advances to offer our patients the best clinical care possible. We also search for new methods of payment which allow our patients the opportunity to receive the greatest amount of quality dental care during any period of time. We have only recently located a company which we feel can help all of our patients.

Enclosed you will find an information brochure and an application for *COMPANY NAME*. This company works with us to offer an extended payment plan to our patients—a plan that lets you receive the necessary treatment, finance that treatment, and spread the payments out over your desired length of time—keeping your monthly payments small and convenient.

One month from the postmark of this letter, we will be forced to initiate a service fee of 2% per month for any past due accounts. If you have an outstanding balance with our practice, you can transfer your existing balance to (name of company) and the service fee is lower. The service fee for (name of company) is 1.75% per month which is lower than ours. In addition, if you transfer your balance, your monthly payments will be smaller and you can take longer to pay.

This is a great program that gives you tremendous benefits. You simply complete the enclosed application and send it or bring it to the office. We will send it to the company for processing and then, once you have received a line of credit, we will transfer your existing balance. Easy. Simple. Beneficial.

In the future, should you or a member of your family need dental care, you will not have to worry about putting off that care. You will have a line of credit established for yourself and your family and it will be there when you need it. You do not have to pay anything for this service. Dr. Jameson has paid all necessary fees for you to become involved. In addition, there is no yearly fee. So, you only pay for it when you use it.

If you have any questions, please feel free to call our office. We feel that this breakthrough is what our patients have been looking for in dental financing.

Sincerely,

John H. Jameson, DDS

Fig. 5–9 Initial accounts receivable transfer letter.

4. Once you have sent your first mailing, begin a telephone campaign to all of those patients who do not respond (Fig. 5–10).

   Track your telephone calls. Make notes of who you have called, those who were sent an application, the date you sent the application, the date it was received back in the office, and any comments relative to the conversation (Fig. 5–11).

   Please note the following: The sooner you can contact someone in person or by the phone, the better. Any time you are in contact with the patient is a good time to encourage them to work with you to transfer their balance. Be faithful with your encouragement of this transfer. The best way to collect is face to face. The second best way is over the phone. The third best way is through the written word.

Telephone Campaign Script

Accounts Receivable Transfer

Business Manager: "Good morning, Ms. Jones. This is Cathy from Dr. Jameson's dental office. Ms. Jones, last month we mailed some information about a new healthcare financing program that we have available in our office. Did you receive that information?

You did? Good. Ms. Jones, my records indicate you have a balance with our practice of $____________. Ms. Jones, we have found that many of our patients are more comfortable with smaller monthly payments that are more convenient. These monthly payments can be spread out over a longer period of time.

Ms. Jones, if you were to apply and be extended a line of credit with (Name of Company) we could immediately convert your balance and your first monthly payment would be approximately $____________. Does this sound like a program that would be of interest to you?

Good. Can you come by the office today to fill out an application? Great! (Or, offer to send the application to her home if she cannot come in.) We can send it in today, and once you receive a line of credit we will make the necessary conversion of your account.

Ms. Jones, we want you to know how much we appreciate your cooperation. We believe that this is one of the best financial services we have been able to offer our patients."

Fig. 5–10 Script for telephone calls for accounts receivable transfer.

ACCOUNTS RECEIVABLES TRANSFER

DATE CONTACTED	PATIENT	PHONE	BALANCE	LAST PAYMENT	HCFP	DATE SENT	APP. RCVD	COMMENTS
1/17	Stephanie Jones	374-5289	$1000	10/03	$50/mo.	1/17	1/22	Glad to transfer balance
1/17	Mike Allen	374-7386	$562	11/03	$37/mo.	1/17	1/30	
1/17	Carol Samuels	278-7439	$754	9/03	$45/mo.	1/17	1/30	Transferred balance

Fig. 5–11 Tracking devices for accounts receivable transfer.

5. At the next statement run—another month has passed—send a follow-up letter with another brochure and another application to anyone who has not yet transferred their account. (Remember that repetition is the key to learning.) Let your patients know that you are serious about this service (Fig. 5–12).

   In this letter, let your patients know that you have changed accounting methods and are offering this financial service to those who wish to extend their payments over a long period of time. Once again, stress the benefits of the program and the benefits to the individuals. Continue your telephone campaign.

6. By now, you should have had a strong response to your efforts—especially if you have followed the recommended regime carefully and with commitment. If you are not going to follow the campaign through to the end—with consistency—don't expect a great response. In fact, if you aren't prepared to take this campaign through all the previously recommended steps, don't even bother to begin. You are obviously not interested in accessing good results if you are not prepared to do this correctly.

7. Continue your telephone campaign until you have negotiated a settlement of the account and/or you have a clear idea of how that account will be reconciled.

Note

If a patient is abiding by a previously agreed upon financial arrangement, go ahead and offer the program to her, but willingly allow her to maintain this agreement if it is comfortable.

• KEY POINT •

Many offices have converted half of their accounts receivable to cash in a three- to six-month period of time. Results are in direct correlation to effort put forth.

I am recommending that—if you are accepting assignment of benefits of insurance—that you maintain an accounts receivable of no more than half of your average monthly production. If you follow the financial protocol outlined previously and if you are managing the insurance system excellently, you should have no accounts receivable other than insurance. Remember the ADA data that shows that the average practice in America has about half of its monthly income coming in the form of an insurance check. That's the half that I am referring to that would be acceptable accounts receivable. If you are using

NAME
STREET
CITY, STATE ZIP

Dear *NAME*:

Last month we introduced a new concept in healthcare financing. The program is called (Name of Company). You have received information regarding this innovative program. We have had an overwhelming response to this convenient method of financing dentistry from our patient friends.

In order to maintain comfortable fees for our patients, our accountant has insisted that we remove ourselves from the banking business. We have found that it is not time or cost efficient to run a banking business within our practice. And so, we have become involved with a healthcare financing program that will allow our patients to have smaller payments that can extend over a longer period of time.

The financial agreement that we previously made with you seems to have been difficult. Since the time of our agreement, there have been occasions when your payments were not made. Since this agreement has become difficult for you to maintain, we would like to encourage you to transfer your existing balance to (Name of Company). This could allow you to lower your monthly payments and give you a longer time in which to pay.

We have enclosed a brochure about the program and an application. We would encourage you to study this information and to call our office with any questions. Complete this application and bring or mail it to our office. We will send the application to the company for processing. Once you are extended a line of credit, we will transfer your balance to (Name of Company).

We look forward to working with you to comfortably convert this account to a method of payment that would be more acceptable to you.

Sincerely,

John H. Jameson, DDS

Fig. 5–12 Follow-up letter #2.

the other options, there would be no accounts receivable. (Using EFT would be the exception.)

Now with electronic processing of insurance claims, you should have an approximate 7–10 working-day turnaround on all your insurance claims and should have no claims 30 days or more past due.

We have been tracking this with the clients of JMI and have found that this is accurate. Practices that are not accepting assignment of benefits from insurance companies have no accounts receivable. In fact, many of these practices have negative accounts receivable because many patients are paying in advance in order to receive the accounting reduction. Practices that have been following our recommended protocol but are accepting assignment of benefits have an accounts receivable that is about half of average monthly production.

If you feel that your accounts receivable is too much, perform an accounts receivable transfer. The money you have been carrying on your own books is converted to cash, and that doesn't hurt when bills have to be paid. The money sitting on your books is doing nothing but losing value every day. Conversion of these accounts is excellent business.

The team will love the accounts receivable transfer, because they are going to get out of the statement and collection business. This gives them more time to take care of other necessary duties within the practice, including taking care of patients. They want to spend their time nurturing relationships with patients, educating them about treatment needs and possibilities, and making good financial arrangements—finding financial solutions for patients—rather than spending time sending statements, calling-past due accounts, or calling insurance companies.

Patients will accept the accounts receivable transfer because most patients would rather owe a financing institution than to owe the dentist. In addition, their payments will probably be less per month.

Put a dam in the river called accounts receivable. From this point forward, no longer offer financing on your own books. You may have to go through the process of cleaning up the existing accounts receivable, but you can do this very successfully. The time spent on converting these accounts is time well spent. These accounts receivable are monies that you deserve to collect. You provided the care in good faith. It is acceptable to ask people to uphold their financial agreement with you.

Will abiding by this financial protocol hurt productivity? No. All the practices we work with increase production significantly and certainly become more profitable. In addition, stress is relieved because the money from production is in the bank and is not sitting out there doing nothing. More time is available for the important activities that build the practice—time is not spent on statements and collection.

Many dentists have said to me, "I am concerned that some patients will be upset with me. I have been carrying accounts for so long that they might get upset and leave."

My experience has been the following: Once you have set a financial protocol and your patients understand that this will serve them better—to offer top-quality dentistry with comfortable financial options—they will be fine. Let them know that you had to get out of the banking business because it was not financially feasible for you to run a banking business within your practice. Maintain your commitment to quality. They will respect this. Presented in this manner, I find that very few people become disgruntled. They understand what you need to do and why. If you have focused your practice on offering quality service, they won't go anywhere else. They will abide by your way of doing things. They will understand and respect your request.

There you have it—accounts receivable transfer. I recommend that you follow this program. Take the concept and individualize it to fit you. No two practices are exactly alike, but these concepts will fit any practice—you just have to fine tune them to make them your own. Get that money into your bank account. That's where it needs to be.

3. Chart Auditing

As I have said several times, most dentists will agree that there is more dentistry sitting in their charts waiting to be done than they have ever done in their practicing days. We now know that the main reason that people do not proceed with dental care is the *fear of cost*. Therefore, going through all of the charts to reactivate people into the practice or to reinforce the need for the dental treatment can be a super practice builder—especially when this effort is combined with the introduction of your healthcare financing program.

I am going to describe a way to fully audit your charts, and then I am going to recommend a way to audit your charts on a daily basis.

Suggested procedure for a full audit of the charts

Set a goal and follow a process of goal accomplishment

Example

- The team sets the goal. They determine the end result they expect and intend to accomplish with the chart audit.
- The objectives and strategies of how the team is going to accomplish the goal are defined as follows: What are they going to do? How are they going to do it?
- The person or persons responsible for each individual task are assigned their specifically detailed duties.
- The time frame is set. Time activate each step.
- Evaluate. You must be able to evaluate your progress and your success. Therefore, the monitor becomes critical. Otherwise, how can you measure your progress?

Let's say that Jan, who, in this example is the clinical assistant, is going to be doing the actual auditing of the charts. Pat, the BA, is going to make the telephone calls. Now, follow along with my example on Figure 5–13. They are going to audit 20 charts per week. They feel that this is a comfortable number for them. They are going to evaluate their progress and give a report at their weekly team meeting to show the entire team the results of these audits. They will be evaluating (1) how many patients were contacted, (2) how many of these patients scheduled an appointment either with the dentist or with the hygienist, and (3) if patients were unwilling to schedule, what were the predominant reasons (Figs. 5–14 and 5–15). Having this vital information gives a practice a wonderful opportunity to learn areas that might need improvement or extra attention.

GOAL ACCOMPLISHMENT

GOAL: Audit all charts to activate or reactivate patients.

Strategies	Person Responsible	Time Frame	Evaluation
#1 Start with A's. Audit 20 charts a week.	Jan	20 charts per week	Week #1– 25 Charts Week #2– 20 Charts Week #3– 10 Charts Week #4– 22 Charts
#2 Go through all charts identifying necessary or desired treatment. Complete tracking sheet.	Jan	20 charts per week	
#3 Contact all people by telephone. Try to schedule an appointment for treatment or for an evaluation and hygienic appointment.	Patt	20 phone calls per week	Week #1– 20 contacts 8 appointments 4 Doctor – 4 Hygiene Week #2– 15 contacts 4 appointments 2 Doctor – 2 Hygiene Week #3– 21 contacts 6 appointments 2 Doctor – 4 Hygiene Week #4– 18 contacts 5 appointments 3 Doctor – 2 Hygiene (People were receptive to the financing program. Time was a barrier for many people. Should we consider extended hours?)

Fig. 5–13 Writing the goal: designing the plan.

Chart Audits

Date Called	Patient	Phone	Last Date Seen	Amount of Dentistry Diagnosed	Ins.	HCFP	Date Sent	App Rcvd	Comments
2/23	Mary Jones	783-4421	12/5	$1000.00	$500	$35/mo	2/24	3/7	Call to schedule when application is approved
2/23	Sam Murray	783-2209	11/1	$495.00	NO	$35/mo	2/24	3/7	
2/23	Joel Coffey	226-4178	12/10	$1500.00	$750	$40/mo	2/24	3/7	Not interested
2/23	Derrick Smith	783-7726	12/5		100%		2/24	3/7	Scheduled appt. with Hyg. Wants to bring in rest of family when application approved. Call

Fig. 5–14 Tracking device for chart audits.

Telephone Campaign Script

Chart Audit

Business Administrator: Good Morning, Ms. Jones. This is Cathy from Dr. Jameson's office. Ms. Jones, Dr. Jameson has been reviewing your chart and noticed that at your last evaluation he had recommended treatment. (Here give a brief description of the recommended treatment stressing the end results and the benefits of treatment.)

Ms. Jones, at the same time that I am calling to reinforce the need for this treatment, I am also calling to tell you about a new financing program that we have available in our practice. It's called (Name of Company). (Name of Company) is a financing program for healthcare that allows people to finance their dentistry, and then to pay this out over a period of time with the monthly payments being very comfortable.

Many of our patients have found this program to be a convenient way to finance necessary and desired dental care.

Ms. Jones, if you were to become involved with (Name of Company) and you financed the dentistry that Dr. Jameson has recommended to you, your first monthly payment would be approximately $50. It is a revolving plan which means that every time you make a payment, your next one is less.

Tell me, Ms. Jones, would this be something that would be of interest to you?

Good. You could stop by the office to complete an application, or, if you prefer, I will mail an application to your home. Which would be best for you? Once we receive your application and when you are extended a line of credit, we will call to schedule an appointment to proceed with your treatment.

We believe that this is one of the best services we have been able to offer to our patients.

Fig. 5–15 Telephone script for chart audits.

Gather the following information on each patient:

- the date the person was called
- the person's name
- telephone number
- the last date seen
- details of any dentistry diagnosed but left incomplete
- if the patient has insurance or not
- details about their policy
- if the patient is a part of the healthcare financing program at this time or not and/or how much their first monthly payment would be if they financed
- if the person is interested in the financing program, the date the application was sent is noted
- the next column is the date the application is returned
- and the last column is for comments

Once the data has been gathered for *this week's charts,* make courteous marketing telephone calls to those patients to (1) express your concern about their care, (2) let them know you have not forgotten them, (3) reinforce the need for treatment, and (4) explain your new financing program.

Don't audit any more charts until these patients have been called. Some people audit all the charts but don't make any phone calls. What's the purpose?

Approach this effort steadily and with a positive attitude. Business tells us that 64% of the people promoting a service or a product never ask a potential customer/client to proceed. You never know what you will get until you ask. You are getting ready to ask your patients to make a decision that is good for them—to get and maintain a healthy mouth, teeth, and gums for a lifetime. The law of averages will work in your favor if you work on your entire set of charts.

Don't become discouraged if everyone doesn't jump at the idea. They won't. If you get a positive response from 20–30% of the people contacted, you will have served your purpose well. Everyone will be a winner—you, the practice, and, most of all, the patient. At this time, you can introduce your healthcare financing program, so that you can clear the way for that patient to come in and say, "yes" to the dentistry.

For example, you audit a chart and find that a person has some necessary dentistry that has been diagnosed but remains incomplete.

> **BA**: Ms. Jones? This is Cathy, from Dr. Jameson's office. How are you? Ms. Jones, Dr. Jameson has been reviewing your records and realized that the dental treatment that he had recommended for you has not been completed at this time and he was concerned. You are missing a tooth on the lower left area of your mouth and the adjacent teeth are shifting and both you and the doctor were concerned about the potential loss of more teeth. He asked that I call you to see if you had any questions about the treatment that he has prescribed.
>
> One of the reasons we're calling is to tell you about an exciting new program that we have available in our practice. Ms. Jones, we have become involved with a program that allows our patients to *finance* their dentistry and pay it out over a period of time with very small monthly payments. Ms. Jones, I see that you have dental insurance through XYZ Company and that is great. Dental insurance has been so helpful to so many of our patients. It serves as a wonderful supplement to their health care budget. Our new program lets you finance your dental care including the balance that insurance does not cover.
>
> In reviewing your record, I see that the fee for the treatment that Dr. Jameson is recommending for you is approximately $2,300. We estimate your insurance company will pay about $1,000. Therefore, we could file your insurance as a service to you and for about $35 per month you could finance your estimated portion. You could spread the payments out over a period of time, keep the payments small enough to be comfortable, not put yourself under any financial stress, and, best of all, you could proceed with the treatment that both you and the doctor believe is best for you. Would this be something of interest to you?

Then she will say, "yes" or "no"or she might have some other questions to ask you about the program. She might say, "Yes, this sounds good to me. I have wanted to have this done, but there was no way I could afford it. I didn't have enough money. But I can pay $35 a month." Then you could say, "Ms. Jones, let me gather some information from you right now. I will transmit this information to our financial partner and within a matter of minutes, we will know if they have been able to extend a line of credit to you. Once they have given us the go-ahead, we can schedule an appointment and begin your treatment. How does that sound?"

If for any reason you don't get the information over the phone and the patient wants you to send them an application through the mail, that is fine. However, any time an application goes out of your office, track the date that the application is sent and follow up consistently.

Again, look at the tracking sheet. Note the date you sent the application. If you notice that you sent Ms. Jones an application but that you have not received the application back in the office, that is an alert. It is time to make a phone call to Ms. Jones.

> **BA**: Ms. Jones? This is Cathy from Dr. Jameson's office. I sent an application to your home regarding our healthcare financing plan and I haven't received that application back in the office. I wondered if you had received it. Oh, you have? Good. Do you have any questions or is there anything I can do to help?
>
> No? Then just drop that back in the mail and we will get it processed. I look forward to receiving the application. When I do receive the information, I will make sure that it is taken care of quickly. Once we find that you have been extended that credit line, I'll contact you and we will schedule an appointment to begin your treatment.

The tracking device will let you know when an application has left the office and when it is returned. Otherwise you can see how a lot of information could fall through the cracks. Evaluation—or monitoring—is like taking the temperature of the practice. If you see that the tracking device indicates negative information, this is a sign of a problem. This measurement gives you a chance to do something about it. If you don't track information about your practice, you lose the opportunity to correct any mistakes or problems.

Track this chart audit and the mailing of your applications. Otherwise the applications will be floating around, and you won't have any idea where they are.

When you do reach a person—whether or not he wishes to become involved with your financing program—you will want to either schedule the patients for treatment with the dentist or with the hygienist for continuous care. Most dentists feel that if the diagnosis has been made in the last six months that it is appropriate to schedule treatment with the dentist. However, if the patient has not been seen in the last six months, he needs to be scheduled for a periodic evaluation with the dentist as well as a professional cleaning with the hygienist. A new diagnosis and treatment plan would be necessary.

Don't try to audit all of the charts at once. Audit on a regular basis, consistently, and with a plan. Then, get on the phone and make contact with those patients. You are going to take many small steps, and pretty soon, you will have completed the long walk. What a fantastic way to expand your practice and to maximize your new financing program.

Daily chart audits through a healthy morning meeting

There are many important parts to a productive morning meeting, but one of those parts is to identify dentistry that has been diagnosed but not completed. Most practices will find that 50–75% of patients coming to the office on any given day need some treatment beyond today—either with the hygienist or the dentist. Instead of spending a great deal of time during the morning meeting talking about what you will be doing that day, identify what the patient needs next. Make note of that. Then when the patient is in the treatment area, have a conversation with him about the next phase of necessary dentistry. Use the intra-oral or digital camera to show the patient the next area of concern. Stress the benefits of proceeding with treatment and discuss any problems that may arise if the person doesn't proceed.

• KEY POINT •

Most practices can schedule more dentistry from any given day than they are providing in that day. In addition to identifying necessary care, become great dental educators to help people understand the benefits of oral health and beautiful smiles.

Your goal is to have more people saying, "yes" to treatment that has been diagnosed but has not yet been provided. Get the dentistry out of the charts and into the mouths of your patients. Remember, your doctor would not diagnose and recommend treatment if the patient didn't need it. You do the patient a great service by continuing to encourage him to proceed.

In essence, by doing this on a daily basis at your morning meeting, the entire team is sharing in the responsbiility of doing ongoing chart audits.

4. Insurance

As you do your chart audit, you may find that many people are putting off their dental treatment in spite of the fact that they have dental insurance. Available benefits are not being used, because these people may not be able to handle the estimated patient portion—or co-pay. If you are taking assignment of benefits, when you contact these people during your chart audit, let them know that you will file their insurance as a service to them. Tell them that if they would like to spread out the balance after insurance pays, that you have a new, convenient way for them to do just that. Then tell them about your financing program.

On an ongoing basis, tell your insured patients about this opportunity to utilize insurance benefits and to also have convenient monthly payments for estimated patient portion. You will find that more of your patients will use their insurance.

If you are not taking insurance on assignment but, rather, patients are paying you in full and being reimbursed by the insurance company directly, terrific. However, some people may choose to finance their entire treatment so that the monthly payments will be comfortable for them. That's fine. Both of you win.

BA: Ms. Jones, it sounds to me like you do want to receive the treatment that the doctor is recommending to you but that you need to spread the payments out over a period of time to keep the monthly payments comfortable for you and your family. That's very understandable. For that reason, we have a financial partner who assists our patients with their financial needs. You can finance the entire treatment that Dr. Jameson has recommended for you, we will file your insurance for you, and you will be reimbursed directly by them. Once you receive your check from your insurance company, you can make a substantial payment to the finance company, which will lower your balance and your monthly payment. Let's fill out the application now. It will just take a couple of minutes, and I will be more than happy to help you.

(See chapter 9 for more information on dental insurance.)

5. Continuous Care

Many people do not stay on a regular program of continuous care in hygiene or they do not involve all members of their family in your program, because the investment is prohibitive. That's the last thing any of you want—for your patients to put off needed or desired care because of the cost.

Introducing the financing program to your hygiene patients or through your hygiene retention program will not only allow more of your patients to receive this valuable service, but it will also help you nurture this lifeblood of your practice, the hygiene department.

If you are involved with a nonsurgical periodontal program or if you are offering sealant therapy, you know that many patients want and need this care but find the financial responsibility difficult. However, if they find that they can obtain these treatments and that the monthly investment will fit nicely into the family budget, many will proceed (Fig. 5–16).

Date

____
____
____

Dear__________________,

Our records indicate that you have not been in for your appointment concerning your professional dental cleaning and oral health evaluation appointment for _____ months/years. We have attempted to schedule this appointment for some time now with no success. We are concerned.

The purpose of this appointment is to prevent the formation or development of dental problems. One problem that can occur is Periodontal (or gum) Disease. Loss of teeth due to bone degeneration can happen quickly and quietly and can go unnoticed without regular dental care.

Please do not ignore this notice!! It is very important to maintain great oral health by visiting our office on a regular basis.

Sincerely,

Special Note: Remember to ask about our new financing program. Finance your dentistry for a small amount each month. There is now no need to put off valuable care for you and your family because of cost.

Fig. 5–16 Hygiene retention letter.

6. Case Presentation

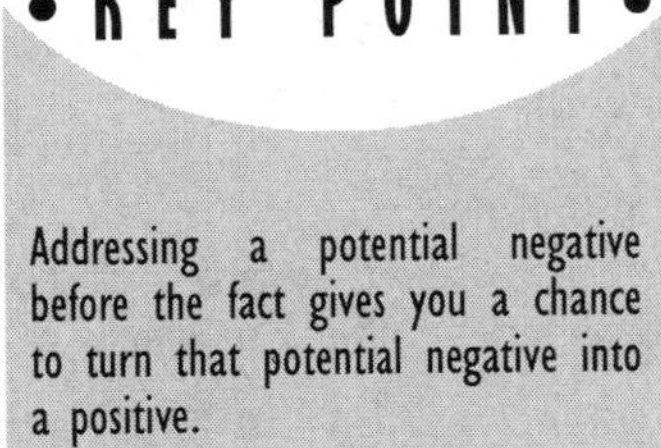

• KEY POINT •
Addressing a potential negative before the fact gives you a chance to turn that potential negative into a positive.

At the time of your case presentation or consultation appointment, introduce the financing program to your clients/patients. Otherwise, as you are trying to educate the patient about the services you are offering, he may be thinking of nothing but the cost. The human mind can only think of one thing at a time. Therefore, if a patient is calculating what they think the treatment will cost, they may not hear a word you are saying.

If you think that something may be a barrier to acceptance, it is better to address this potential barrier before the patient brings it up.

Example

Dr.: Mr. Jones, before I tell you what I have diagnosed and before I explain the treatment that I believe would be best for you, let me tell you that if you have any concern about the financing of the dentistry, we have convenient financial options right here in our practice. Before we proceed with treatment, we will make sure that you are comfortable with the financing of the treatment.

But for right now, I would like to discuss the treatment I feel would be best for you. Let's focus on those recommendations, and then we will discuss the financing thoroughly. Does that sound good to you?

Or, if a person walks into a consultation room and before you even open your mouth to start making recommendations, they look at you and say something like, "Hey, Doc, just get to the bottom line. Just tell me how much this is going to cost me."

Respond in the following way: Answer his question with a question to clarify what they are asking.

Dr.: Are you concerned about the financing of your dental care?

Patient: Sure. I'll bet this is going to cost an arm and a leg.

Dr.: Are you concerned about the total investment or finding a comfortable way to finance your care?

Patient: Well, a bit of both, I guess.

Dr.: That's why I have asked Jan, my treatment coordinator, to join us today. She will discuss the total investment and the options for payment that we have available right here in our practice. I am sure Jan will be able to work this out with you. But for now, if it's OK with you, I would like to focus on the clinical aspects of treatment—what I believe would be the best possible treatment for you. Then, Jan will spend some time with you discussing the finances. Is that OK?

Then, once the patient has agreed, proceed with your clinical presentation. You will defuse the fear of cost. The patient will be able to focus his attention on your clinical presentation. He will appreciate your empathy to his concern, and you will put the money questions where they belong.

For the entire clinical team, let me make this strong recommendation. All of you have an essential role in the making of a financial arrangement. What do I mean by that? When a patient asks you a financial question in the clinical area, you must answer professionally and excellently. Without meaning to do so, you can undermine the TC's efforts to obtain a financial agreement by avoiding financial questions or by insinuating that discussions of money are taboo. (See chapter 6.)

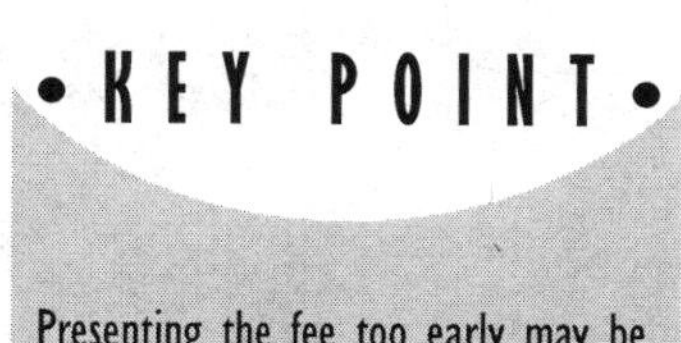

• KEY POINT •
Presenting the fee too early may be worse than not presenting the fee at all.

Offer the best treatment possible, make the financing of the dentistry comfortable, and then get out of the way. Let the patient make the decision of whether or not to proceed (Figs. 5–17 and 5–18).

Create A Win/Win Situation

Benefits to Patients

- An alternative payment method
- Small monthly payments, longer to pay out
- No large amounts due at one time
- Needed or desired care does not have to be delayed
- Supplement for insurance

© Jameson Management, Inc.

Fig. 5–17 Providing a win/win situation.

Benefits to Practice

- Greater cash flow—accounts are paid at the time of service
- Less time and effort is put into collection
- Fewer complaints
- Money it not tied up in A/R
- Greater case acceptance

© Jameson Management, Inc.

Fig. 5–18 For the patient and the practice.

Summary

As a team, spend time going over all of this financial information—how the programs work, the benefits to the patients and to the practice, and the integration of a financing program into the practice. A strategic plan of action for maximizing your financing program needs to be determined, written, and implemented.

By becoming involved with and by maximizing a healthcare financing program, not only do you win by running a more cost-effective practice, but your patients win, because they are able to have the care that they want and need. One more benefit is that dentists are able to do the dentistry they were taught to do and love to do. Plus they will be able to schedule longer appointments doing more dentistry per appointment, which is a productive, profitable and stress-controlled way to practice.

Making the financing of the dentistry comfortable for the patient by defusing the fear of cost makes it possible for people to receive quality, optimum, and complete dentistry rather than partial, incomplete, or patchwork dentistry.

Gather information about these financial programs and study this information together as a team. (See the appendix for a list of programs.) Decide which one will work best for you. Which one can you get behind, get excited about, and really support? Which one do you think will help build your practice and serve your patients best? These programs offer firmness while at the same time incredible flexibility.

Once you have determined the program that is best for you, the entire team will need to work on how to communicate with patients about the program. This will include addressing and overcoming any barriers that patients may present. Don't be afraid of the objections, they are a gift. These questions that arise indicate that the person is seeking additional information. That's good. Let's look at that now.

• CHAPTER • 6

Presenting a Healthcare Financing Program

An objection is a request for further information, indicating that the person is interested in your proposal.

– Tom Hopkins
How to Master the Art of Selling Anything

The presentation of a healthcare financing program makes all the difference in the world. The program will work in direct proportion to your belief in the program as an asset to your practice and to your patients and in direct proportion to your ability to present and market the program. How you communicate these programs will make them work or will leave you with little success. (Refer to my book, *Great Communication = Great Production,* also published by PennWell Books, for further information on communication, including overcoming objections.)

You will need to spend time, as a team, going over these communication skills so that everyone is comfortable with them. When patients ask questions, everyone on the team must be able to answer questions enthusiastically and competently. The more excited you are about this new financing program, the more excited your patients will be, and the more receptive they will be to your suggestions. The patients will be a reflection of you. Your success will be in direct proportion to your enthusiasm.

How to Present a Healthcare Financing Program

Pay close attention to the following presentation script. Count the number of benefits I stress to the patient. A person's behavior will be driven by *what's in this for me*. If you intend for a person to accept your offer to become involved with a financing program, you must present the program in terms of how that program will benefit the patient. Memorize this script. Practice it with one another. These verbal skills have worked for thousands of people—hundreds of practices. I would give it a try, if I were you.

> Ms. Jones, I am glad to tell you that we do have a wonderful method of long-term financing right here in our practice. The program is called ABC Financing Program. ABC offers financing for healthcare—dentistry in our case. You apply right here in our office. You don't have to go anywhere. The application is very easy to complete and will take only a few minutes. I'll be more than happy to assist you. We will send your application to the company through the Internet and will know immediately if they are able to offer you a line of credit. Once you have received a line of credit, we can schedule an appointment to begin your treatment. You can finance your treatment with ABC and can spread the payments out over a designated period of time, thus making your payments very small—payments that will fit nicely into your monthly situation.
>
> Dr. Jameson has paid all necessary fees for you to become involved with the company, and there is no yearly fee. Ms. Jones, based on the treatment that Dr. Jameson is recommending for you, your first monthly payment would be approximately $30. It is a revolving payment program, which means that every time you make a payment your next one is less. In other words, for about $30 per month, you can receive the very best treatment we can provide. Does this sound like something that would be of interest to you?

Overcoming Objections

At the same time that you are learning to present the program, you will want to learn how to defuse negatives that might come up during the presentation. You will want to defuse the negatives associated with this new payment option, and you will want to build a patient's confidence in the fact that the program will help them. Patients must understand the benefits of the program, or they will not accept.

Here are some common situations you will probably encounter and suggested verbal skills for addressing these situations.

Example

You have been practicing dentistry for a while and your patients have been paying you small monthly payments for ever—and ever—and ever.

BA: Mr. Jones, let me tell you about a new program we have in our office. We have found that many of our patients need long-term comfortable financing to handle the financing of their dental care. So, we have listened to our patients and have responded. We now have available in our practice a method of long-term financing called ABC Financing Company. This company has joined our team as our financial partner.

Mr. Jones, you can apply for the financing program right here in our practice. You don't have to go anywhere. Once you are extended a line of credit, we can finance your dentistry, and you can pay it out over a period of time, and your payments will be very small.

Mr. Jones: What are you talking about? I have been paying Dr. Jameson forever! Why can't I just keep paying him out the way I always have? Doesn't he think I'm good for the money anymore?

BA: Of course he does. We are still offering long-term payment, just as we have in the past. We are just doing it in a better way. We have been advised by our accountant that it is neither time nor cost efficient to run a banking business within our practice. We decided it was better for our patients if we concentrated on what we do best, and that is providing excellent dental care.

We have become associated with a reputable company that offers long-term extended payments to our patients. This company works with us to offer this convenient financing. In addition, Mr. Jones, we are committed to maintaining comfortable fees for our dental services, and so we have searched for a better, more cost-efficient way to offer long-term payments so that we can keep our fees at a comfortable level.

Mr. Jones: Well, what is this program? How does this work?

BA: It is a financing company that features an extended payment plan for healthcare. By having a line of credit established for your healthcare, you can conveniently budget this vital service into your monthly income.

Mr. Jones: I don't know about this. Is it hard to apply or to get accepted?

BA: You ask a good question, Mr. Jones, and I am glad to tell you that the application is quite easy, and the acceptance rate is quite high. In fact you apply right here in our office. The application will be similar to any application you have filled out previously. However, if you do have any questions, I'll be more than happy to help you. In a matter of minutes we can complete the application and send it to the company over the Internet and receive a response immediately.

(**Note**: Some companies may require a telephone call or a faxed application. Alter these particular verbal skills to fit the requirements of your company.)

Mr. Jones: Well, are they going to charge me interest?

(Response #1 for the revolving payment plan.)

BA: There is a service fee, Mr. Jones, just as you pay with any other financing program. The service fee is 1.75% a month or about $1.75 per month for every $100 that you finance, and Mr. Jones, I'm sure that you will agree, that is not much considering the fact that you can receive the treatment that the doctor has recommended to you, and you won't have to make a major investment all at once.

(Response #2 for the interest-free plan.)

BA: There is no interest to you, Mr. Jones. Dr. Jameson has paid all necessary fees for you to participate in this program so that you can spread the payments over a designated period of time, and you will not be charged any interest. That's great, isn't it?

Mr. Jones: Well, I don't know about this. I just wish I could pay Dr. Jameson the way I used to.

BA: I know how you feel. We have other good, long-term patients that have felt confused about the changes we are making until they found out that they could still spread out the payments for their dental care. However, their monthly payments are usually smaller, and they can take longer to pay out their balance. Mr. Jones, we have many families using this program, and they just love the convenience. These families seem to be happier because with their available line of credit, they are better able to take care of more members of their family on a more regular basis.

Mr. Jones: Well, how much will my monthly payments be?

(Response #1 for the revolving payment plan.)

BA: You are only required to pay 3% of the outstanding balance. The fee for the treatment that Dr. Jameson has recommended for you is $1,000. Your first monthly payment will be approximately $30. It is a revolving program, which means that every time you make a payment, the next payment will be less. Would that be comfortable for you?

(Response #2 for the interest-free program.)

BA: You will be required to make a small monthly payment of 3% of the total balance which would be $30 for your case. Then you can take care of the balance in any manner you wish as long as the total balance is paid by the end of your agreement. You can have 3, 6, 12, or 18 months to pay. The length of time you select is up to you.

(**Note**: Most companies determine the length of time they will give a patient to pay in full by the size of the charge. For example,: for charges of $300 or less; 3 months is maximum, $700, 6 months; and $1,000 or more, 12 months. There are companies today that will go longer—up to 24 months. The point here is to check carefully into the programs and requirements of the various companies and find the one that fits your needs.)

In the previous example, I have used a particular set of percentages for illustration purposes. You would have to supplement the percentages, service fee rates, and monthly rates according to your own program. But study these verbal skills and scripts. Put these skills into your own words and become comfortable with them. Insert the appropiate numbers. The presentation of the program is three-fourths of it.

Again, everyone on the team must have confidence in the program and know how to present the program as well as how to address and overcome objections.

Once your financial system is in place, everyone on the team must provide support for the program. It is very difficult for a business administrator to make financial arrangements with the patients based on the financial protocol only to have exceptions made on a regular basis.

I am not suggesting that the dentist does not have the option to make an exception to the financial protocol. She should certainly have that option. However, the business administrator must know that he will be supported and backed up by the dentist and the entire team.

If a patient asks a question about financing or money or cost in the clinical area, here is how I recommend you handle those kinds of questions.

Example

Patient: The doctor says I need a crown. How much is that? And how can I pay for that ?

Dr./Clinical Assistant/or Hygienist: Ms. Jones, are you concerned about the financing of your crown? Will that make a difference as to whether or not you go ahead with treatment?

Patient: Well, yes.

Dr. /Clinical Assistant/ or Hygienist: I can appreciate your concern. We have several excellent financial options available for our patients. Joe, our Business Administrator, handles all financial arrangements, and he is terrific. I will let him know that you are concerned about the financing of your treatment. He will tell you the total investment and the options we have available for payment. We have some very convenient methods of financing. I am sure that he will be able to work something out for you.

In the previous dialogue, the clinical team did not close the door on the financial question. They left the door open for the patient and for the BA. They gave a very positive introduction to the financial options, and they gave a professional compliment to the BA. A compliment of this kind from the clinical team can make the financial discussion go much smoother.

Clinical team, you must be careful not to close the door to a positive financial discussion, and you must not give the patient the idea that a discussion of money is a taboo thing or that the fees are so high that you wouldn't want to touch such a discussion with a 10-ft pole.

Your confidence will give the BA a smoother path. Get the previous verbal skills down pat and use them whenever you are asked a financial/money question in the clinical area.

Summary

There is no question in my mind that the way you communicate makes all the difference in the world. In fact, I believe that communication is the bottom line to your success—or the lack of it. Communicating financially with your patients is a very personal and private conversation. Be gracious while, at the same time, enthusiastic.

Once you become involved with a patient financing program, learning how to present it, explaining the benefits, and overcoming the very normal objections could make the difference as to whether or not patients accept the program. It will be worth the effort to learn these communication skills. Communication skills can be learned. You can do this. It will take careful planning and practice. The end result of your efforts will be higher levels of case acceptance and greater personal satisfaction.

•CHAPTER•

7

The Financial Agreement: Getting Ready

It isn't only what you do, or even how you do it—but also when you do it.

– **Mark McCormack**
The 110% Solution

Now you have a financial protocol in your practice. You have carefully and caringly selected the options you are going to make available to your patients. You have become involved with a healthcare financing program. You have put a dam in the river called *accounts receivable*, and you are no longer carrying accounts on your own books. You have spent time, as a team, discussing and developing the financial system in your practice and studying how to communicate about finances. You are ready to go.

In order to be effective at coming to a financial agreement with a patient, you have to start with the right mind set. You must be totally committed to the belief that the patient needs the dental care, and that he will benefit tremendously from your services. Everyone on the team must believe that if a patient walks out the door not scheduling an appointment—that the patient loses just as much as you do or more.

Synonyms for the word agreement are as follows: accord, harmony, union, concurrence. Nice, huh? Isn't that what you are trying to do? Come to a harmonious accord with a patient where you can develop a union between your practice and the patient—where both of you win? When you arrive at an agreement with the patient about the equitability of the fee as it relates to the service—the end results they will obtain—and when you *concur* on a method of payment that works for both of you—that's an agreement. That's what you want. Clarity, understanding, agreement.

If your attitude is in the right place and you have this type of commitment, then you will see the making of the financial arrangement—coming to a financial agreement—as a constructive challenge to determine each patient's financial situation and her concerns, if any. Your job, then, will be to find a *solution* to every patient's financial needs.

There are three essential elements of *getting ready* to determine to a financial agreement with your patients (Fig. 7–1).

To Lead a Person To a Buying Decision, One Must Have:

1. Knowledge of product or service
2. In–depth knowledge of money and financing
3. Ability to complete any necessary paperwork

Fig. 7–1 The key elements of a buying decision.

As I describe the key elements of making a financial arrangement and securing an agreement, I will refer to the person or persons carrying out this responsibility as the business administrator (BA), the treatment coordinator (TC), or the financial coordinator (FC). I am fine with all three of these descriptions for this role.

What I am not comfortable with is calling the person administering the business portion of the practice as the *front desk*! "Oh, Mr. Jones just ask Susie, she's my front desk!"

These awesome professionals who are administering the complexities of a dental office are not front desks. They are not made of wood! If you want your patients to respect the person making this critical arrangement, address her with respect. Your patients will reflect that respect. (It goes without saying that the person must deserve this type of respect by doing a great job. Never stop working on and making effort to improve the skill level here—just as you work on improving your clinical skill level.)

Let's look at the following three areas:

1. **Knowledge of Product and Service**—You must be comfortable answering questions about the treatment itself. This does not infer that you have to be a dentist to make a financial agreement, but you need to be aware of what the doctor is recommending, why he is recommending certain procedures, how long this will take and, of course, the financial responsibility. The person discussing the financial responsibiltiy needs to be able to give the doctor third-party backup support. We all know that patients may ask a team member things they will not ask the doctor. The last thing you want is to be totally *clueless* about the procedure.

When a person asks things like, "Do you think I really need this?" or "Would you have this done if it were you?" or "Do you think this will hurt?" or "How long will this last?" or "Is there any other way I could get this done?" and so on, the FC must be able to confidently and sincerely answer those questions.

In my book, *Great Communication = Great Production*, I make the point that just because a patient tells the doctor that this is the type of treatment she wants and that she doesn't have any questions doesn't necessarily mean that this is true. She may have all kinds of questions—but she is embarrassed or uncomfortable asking the doctor. Patients don't want to look stupid in the eyes of the doctor, and/or they don't want to make the doctor think that he didn't do a good job of presenting the recommendations.

In addition, just because the patient says yes to the clinical dentistry, this doesn't mean that the case is *closed*. Not so. The presenter of the clinical aspects of treatment will do the initial close—but the final close comes at the financial presentation. When a patient and the practice come to a financial agreement—an agreement on the total investment and on the method of payment, that's the final close. All consultations have two parts: the clinical presentation and the financial presentation.

2. **In Depth Knowledge of Money and Financing**—The FC must know all about the financial options of the practice—what they are, how they work, and the benefits to the patient. She must be able to discuss money comfortably, handle objections, and not give up until a financial agreement has been concluded.

You do not want to get into a financial discussion only to find that you don't have the materials or the knowledge you need. Your ineptness will come across loud and clear to the patient. And then, no matter how great your doctor may be, you could absolutely blow this agreement. Much relies upon the financial discussion. In surveys I do with my audiences, I often ask this somewhat obvious question—but a good one for us to ackowledge—"If someone wants the treatment that the doctor has recommended but they do not proceed with treatment, what's the reason?" Of course, we all know—and the audiences ackowledge—*money*!

Doctors, do not turn your head to this imperative aspect of practice health—and of your ultimate success. Place the importance of making financial arrangements where it belongs—as one of the most important *moments of truth* in your relationship with a patient. Remember: If one patient per day goes ahead with treatment that might not otherwise do that, this could make a minimum of a $100,000 difference in your practices.

Example

Today, one of my consultants and I were speaking of one of our clients—a great lady, practicing in the midwest. She is a great practitioner and a lovely person. Her practice has done very well under our guidance but has in the past two months taken a downturn—a trend that we rarely see in our practices and one, of course, that distresses us, as well as the doctor.

In speaking with the doctor, the only identifiable event that has shown up as a potential causative for the drop in production was a recent change of staff in the business office. The person we had trained at the outset had moved, and a new person was on board. At a monthly teleconference with her team, my consultant quickly discovered that this new person had not been well-trained by the departing team member and/or the doctor, so step one was for us to do an intensive training to bring her *up to snuff*. However, in addition, this person—this new person—did not think the doctor's fees were equitable, that they were much too high, and she felt that this was why people were not accepting treatment.

Obviously, this was not the fact because people had been accepting treatment before her arrival. She was using the *excuses of fees too high, not being lenient enough in financial option*, etc. to cover up her own inability to make a good financial arrangement.

With excellent training, we were able to work this out. However, this example is a *heads up* for all of you. With no other major change in this practice, the overall productivity dropped because of a FC who did not have in depth knowledge of money and financing and who did not have knowledge of product or service. Luckily, we caught this early and turned it around.Too much is as stake—too much is at risk—not to have this position honored and managed with superior ability.

3. **Ability to Complete Any Necessary Paperwork**—Your FC must be able to complete the written financial agreement, handle any insurance issues, manage your healthcare financing program or programs and do so with confidence and ability. The last thing in the world that you want is to have your FC falter at the last minute—not being able to quickly and succinctly complete all paperwork to finish. Remember: You falter, you lose. Be prepared.

To Be Effective with Your Financial Arrangements

To be truly effective in making financial arrangements or to come to a comfortable financial agreement between you and a patient, there are several parameters that will make this transaction with your patients as positive as possible. Consider including the following in your financial protocols:

1. **Privacy.** Remember, the oral cavity is an intimate zone of a person's body and so is the pocketbook. Therefore, you need to be in a quiet area that provides the necessary privacy. Do not try to make a financial agreement at the front desk in front of everyone for the following reasons:

   A. A person may become embarrassed and may schedule the appointment but have no intention to come to the appointment. She may not feel comfortable telling you that she has a concern about the fee, and she may not want to ask you for financial options for fear that other people will overhear the conversation.

B. Patient privacy is protected when conversations about treatment and about finances are done in private. If you do not have a formal consultation area, find some place in the office where a small but neat area can be prepared for the consultations, like the dentist's private office. Some offices are constructed to have an area in the business office where discussions of money can take place. This is great. You must evaluate your own facility and determine what works best for you.

C. The FC may be interrupted by people checking in or by the telephone or by another person coming to the front desk to check out. If there are interruptions during the conversation regarding the fee, mistakes can be made easily. Attention cannot be focused on the person with whom she is having the discussion. Or, if there are too many interruptions and the conversation becomes impossible, there may be no financial agreement made whatsoever. This, of course, can lead to poor collections and, sometimes, disgruntled patients who were not informed of their financial responsibility in advance.

Personal Note

In our office, we removed an unnecessary couch from my husband's, John's, private office and now we use his office for our consultations. This area is used for consultations—both clinical and financial. All necessary paperwork is within reach for the TC. A 19-in. flat screen monitor is in the consultation room. We have access to all patient information, including stored and retrievable digital images of the patient to whom we are presenting and a *library* of all of our cases so that patients can see similar situations. (Obviously, these are shown with that patient's written permission.)

John's treatment coordinator joins him as he is designing treatment plans. We schedule time during the week for case planning. He wants to make sure that his treatment coordinator is clear about the treatment plan he has created before the consultation appointment so that she knows what he wants to do, why and how he wants to proceed—what he wants to do first, second, and so on, and how long he needs for each appointment. She will do a better job of giving him backup support and will be more prepared for that critical financial presentation if she is fully informed (Fig. 7–2).

John makes his presentation of recommendations with his TC present. Once he has completed his presentation and is sure that the patient has no further clinical questions for him, he turns the consultation over to the TC and excuses himself.

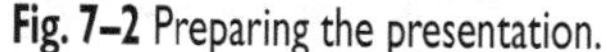

Fig. 7–2 Preparing the presentation.

Fig. 7–3 Presenting the dentistry.

The TC has heard everything John has said to the patient—and the questions or concerns expressed by the patient to the doctor (Fig. 7–3).

She is fully prepared to give the doctor *quality* third-party reinforcement. She will be able to answer possible clinical questions that the patient may not have been comfortable asking the doctor. (The person presenting the financial consultation needs to have clinical knowledge so that she can give this type of backup and so that she can answer—in layman's language—questions that *will* come up during her time with the patient.)

Once the doctor has excused himself, the TC takes over. She needs to ask the following question before the discussion of finances begins:

> Ms. Jones, I know that Dr. Jameson asked if you had any questions and you said no, but I thought there might be something you would like to ask me.

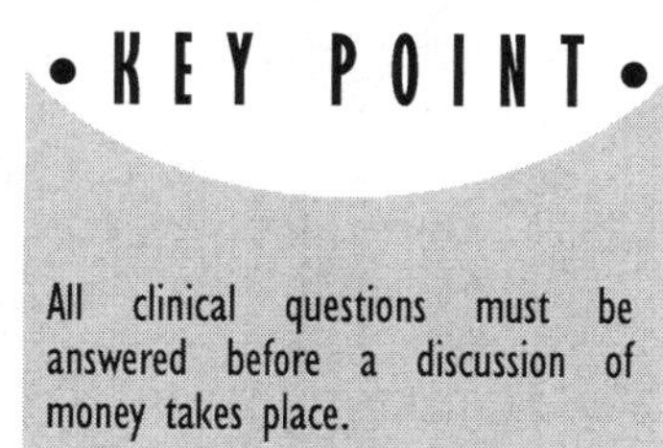

• KEY POINT •

All clinical questions must be answered before a discussion of money takes place.

Clear any questions about the procedures/ treatment, the course of action to be taken, and give statements related to the benefits of the treatment. Sell the person on the treatment first—then discuss the fee.

Do not be in a rush. Have time to answer questions and discuss any concerns. Know that the discussion with the TC might be longer than the discussion with the dentist about the treatment. That's OK. This is a person who wants or needs your care. Your responsibility is to make a financial arrangement that will allow him to go ahead. You want a clear, written financial agreement before the discussion is complete, and you will want to have scheduled at least the first appointment.

Trying to close too fast may be worse than not trying to close at all. How can a patient make a decision about his financial responsibility before he even knows what he is buying?

• KEY POINT •

Quoting a fee too early may be worse than not quoting a fee at all.

If you are in an office where there is a small team and only one person in the business office—the BA—you can still do this. Pre-block your appointment book for the dentist's consultation time and the BA's time. Knowing in advance that the BA will be occupied with a patient discussing finances makes it possible for other team members to cover the front desk. The clinical assistant can check people in and out during that time. Put a bell or chime on your front door so that she will hear when a patient arrives and, if need be, place a special message on your telephone so that you can gather necessary data from incoming calls and can return the calls immediately.

If you have more than one clinical assistant, she can answer the telephone. Make sure that all people are cross-trained. It is imperative that the right hand knows what the left hand is doing. Crossover is a key element of every job description.

What you don't want is for the BA to be interrupted to handle front desk responsibilities or to answer the telephone while she is having a private financial conversation with a patient. That's a great way to lose the patient and to lose the case.

2. **Professional Image.** The person making the financial arrangement needs to be dressed in business attire and presenting a very professional image. She is going to be making a financial/business arrangement with the patient. She has a totally different relationship with the patient than does the clinical team. Sitting down with a person talking about the financial responsibility for dental care needs to be done in a business-like atmosphere. That includes the atmosphere or aura created by the person making that arrangement.

3. **Introductions.** In most instances, the patient will already know the person who is going to be making the financial arrangement. The patient would have met him on the telephone and in the business office. Or, if a member of your clinical team is serving the role of TC, the patient may have met him during the initial comprehensive oral evaluation appointment.

However, if you are in a large office where a person is handling all of the financial aspects of the practice, including making the financial arrangements, the patient may not have met this team member. Make sure that appropriate introductions are made.

> Ms. Jones, this is Jan Davis, my Treatment Coordinator. I have asked her to join us today for our consultation. Jan will be working with you to make the financial arrangement, and she will be helping with the scheduling of your appointments. I felt that it was very important that she hear what I am recommending for you. Is this all right with you?" (No one in our own practice has ever said, "no" to that question.)

Note that the dentist not only introduced Jan, but he also told Ms. Jones what her role was in the consultation. He also stressed how much he wanted to make sure she knew exactly where they would be going with the treatment.

4. **Body Language—Watch for Buying Signs.** All of the previously mentioned reasons for having the TC join you for the consultation are excellent ones. However, one more significant reason is that she can watch the patient's body language for visual buying signs, or signs of discomfort. She can also hear the exchange between the doctor and the patient and will know what part of the treatment plan she may need to revisit. In addition, the patient will not be able to say, "Oh, no, the doctor said I could do this—or that." If she is sitting in the room, she will know exactly what the doctor did or did not say.

The TC needs to be in the room—with the patient's permission, but needs to be noninvasive during the doctors' discussion. She does not want to interfere during the consultation, unless the doctor or patient addresses her with a question. However, she does need to make notes that she will refer to during her time with the patient.

5. **Call the Patient by Name—Frequently.** During your financial discussion, refer to the patient by name from time to time. The sweetest sound to a person's ear is the sound of his/her own name. Plus, patients will feel that your time with them is more personalized. This *Ritz-Carlton* type of quality customer service is appropriate throughout the office by all members of the team but is critical during the intimate discussion of money.

6. **Have All Necessary Information.** Be prepared. All of the appropriate information needs to be complete and in the consultation room during the financial consultation. The TC will have had the treatment plan in hand prior to the consultation so that she can calculate the fees, including the expected insurance coverage, if appropriate. She also needs to know what the first monthly payment will be if the patient chooses to participate with the healthcare financing program (Fig. 7–4).

FINANCIAL AGREEMENT
Non-Insurance Patient

Patient name:____ **Date:**__________

We are concerned about your dental health. We look forward to helping you with your dental care.

Area/Appt	*Recommended Treatment*	*Fee*
		TOTAL

Financial agreement for your treatment:

_____Fee reduction _5_% is available if payment for treatment is made in full prior to treatment. $______________- $______________ = $____________

_____Cash or check at time of service ______________________________________

_____VISA, MC, AMEX or DISCOVER

________ Healthcare Financing Program ______________________________________

I understand and accept the TREATMENT PLAN above:_______________Date:______

I agree to the FINANCIAL RESPONSIBILITY for the total fee. The fees listed on this treatment outline will be honored for 90 days from the above date. After that time, the fees are subject to adjustments.

REMARKS:____

Jameson Management, Inc.

Fig. 7–4 Written financial agreement.

If a patient expresses a concern about money on the phone, send him information about your patient financing program. Make effort to get him preapproved before he walks into the office. Or, at the initial appointment if he expresses financial concerns, then have him complete an application for your financing program while in the office. You can send the information over the Internet, by fax, or on the phone. In fact, certain companies have developed relationships with some of the major dental software companies, and you can gather the financing information within your software. From there, you can complete all necessary information, send the information through the Internet so that you will receive immediate response regarding approval and amount of credit.

You want to be so well prepared for the consultation appointment that you do not have to figure information while the patient waits for you. You want to have all the necessary information to make any kind of financial arrangement. You want to have your *ducks in a row*. Being well prepared says, "We want to take care of you—physically and financially." Being prepared says that you are professionals and handle all aspects of your relationship with a patient in a professional manner (Fig. 7–5).

Fig. 7–5 Making a financial arrangement.

Know that patients make decisions about your quality of care by everything, including how you handle their business relationship. You must be organized in order to give excellent, *state-of-the-art care*.

Summary

Have a team meeting to determine the who, what, how, when, why, and where of your financial arrangements. Make sure that you incorporate all the previous six criteria in your discussion and in your protocol. Get your paperwork in order. Make sure that you have the location arranged and that it is conducive to a professionally presented financial discussion.

The person making the financial arrangements will be making the final close of the presentation. She has a critical responsibility. If a patient sees the benefits of treatment as presented by the dentist, then the only thing that may prevent the patient from going ahead may be the financing. Have everything work toward the goal of gaining a high rate of case acceptance, including financial acceptance.

• CHAPTER • 8

Establishing a Financial Agreement: Communication and Verbal Skills

Communication skill is the bottom line to your success.

– **Cathy Jameson, PhD**
Great Communication = Great Production

The environment has been prepared, the appropriate paperwork has been made available, the format of the financial presentation has been determined. Now you are ready to prepare for the face-to-face presentation. In *Great Communication = Great Production,* I said, "communication skill is the bottom line to your success." Certainly, in the area of making financial arrangements, how you communicate with a patient will make or break the situation.

People want you to help them find a solution to their financial situation, no matter what that may be. You must be a good listener. Identify wants and needs. The only way to do this is to ask questions and listen. Identify objections or problems to treatment acceptance. You must be able to peel the layers of the problem to determine the core or center of the problem. Then—and only then—can you come to a cooperative decision as to how to solve that problem. Be aware that you

> **• KEY POINT •**
>
> A problem is only a problem until it becomes defined. Once it becomes defined, it becomes manageable.

may need to offer *alternatives*—different ways to solve the problem whether that be a problem of time, money, or treatment option (Fig. 8–1).

There's your challenge. Define the problem. Consider it a challenge—one that can be solved.

Communication:
The Bottom Line To Your Success

Presentation Skills

1. Ask questions to better understand the situation
2. Overcome objections to motivate the patient to pay
3. Offer options to gain commitment

Fig. 8–1 Communication is the key.

Build a Relationship of Trust and Confidence

Dentistry is a relationship business. I am sure we will all agree on that fact. You are in the business of working with people emotionally, physically, and financially. You are interacting with their behaviors—their needs and wants as well as their individual differences.

Because a discussion of money is such a personal discussion, focus on establishing a relationship with the patient before presenting your recommendations—clinical or financial. Business experts tell us that people will never buy your product or service unless they have a strong relationship of trust and/or confidence with you. Without question, if people are going to invest in your services, they must have that trust. After all, you are going to be *in their mouth*—that intimate zone. Plus, you are going to be helping the patient to get healthy again—or you are going to be changing their smile.

Therefore, from the minute the telephone is answered, to the mailing of the welcome packet, to the initial appointment, to the making of the financial arrangements, and through the completion of treatment, each person on the team has what business calls a *moment of truth*. Each person on the team has a chance to make or break a relationship with a patient. Each step of the patient's path must be based on the establishment and the continuation of trust.

If too many patients are saying, "I'd like to think it over," or saying, "no," there may be weakness in the area of personal/patient relationships. If you analyze your case acceptance ratio and are displeased with the level of acceptance, you may find that a trust level is not established before the financial responsibility is discussed. There is no reason to talk about money if the patient doesn't see the benefit of the treatment or doesn't have a solid sense of trust with you.

When a person comes to you as a personal referral, that person will already have a certain level of trust and confidence. However, once they decide to come to the office, your *people skills* take over.

In developing a relationship with an existing or a new patient, ask questions and listen to understand their concerns, their likes and dislikes. The most important thing you will do during your initial interview is establish the patient's motivator—his emotional *hot button*. Know that a person will make a purchase based on *what's in this for me* or *how will this benefit me* or *how will this purchase help me*.

Remember to be flexible. Sense the patients' needs. Meet her *where she is coming from*. Don't be too directive; don't be judgmental. Don't X-ray a person's pocketbook. Listen. Present the dentistry that you believe will meet the patient's needs. Make the financing of the dentistry comfortable by offering several options. Then get out of the way, and let the patient make her own decision about health, well-being, and appearance.

If the patient doesn't say, "When do we start," you may have presented the fee too soon. You do not present the fee until motivators are determined, all clinical questions are answered, and the person wants the dentistry.

A person will buy what they want long before they will buy what they need. You *must* determine the motivators and present to that motivator. Trying to *close* too early is as nonproductive as not closing at all.

Listen Your Way to Financial Acceptance

Listen your way to financial acceptance? How? Is this possible? Don't you have to talk and talk and talk before a person will understand things well enough to say yes? No. Listening may be the single most important communication skill that you can access when you are trying to establish a solid relationship with a patient and when you are trying to gain insight into his personal concerns. Listening can make a positive difference in your dental practice.

Four different activities that a person does with language are the following:

1. reading
2. writing
3. speaking
4. listening

Most people believe that listening is the most powerful of all these skills. I would agree. However, most people also agree that of these four communication skills that listening is the skill that is the most difficult and the one that needs the most work and attention. Again, I agree.

Kevin Murphy, President of CDK Management and Consulting Associates, says that listening is

- the accurate perception of what is being communicated
- a process in perpetual motion
- a two-way exchange in which both parties involved must always be receptive to the thoughts, ideas, and emotions of the other

Mr. Murphy also says, "Listening is a natural process that goes against human nature!"

What Gets in the Way of Effective Listening in the Dental Office?

Some of the prevalent deterrents to good listening in your office may be as follows:

- time pressure
- stress — not being able to relax
- mind set — being rigid in thought processes
- talking too much — dominating the conversation as the *authority*
- thinking what to say in response instead of listening
- lack of interest

Before you can learn how to listen effectively, you must develop an understanding of the attitudes necessary for listening to take place. An open mind is necessary for the skill of listening to be considered a true avenue of communication.

By listening to your patients, you will learn how they feel about their situations and you will learn what it is they want. Then you will be better able to satisfy those wants. The patient wins by receiving needed or desired treatment; and you, the dental team, win with increased productivity.

What Attitudes Are Required for Successful Listening to Take Place?

1. **You must want to hear what the other person is saying.** This takes time. Scheduled time for discussion of financial issues lets you and the patient focus on this intimate discussion without interruption. The patient won't feel rushed and neither will you. You must have time if you are going to listen well enough to determine a person's questions, concerns, and particular needs. The point here is vital: you must be able to hear the other person's point of view—determine what she wants, then be able to communicate well enough to address those wants.

2. **You must sincerely want to help the other person with the problem.** The position of FC/TC must be assigned to someone who *wants* to deal with this area. This takes a confident person; one who (a) believes in the benefits of dental care, (b) has faith in the dentist's ability, (c) can quote total treatment fees without flinching, and (d) is an excellent communicator—one who can *listen.*

3. **You must be able to accept the other person's true feelings.** Other people will have feelings different from yours. Sometimes these feelings may be different from what you think they *should be.* Learning to accept these differences and not letting them affect your relationship to that person. may take both time and effort.

In the area of financing, you may hear statements from patients that could be offensive. For example, "This fee is ridiculous. What does that dentist want to do—go to Hawaii on my mouth?" and so on.

I've heard everything—you probably have, too. It may be difficult to accept another person's opinion at first. As difficult as it may be to listen to the person, letting the patient get things out on the table and making sure you are clear on where that person is coming from is the first step to coming to a financial agreement.

4. **You must trust that the other person has the ability to handle his/her feelings.** You cannot make another person feel differently. However, you can influence a person's opinion. That's what you want—the opportunity to influence a person's opinion. You want to get the patient to a place where he/she will listen to you—listen to the options you have available for payment.

• KEY POINT •

The best way to get a person to listen to you is to listen to that person first.

The goal of determining open lines of communication is to develop a win-win solution—one that is good for the patient and one that is good for the practice. In order to develop a financial solution with a patient, you must establish the needs of both parties—what does the patient need? What does the practice need? A good solution is one that works for both parties. In a true win-win solution, the needs of both parties are met.

5. **You must know that feelings can be transitory.** Be accepting of the *human nature* of changing feelings. Don't make judgments about a person based on your automatic reaction. Take the time to truly define the problem, design a plan for the resolution of the problem, and to implement the solution.

Don't prejudge anyone. You may be surprised at which patients accept the full treatment plan. If you go into every financial presentation with a positive mindset and if you *think* that the person will accept the treatment, you will have a much greater acceptance rate.

6. **You must be able to actually listen without becoming self-stimulated or defensive.** Allow for a *separateness*. The other person is unique from you and responds in his/her own way. Respect this separateness (i.e., often, when you *hear* what another person says, you *do* become defensive and, thus, close the door to *good communication*). A more effective way to truly *listen* to another is to reflect back to the person what you think you are hearing. By *actively listening* to a person, you are able to get to the center of the message—what the sender really means.

Saying nothing at all is just fine, if you are truly *listening attentively*. Silence is a nonverbal message that, when used effectively, can make a person feel genuinely accepted. Ask a question. Then give the patient your full attention.

- **Body Language:** Body language accounts for approximately 60% of the perception of a message whether you are sending it or receiving it. Examples of good body language are eye contact, being on the same level, slightly leaning forward, arms and legs uncrossed. If 60% of the perception of a message is body language, then I would encourage you to pay close attention here. Videotape yourselves in your various roles and see how you can improve. Coach one another. The great athletes, performers, and presenters of the world have coaches and are constantly trying to improve.

- **Tone of Voice:** Tone of voice accounts for 30% of the perception of a message. Be willing and able to reflect the personality of the patient. If they are high energy, step it up a notch. If they are quiet and serene, you may need to soften your conversations. In addition, listen to yourself sometime. Record yourself. Are you being enthusiastic? Are you interesting? Are you organized in your presentation? Critique yourself and work on improvement.

- **Words:** The words you speak account for 10% of the perception of the message. I, certainly, am interested in the verbal skills—as is evidenced throughtout this book. But no matter how excellent your verbal skills, 90% of the message you are sending or receiving is everything but the verbal skills. Remember, you want information so that you can determine where the person is coming from. Let the patient give you the lead. Then engineer your presentation to follow that lead.

Passive Listening

When a person begins to share information with you, encourage her to continue, to go on, to provide more information to you by sincerely saying such things as, "Oh," "I see," "really," "uh huh," and so on. These simple, nonjudgmental responses are called "passive listening" by Dr. Thomas Gordon. This passive listening, along with attentive body language will (1) make the patient comfortable, (2) motivate the patient to share information, and (3) develop a trusting relationship that leads to mutual respect.

Active Listening

When a situation or problem warrants a more active participation by both parties, the communication skill called *active listening* is appropriate. The term and concept of active listening was also developed by Dr. Thomas Gordon. Active listening is the restating in your own words what you understand the other person to be saying. When actively listening to someone, you need to give careful attention to both the content of the message and to the feeling that is being transmitted.

Example

FC: Ms. Jones, the fee for the recommended treatment is $800. Let's discuss our available methods of payment so that we can find the one that best suits your needs.

Patient: $800! You have got to be kidding! For one tooth?

FC: You seem surprised with the fee.

Patient: I am. I can't believe that it costs that much to fix this tooth. I just think I'll have him pull it out.

FC: Sounds like you feel that the fee is too high to save your tooth.

Patient: I'd like to save this tooth, but I had no idea it would be this much.

FC: Are you concerned about the total fee or about finding a way to pay for this?

Patient: Finding a way to pay, I guess.

FC: So, what we need to do is find a way for you to save the tooth and, at the same time, find a way for you to finance this so it will not be stressful to you.

Patient: Yes. If I'm going to be able to get this done, I need a way to pay it out.

Feed back to the person your own understanding of their message. This type of listening helps to establish clarity. You must know the concern of the patient. In the previous example, the FC is determining if the patient is not interested in her health or if she is concerned about that fee and if she needs a way to spread out the payments.

You will shoot yourself in the foot if you begin answering questions before you determine the real problem. Often the opening remarks are only the peripheral issue. Listening lets you peel the layers of problem to get to the core, the real issue.

Don't Become Defensive

Although there are many roadblocks that get in the way of good listening, becoming defensive toward the other person is, perhaps, the greatest barrier. When a person becomes defensive, the lines of communication close. Therefore, when discussing possible treatment—and certainly when discussing financing—becoming defensive is detrimental.

In order *not* to become defensive, the single best skill you can use is listening. According to Dr. Gordon in his book, *Making the Patient Your Partner,* the following three characteristics describe a good listener:

1. Empathy
2. Genuineness
3. Acceptance

Native American lore says, "You can't walk a mile in another person's moccasins unless you first take off your own." That's a good way to describe *empathy*. The only way to let a person know that you are really interested in him, without judgment, is to listen to him. A person feels important, respected, and validated when you listen.

Genuineness means that you are congruent or sincere in your willingness to hear what another person is thinking and feeling. It also means that you are willing to be honest with your own feelings.

Acceptance. You may not agree with what another person says, but you must be able to accept his opinion or, at least, accept his right to express his opinion.

However, if you listen to, validate, and respect the other person—he will be more likely to listen to you when the time comes. In order for the patient to listen to your financial presentation, he must respect you. In order to gain respect, you must have first shown respect for him through listening.

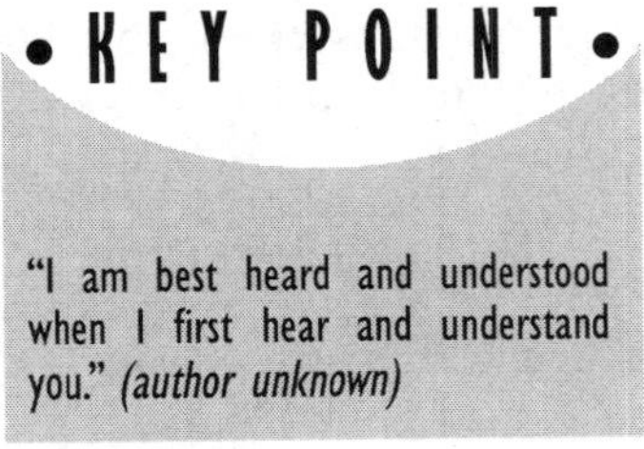

• KEY POINT •

"I am best heard and understood when I first hear and understand you." *(author unknown)*

When you learn to integrate active listening into your repertoire of communication skills, you truly involve the mind in a dynamic process rather than using only the ears in a physical process. You reach out to the sender of the message with your own message of caring and acceptance. If you use only your ears to *hear* the words but do not use your mind actively to understand what is really being said and felt, then you do nothing to advance communication. The result is *failure to communicate*.

From active listening feedback, the sender gets tangible evidence of how the receiver deciphered the message. The sender can either confirm the accuracy of the message (yes, that is just what I meant) or can deny the accuracy (no, that is not what I meant at all...it is like this...). This kind of continual feedback allows a you to be absolutely sure that you understand what is being said. This also provides a sense of *empathy* and *acceptance* for the one delivering the message.

Listen, Listen, Listen

You have heard the saying,"God gave you two ears and one mouth so that you could listen twice as much as you talk." Pretty good advice.

No matter what the specific goals and objectives of your practice, every one of your days is an exchange of content and emotion—both verbal and nonverbal. That is communication. If you choose to ignore or underplay this constant exchange of data, you will be missing an incredible opportunity to expand your practice by utilizing numerous information sources, by solving everyday problems constructively and painlessly, by drawing upon the talent that penetrates your practice every day. Put the greatest single management tool you can possess—listening—into effect. Put it to work for you.

Presentation of the Fee

How do you move from the clinical presentation to the financial presentation? How does the dentist keep the doors open for a good financial discussion—but not get involved with that discussion?

Once the dentist has presented the clinical recommendations, she needs to ask the following question:

Dr.: Mr. Jones, do you have any questions regarding the treatment that I have just presented to you?

(The patient may say no. However, if he says anything about money, like the following:)

Patient: Well, yes, I do have a couple of questions. How much is this, and how can I pay for it?

(Then, the dentist should answer in the following way:)

Dr.: Mr. Jones, are you concerned about the financing of the dentistry?

Patient: Yes. It sounds like a lot of treatment, and I'm not sure I can afford it.

Dr.: I certainly understand how you feel. Many patients have felt the same concern until they found out that we do have several excellent payment options right here in our practice. Jan, our Treatment Coordinator, will discuss the total investment and will tell you about those options. She is excellent, and I feel confident that she will be able to work things out with you. Once the two of you develop a financial agreement that works for you, is this the type of dental treatment you would like to receive?

Patient: Yes. I know I need this. And I want to do it. I just need to see what it's going to cost.

Dr.: OK. Then, I will excuse myself and let you and Jan work together. I am certain that you will find a comfortable option, and I will look forward to working with you to get you healthy again.

The previous discussion is a closing sequence by the dentist that clarifies whether or not there are clinical questions that need to be addressed. It also leads nicely into the financial discussion. It paves the way for the TC to take over and to do so with the professional compliment of the dentist, thus building the patient's confidence in her and in her ability. The dentist acknowledges the patient's concern but does not get involved in the financial presentation.

I do not have a problem with the dentist quoting the fee. However, the TC needs to be the one who works toward the financial agreement.

Notice that the dentist *did* open the door for the discussion by telling the patient that there were several financial options available, but the dentist *did not* discuss those options. The dentist needs to get back to the chair. Also, the business person will do a better job, and she will be less vulnerable than the dentist to requests by the patient to let them pay out their dentistry at $2 per month for the rest of their lives.

Now the TC changes her location. She can sit where the dentist was sitting before her departure. She needs to be sitting on the same level with the patient and there should not be anything between them like a big desk. Sitting next to each other or sitting at either side of a corner of a table is ideal. Body language is critical. Again, you want everything to be advantageous for the very best presentation/discussion to take place.

TC: Mr. Jones, I know the doctor asked if you had any questions about the treatment that she recommended and you said no, but I thought that there might be something you would like to ask me about the treatment before we discuss the financial responsibility.

Patient: No. She explained everything just fine. And I could see the problems on that camera. So, hit me with the tough stuff.

TC: The fee for the treatment that the doctor has recommended is $3,000. How would you like to take care of that?

(This is exactly how to present the fee: the statement of the total investment followed by the *qualifying question*: How would you like to take care of that? Let your patient give you the lead. You stay in control of a conversation by asking questions. Ask this question, then, be quiet and listen to the patient's response. The patient will give you the direction you need to find the right solution.)

Patient: $3,000! You have got to be kidding?

TC: It seems that you are surprised with that figure.

(Actively listen to the patient to see if you are hearing them accurately. Remember, *active listening* is reflecting back to the person your perception of the message he has just sent. This gives you a chance to clarify. Do not overreact. Do not start back pedaling. Just listen.)

Patient: Surprised isn't the word for it. I'm shocked! I had no idea it would be that much. That's way too much money for teeth!

TC: How much too much is this for you?

(The answer to the statement, "That costs too much," needs a responsive question. The TC wants to know if the whole thing is too much—or if the treatment is just more than had been expected. And she will begin here to determine if the patient wants the treatment but needs a way to pay. Again, with a qualifying question, she gains necessary information to move ahead.)

Patient: Oh, about twice too much! I knew it would be quite a bit. I thought it might be around $1,500 or so—but $3,000! WOW!

(Here the question asked by the TC led to the patient's response that the total investment was not the shock, it was the amount more than what he was prepared to pay. In addition to clarifying how much too much he felt the investment would be, the TC made note of the fact that the patient had come in knowing that there would be quite a bit of treatment and that there would be an investment. But he thinks it is about twice too much—about $1,500 too much.)

TC: Mr. Jones, if I am hearing you correctly, you are saying that you were prepared to pay approximately $1,500 for your treatment and that the additional $1,500 is the real stumbling block. Am I right about that?

(Clarification through active listening.)

Patient: Yeah. I guess so. I had some money saved for this, but not that much.

TC: Mr. Jones, since you are prepared to pay $1,500 of the treatment from your savings account, if we are able to finance the other $1,500 so that the investment is not a financial burden for you, would that make it possible for us to go ahead?

(Here the TC is trying to get back to an open line of communication with the patient. She is trying to get past the issue of the total investment and have the patient start thinking of a method of payment that would let him proceed with treatment. If the patient's mind is closed, he can hear no further discussion. The mind must be reopened so that a logical discussion can take place. If a person is overwhelmed with emotion, he cannot think logically.)

Patient: Well, maybe. What can you do?

TC: I do want to make you aware of one option that would help you save some money. If there were any way that you could pay for the treatment in advance, we would reduce your fee by 5%. We would not be involved with any bookkeeping, that would save us time and money, and we would be able to pass those savings on to you. In your situation, that would save you $150. That's quite a bit of savings. Does that sound like a possibility?

(You will notice that she closes her statements with a question to get the patient's response and to keep the patient involved.)

Patient: No. I have the $1,500 cash, but no more than that.

TC: You could pay the $1500 that you have saved and then we could spread the $1,500 balance equally throughout your treatment. The doctor will be seeing you for three separate visits. We could accept three $500 payments with one payment being due at each of your three appointments.

Patient: No. That is still too much for me. I have a limited income and can't do $500 at a time. Can I just make payments to you for a while?

TC: You would like to do is take care of the $1,500 right now and then spread out the remainder of the fee over a period of time and keep the payments small.

(Active listening.)

Patient: Yeah. That's the only way I could do it.

TC: How much per month would you be willing and able to invest?

(This is a critical question. The TC is, again, qualifying. She needs to ask this question to see which type of payment option she will offer in order to satisfy the patient's need.)

Patient: Oh, I was thinking about maybe $40 or $50 per month.

TC: I am happy to tell you that we do have a couple of options that will let you do just that. We accept all major bankcards. We could place the $1,500 balance on one of those bankcards—whichever one you choose—and then you could pay however much you want every month. Does that work for you?

Patient: No. I already have those maxed out. I don't want to use a credit card.

TC: Then, Mr. Jones, let me tell you about another option that many of our patients have chosen to use. We have an arrangement with a financing company called ABC Financing Company. They offer a financing program for healthcare. You apply right here in our office. You don't have to go anywhere. The application is easy to complete, and I will be more than happy to assist you.

We will send the information to ABC. Once they have extended a line of credit to you, we can go ahead with your dental care, finance the $1,500, and your monthly payments will be around $35–40 per month. So, what I am saying is that you can receive the care that the doctor has recommended, and you will be able to comfortably fit the monthly payments into your family situation. How does that sound?

Patient: OK. That sounds pretty good.

TC: Great. I have an application right here. Let's work together to fill this out.

Study the verbal skills that I have outlined here and throughout the book. Learn how to present a healthcare financing program—and how to overcome the normal objections that will come up. Practice. Practice. Practice. You should be able to answer any objection. The verbal skills should roll off your tongue because you have learned them so well.

Do not let yourself be placed in a position to become flustered because you don't know how to respond to a patient's objection. If you believe in your services, in the payment options you have available, and if you have the verbal skills mastered, you will present confidently, and you will receive more positive results.

Once the financial agreement has been made, write it down. The patient may keep a copy for his own reference and records. You file one in the patient's chart. Know that just because someone tells you he understands—or that he will remember—doesn't mean that he does or will. Your records will become vital.

Every time a person comes to the office, you will be collecting the agreed upon amount of money. You will, also, know the method of payment selected and be prepared for the collection process. Once the fee for the day has been collected, remind or reconfirm the patient's financial responsibility for the next visit.

Plus, anyone in the office should be able to access the record of the financial agreement so that if the FC is on vacation, out with an illness, or in a private area making a financial arrangement, anyone should be able to note—quickly and accurately—how much is to be collected on each patient and the method of payment that has been agreed upon.

No one should ever walk out of your door without an appointment either with the hygienist for continuous care or with the dentist for the next phase of restorative care—or in some cases, both. In addition, no one should ever walk out your door without paying for the day's service and being very clear about their financial responsibility for the next visit.

Sample Scripts for Handling Financial Questions

You need to be ready for patient's questions regarding your financial program. Here are some suggested scripts for such questions, as well as some suggested responses to challenging financial situations.

Example

You are no longer handling long-term accounts on your own books.

Ms. Jones, we are no longer able to carry accounts here within our office. Our accountant no longer will allow us to manage a banking business within our practice. We have found that in order to maintain comfortable fees for our patients that we must be able to concentrate our time and money on our dental care.

Example

Patient wants to wait until after insurance has paid to make any private payments.

Ms. Jones, I can understand that you want to see what your insurance will pay before you make any investment yourself. However, because we have accurate information on your insurance benefits, we are able to estimate very closely what your insurance probably will cover and the portion for which you will be responsible. Therefore, in order to cover our laboratory and operating expenses, we ask that you take care of your part at the time of the service.

We will file your insurance as a service to you. However, if for any reason your insurance company does not pay what we expect, then you will be responsible for the balance.

Example

Patient says that she doesn't get paid until next week. Can she send you a check?

Ms. Jones, for your convenience we do accept all major bankcards. You can place your payment on a bankcard today and pay it off next week so that you do not incur any interest.

Or, if you so choose:

I can accept a postdated check. I will keep it here and will not deposit the check until next Friday.

(Collection experts, bankers, accountants, and attorneys that we have contacted all agree on the legality of doing this. Collection experts say that 95–98% of all postdated checks clear the bank.)

Example

Patient doesn't have her checkbook.

Oh, I see. Well, that happens sometimes, doesn't it? We do accept all the major bankcards. Which would you prefer?

You don't use bankcards? Well, then I will give you a statement and a self-addressed, stamped envelope. You can send us a check as soon as you get home. We will look forward to receiving that check in a couple of days. I will make a note to myself that we can expect your check. I will inform the doctor of our agreement.

(Make a note in the tickler file. If you don't get the check in a few days, call.)

Example

You have made financial arrangements with a person. He comes in the day of the preparation appointment. When he is being excused from the clinical area, he informs you that he does not have the agreed-upon payment.

Mr. Jones, I am confused. We discussed your financial responsibility for this appointment and came to a comfortable agreement. However, since we do not carry accounts on our own books, I would be able to accept a credit card payment today. Then, we will be able to send the models of your case to the laboratory.

(If he doesn't have a bankcard, tell him you will hold the case, and as soon as he brings in payment, you will send it to the lab. You will need to complete the treatment, obviously, but consider holding the models for a brief period of time as a motivator for payment.)

Example

A financial arrangement is made for treatment. The patient is in the middle of the treatment but is not abiding by the financial agreement.

> Ms. Jones, I became concerned when we didn't receive your payments as scheduled, because this may force us to delay your treatment. I know you want to proceed with your treatment . And so, it is critical that we come to an agreement so that you can go ahead with your dentistry. How may I help you?

Example

You have made a financial arrangement that is comfortable for your patient and for you. However, the patient has not fulfilled his obligations. You have made consistent efforts to negotiate an agreement but have not received cooperation from the patient. Now you are making your last telephone call before you turn the patient over for legal action. You wish to make one last effort to prevent such action.

> Mr. Jones, I will be forced to turn your account over for legal action unless I receive your payment in full immediately. I am calling today to discuss this with you in the hopes that we might be able to do something about your balance. I know you want to avoid this legal action. So do we. I'm sure you would agree with me that avoiding such action would be better for both of us.

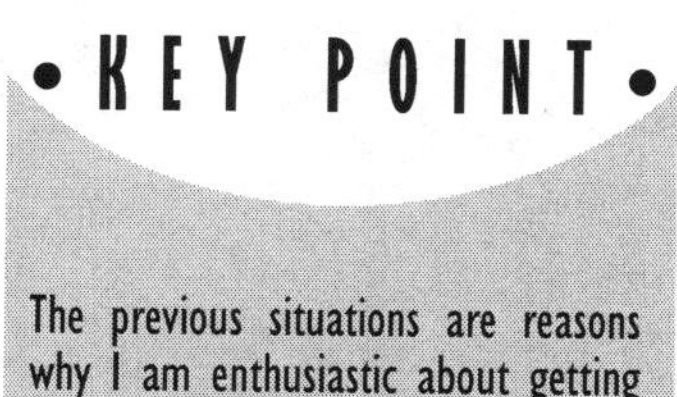

• KEY POINT •
The previous situations are reasons why I am enthusiastic about getting payments in advance.

Verbal Skills to Use When Discussing Financing

As I have said throughout this book, the way you say something makes all the difference in the world and your success will be in direct proportion to your ability to communicate. There are some words that bring about a positive response and some that seem to stimulate a negative response. Several of these are listed. Use the positive words and phrases and eliminate the others. This will take practice, but it will be worth the effort.

Words and Phrases

Negative	Positive
money, dollars	fee for the service
charge, cost	financial responsibility, total investment, monthly investment
bill	statement
discount	cash courtesy, fee reduction or accounting reduction
sign here	please initial, may I ask for your signature?
policy	financial options, financial protocol
deposit	initial investment
Do you want to pay today?	Ms. Jones, your fee today is $55. Will that be cash, check, or do you prefer to use a bankcard?

Summary

Establishing a financial agreement is one of the most important moments in your time with a patient. Without question, a person's willingness to *go ahead* may depend on your ability to define that person's situation and/or problems and to work out a solution.

CHAPTER 9

Insurance Management

Be insurance aware but do not be insurance driven.

– Cathy Jameson, PhD

Dental insurance has been an asset to many people and to many practices for the last few decades. Many people have been able to receive dental care who might not have been able to do so without dental insurance. Or they may not have even considered going to the dentist until they received this benefit from their employer. For many, the insurance served as a stimulus. This has been a major factor in the increased number of people who are seeking dental care. Plus, many doctors have increased the amount of care they have been able to provide because patients had insurance and wanted to use their benefits.

However, over time, insurance has played less and less of a role in the productivity of dental practices due to many issues.

1. Inappropriate increases in yearly maximums by the insurance companies or no increases at all. Thus, a patient's insurance plan covers less and less care.

2. Dominance of insurance companies trying to dictate fees, treatment modalities, and/or types of treatment to be covered in the first place.

3. Difficult, if not detrimental, communication with the patient about the dentist's fees.

Whether or not you are accepting assignment of benefits from insurance companies, the way you handle patients' insurance is important. (I am not addressing managed care programs here. This applies to private indemnity programs.) This is a benefit they have paid for or received from their employer. Dealing with and conversing about their insurance can be very personal. If you are filing insurance as a service to your patients, know that it is just that—a service. You don't have to do that. But if you are, you are providing a generous favor—an added-value service. Handle this well.

The handling of insurance is a system. It is a system that needs and deserves special attention because, as I said earlier, if you are accepting assignment of benefits, approximately 50% of your revenue is probably coming in the form of an insurance check. Whether you are computerized or not, there are certain criteria that must be in place in regard to insurance.

Before a patient receives treatment in your office, verify his insurance program (Fig. 9–1). Gather relevant information about the benefit package from a patient's insurance plan. Necessary information to be gathered is as follows:

1. the employer
2. the carrier
3. the phone number
4. the address
5. the contact person
6. the deductible
7. maximum per year
8. policy holder and policy number
9. ID number
10. the coverage types—preventive, basic, major, ortho, and others
11. frequency limitations
12. when he became eligible for benefits
13. the information on the patient/policy holder

VERIFICATION OF INSURANCE

Patient's Name: ____________________ Insured Name: ____________________

Patient's Birth Date: ________________ Insured's Birth Date: ________________

Social Security Number: _____________ Social Security Number: _____________

Insurance Co. Name: _______________ Group Name: ____________________

Group #: _____ Mailing Address: _________________

Phone #: _________________________ Contact Person: __________________

Employee ID#: ____________________ Eligibility Date: __________________

Web address: _____________ Verification Date: _____________

COVERAGE

Benefits paid on:____

Calendar Year: _______ Fiscal Year: _______ Anniversary Date: ______

Individual Deductible: _______________Family Deductible Max.: _______________

If Fiscal Year, Dates To and From:______________

Dental deductible met? Yes _____ No_____

Medical Deductible: ___________ Deductible met? Yes _____ No _____

Deductible for preventive? Yes _______ No _______

Coverage based on UCR? _______________ Or set fee schedule? _______________

Are X-Rays covered under preventive? Yes _______ No _______

Are periodontics covered under dental? ___ Or medical? ____ % of coverage? ______

Is D4381 a covered procedure? Yes ___ No ___ Special limitations: ____________

Are endodontics considered basic? __________ Major? __________

Orthodontics covered? Yes _____ No _____ Lifetime max: _______________

Oral surgery covered under dental? ___ Or medical? ___ % of coverage: __________

IV Sedations covered under dental? ___ Or medical? ___ % of coverage: __________

Implants (by report) covered under dental? ___ Or medical? ___ % of coverage: _____

Implant crowns covered? Yes ___ No ___ % of coverage: _____

Coverage Percentages

Preventive: ______ Basic: _________ Major: _________ I.V. Sed.: _______

Fig. 9–1a Insurance verification form.

FREQUENCIES & LIMITATIONS

Prophylaxis: ____________________
BWX: ____________________
Sealants: ____________________
Fluoride: ____________________
Molars only: ____________________

Evaluations: ____________________
FMX or Pano: ____________________
Age limit: ____________________
Age limit: ____________________

Missing tooth clause? Yes _____ No _____
Replacement clause? Yes _____ Time Period? _____ No _____
Waiting period for major services? Yes _____ Time Period? _____ No _____
Initial placement only? Yes _____ No _____
Other exclusions or limitations?

____
____
____

General Information

Plan allows signature on file? Yes _____ No _____
Plan allows assignment of benefits? Yes _____ No _____
Plan requires specific company form? Yes _____ No _____
Plan accepts standard ADA claim form? Yes _____ No _____
Plan requires a predetermination of benefits? Yes _____ No _____

Coordination of Benefits:

Does plan honor the following rules?

Birthday Rule? __________
Gender Rule? __________
Non-duplication of benefits? __________
Standard Method? __________
Is 100% possible? __________

Additional or Unusual Comments:

____
____
____
____
____

Fig. 9–1b Insurance verification form. *(continued)*

There is no question, you want to diagnose comprehesively, treatment plan thoroughly, and present the best dentistry possible. We recommend you do this with all patients. We recommend that you offer our financial options and try to get all the money up front before you even pick up a handpiece. The same is true with insurance patients. We would prefer that you collect the entire fee before you begin, file the insurance as a service to your patients—if you choose—and let the insurance company reimburse the patient. If a patient becomes involved with your healthcare financing company, she can finance the full amount: you can file her insurance and ask for a direct reimbursement to the patient. More than likely the patient will receive her insurance check before her first payment to the financing company comes due.

Predetermination of Benefits

Insurance experts say that unless an insurance company *requires* a predetermination of benefits, do not do one. Most patients who ask for a predetermination do so because dental practices have taught them to do so. Some people in practices are so apprehensive about asking for money that they put this off by saying, "Oh, let's see what your insurance is going to pay, then we can see what we need to do—or see how much you will owe." That's a stall tactic on the part of the team.

Insurance companies also like stall tactics. Do predeterminations only when they are to your advantage. According to insurance expert, Tom Limoli, Jr., the three times to do a predetermination of benefits are as follows:

1. If an insurance company requires it.

2. If a patient requests it (but try to coach them out of needing this).

3. If the patient refuses to accept accountability for the strengths and weaknesses of his dental plan.

Do not introduce this concept to your patients. Do your best to file the insurance to maximize benefits, but do not let this deter your resolve to help a patient get healthy.

Of course, we all know that just because a patient receives a predetermination of benefits does not necessarily mean—in the end—that the insurance company will pay.

If a patient has an extensive treatment plan that includes resorative and crown and bridge and if the patient insists on a predetermination, consider filing the predetermination but go ahead and start the restorative. By the time the response is received, you would be ready for the crown and bridge (or whatever).

Make sure that you are tracking the predetermination of benefits as carefully as filed claims.

If you are accepting assignment of benefits, consider the following:

1. Quote the entire fee and let the patient know that she is ultimately responsible for the entire fee, regardless of insurance payment or lack of it!

2. File her insurance as a service. Take the assignment of benefits.

3. Collect the estimated patient portion at the time of the service. **Do not—under any circumstance—file the insurance and wait to collect the estimated patient portion after insurance has paid.** This is financial suicide.

4. Let the patient know—right up front—that she is responsible for this account—that the contract is between her and the insurance company. Verbalize and put into writing that if for any reason insurance has not paid in 45 days that the patient will need to pay for the balance in full. Or, if the insurance company does not pay at all, she will be responsible for the total amount.

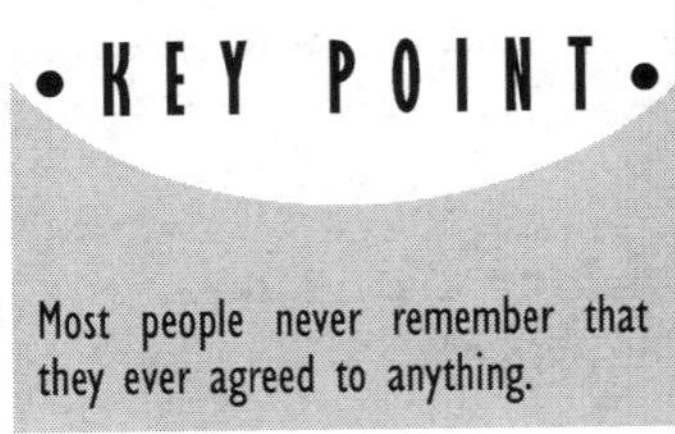

• KEY POINT •
Most people never remember that they ever agreed to anything.

   We recommend a written financial agreement.

   Do not put yourselves into a position for a dispute of money (Fig. 9–2).

5. Then, keep track of this. If insurance has not paid in the agreed-upon time frame or if insurance pays but does not pay what is expected and a balance remains, send a letter to the patient indicating the situation and make a telephone call to her. The purpose of both of these contacts will be to collect the money due to the practice (Fig. 9–3).

FINANCIAL AGREEMENT

Patient name:____ Date:__________

We are concerned about your dental health. We look forward to helping you with your dental care. Please remember that your dental insurance is your responsibility — but we can help. Regardless of what we might calculate as your dental benefit in dollars, we must stress the fact that you, the patient, are responsible for the total treatment fee. As a courtesy to you, we can accept assignment of benefit payments from most insurance companies. This will reduce your immediate, out-of-pocket expenditures. The outlined estimate is based on limited information obtained from your insurance company. We allow 45 days for your insurance company to make a payment. After this time all inquiries (follow-up) on payments due become your responsibility.

Area/Appt	*Recommended Treatment*	*Fee*	*Est. Ins. Pmt.*	*Est. Pt. Pmt.*
		Total		

Financial agreement for your treatment:

____Fee reduction __5__% is available if payment for treatment is made in full prior to treatment. $_______________- $_________ = $____________

____ Cash or check at time of service ______________________________

____VISA, MC, AMEX or DISCOVER

____ Healthcare Financing Program ______________________________

I understand and accept the TREATMENT PLAN above:____________________Date:______

I agree to the FINANCIAL RESPONSIBILITY for the total fee. The fees listed on this treatment outline will be honored for 90 days from the above date. After that time, the fees are subject to adjustments.

REMARKS:____

Fig. 9–2 Financial agreement—insurance.

DATE

NAME
STREET
CITY, STATE ZIP

Dear *NAME*:

Your insurance company has paid its portion on your dental services, leaving a balance of ______________________________.

Please indicate below your option for handling your balance due:

1. Enclosed is payment in full.
2. Please transfer my balance to:

_____ Healthcare Financing Program # __________________
_____ Visa/MC # ______________________________
_____ Discover # ______________________________
_____ Amex # ______________________________

Expiration Date: __________________

Signature ____

Please respond upon receipt of this letter. If you have any questions, please call our office.

Sincerely,

Jan Smith
Business Administrator

Fig. 9–3 Patient portion letter after insurance.

6. Use pre-authorization forms—consistently (Fig. 9–4). You can do the following things with this form:

   A. Place any balances after insurance pays onto a healthcare financing program or on a bankcard.

   B. Place the full balance onto the financial program or a bankcard if insurance doesn't pay at all.

   C. Place regular payments on the program if the patient is on a regular program of therapy or treatment, such as orthodontics. Or, this could be used during your accounts receivable transfer if you negotiate regular monthly payments to service the debt.

You may create your own Pre-Authorized Health Care Form or reproduce this one onto your letterhead

Pre-Authorized Health Care Form

I authorize ______________________________

____

(name of health care provider)

to keep my signature on file and to charge my ____________ account for:

_ Balance of charges not paid by insurance within 45 days and not to exceed $____ for:

_ this visit only
_ all visits this year

_ Recurring charges (ongoing treatments) of $_________

every______________________________
(frequency)

from ______________________ to ______________________
(date) (date)

I assign my insured benefits provider listed above. I understand that this form is valid for one year unless I cancel the authorization through written notice to the health provider.

Patient Name: ______________________________

Cardholder Name: ______________________________

Cardholder Address: ______________________________

City: ______________________________

State: ______________________ Zip: ______________________

Card of choice: MC ___ VISA: ___ Amex: ___ Discover: ___ HCFP: ___

Account Number: ______________________________

Expiration Date: ______________________

Cardholder Signature: ______________________________

Date: ______________________

Fig. 9–4 Pre-authorization form.

Clearing Up Misconceptions about Dental Insurance

I am sure that many of you shake your heads on a daily basis as patients come to you with thought processes about insurance that are totally *off the wall* or misconceptions presented to them by their employer. So, you may have quite a job ahead of you clarifying those incorrect ideas. We have found in our own practice that the following sheet of information was very enlightening to patients and offset many future misunderstandings. We use this during the financial consultation or any time patients express confusion about their insurance. This doesn't indicate that we don't address their confusions verbally. We do. But this written support is valuable.

This form—"Facts About Dental Insurance" has been around longer than me. I don't know who originally wrote this, so I can't give credit where credit is due—but it's great. Consider Figure 9–5.

FACTS REGARDING DENTAL INSURANCE

Dental insurance plays a large role in helping people obtain dental treatment. Since we strongly feel our patients deserve the best possible dental care we can provide, and in an effort to maintain this high quality care, we would like to share some facts about dental insurance with you.

Fact #1: Dental insurance is not meant to be a pay-all. It is only meant to be a supplement.

Fact #2: Many plans tell their insured that they'll be covered "up to 80% or up to 100%." In spite of what you're told, we've found most plans cover less than the average fee. Some plans pay more, some less. The amount your plan pays is determined by how much your employer paid for the plan. The less the employer paid for the insurance, the less you'll receive.

Fact #3: It has been the experience of many dentists that some insurance companies tell their customers that "fees are above the usual and customary fees" rather than saying to them that "our benefits are low." Remember, you get back only what your employer puts in, less the profits and administrative costs of the insurance company.

Fact #4:Many routine dental services are not covered by insurance plans.

Please do not hesitate to ask us any questions. We want you to be comfortable in dealing with these matters, and we urge you to consult us if you have any questions regarding our services and/or fees. We will fill out and file insurance forms at no charge. We will do this as a service to you.

If we take assignment on your insurance, we feel that 45 days is a reasonable length of time for us to wait for payment from your insurance company.

Thank You!

Fig. 9–5 Information on dental insurance.

Insurance Objections

People must want the dental care that you are recommending before they will be willing to make the investment. Your presentation of recommendations is critical to overcoming any fee objections—including objections regarding dental insurance. However, when insurance objections do arise, communication skill is the bottom line to your success.

The following are some normal objections/questions about dental insurance and appropriate responses:

1. **Does my insurance cover this? If it doesn't, I'm not sure I want to get this done.**

   BA: Mr. Jones, we'll do the best we can to maximize your insurance benefits. We want to work with you to find a comfortable way for you to finance your dental care. We have several excellent options. I am sure that one of them will work well for you. Let's discuss this.

   Patient: OK.

   BA: First of all, let me ask you this, if we can find a way to handle the financial aspect of your treatment, is this the type of dentistry you would like to receive?

   Patient: Yes. But, I don't think I can afford it if my insurance doesn't cover it.

   BA: How much could you afford to invest per month?

   Patient: Oh, I could pay maybe $30 or $40 per month, but no more.

   BA: OK. With the information we have from your insurance company, we estimate that they will cover approximately $1,000. That's your yearly maximum. Then your estimated portion at the time of the service would be approximately $1,000. We will contact our financial partner, provide them with appropriate information and see if they can establish a line of credit for you. Once they have established that line of credit, for about $30 per month, you can go ahead with the treatment that the doctor has recommended. Does that work for you?

   Patient: Yes. That would be fine.

2. **If my insurance doesn't cover this, why do you say that I need it?**

   BA: Dental insurance is a supplement to your healthcare. It is not a pay-all. The benefits that are available to you are based on the amount your employer paid for the policy. The less the employer pays—the less you receive. Predefined benefits have nothing to do with necessary treatment.

3. **My insurance covers 100% of my dental care. My employer said it did.**

   BA: Many insurance programs say that they will pay 100% or 80% . What they don't say that this is a percentage of their fees—not ours.

4. **My insurance company says that your fees are above the usual and customary. Why are your fees above average?**

   BA: Our fees reflect our commitment to quality. Insurance companies provide a great service by supplementing your healthcare, but their benefits are not determined by the quality of the care, only on the amount of premium paid.

   Or

   BA: Thank you for noting that, Mr. Jones. We do our very best to provide quality, above-average dental care. The last thing in the world that we would want to put into your mouth or the mouth of any of our dental patients is average dental care. And our fees reflect that.

5. **This costs too much.**

   BA: Today, most things do. Tell me, how much too much is it?

   (Most of the time the patient will give you an amount that he feels is too much—the amount that is more than he was prepared to pay. If he does this, you will know what amount has become difficult for him—what amount you need to help him with.)

Example

Patient: Oh, it's about $1,000 more than I thought. I knew it would be a lot—but $2,000?

BA: Sounds like you were prepared to invest $1,000, but the fee for your recommended treatment is $2,000, so what we need to work on is a way for you to handle the other $1,000 without having you be financially stressed. Is that correct?

6. **I have to think this over.**

BA: Mr. Jones, I know you wouldn't take the time to think this over if you weren't seriously interested. Tell me what is it that you need to think over. Is it the dentistry itself? Are you wondering whether or not this type of treatment will help solve your problem?

Patient: No, I know I need this.

BA: Then let me ask you, are you unsure if Dr. Jameson is the right doctor to provide our care?

Patient: Oh, no. I know he's the right doctor. That's not a problem.

BA: Then, let me ask you this. Is it the money? Are you concerned about the financing of your dental care?

Patient: Yeah, that's a lot of money. I just don't know if I can handle this right now.

BA: I can appreciate that. Let me ask you this, if we were able to finance your dentistry, spread the payments out over a period of time and keep the payments small, would that make it possible for you to go ahead?

Patient: Probably. What do you have in mind?

7. **I can't believe I need this much. How in the world did this happen?**

BA: I understand your concern. Many factors may have affected your oral health. We can't change what's happened up to now, but we can change the situation that exists and restore your mouth to health again. Then, let's mutually commit to keeping it healthy. You'll make an investment now, and then we'll work together to ensure that investment with an excellent program of maintenance and home care.

More about Insurance Management

As I have said, for most dental practices, 50% of revenue comes in the form of an insurance check—approximately half of the collections of the practice. Your insurance system must be managed and monitored with extreme dedication. What do you collect per year? What is half of that? Your management of this much money is a critical factor of the business of your practice and must be handled with respect and care.

Management systems in the dental practice need to be both time efficient and cost efficient. The insurance management system is no exception. Insurance has been (and will remain) an asset to many dental practices. The following graph illustrates data related to dental insurance coverage (Fig. 9–6).

Who Has Dental Insurance?

- 58.5% of the population has dental insurance
- 56% of their dental bill is paid by insurance
- 44% of their dental bill is paid out of pocket

*adjusted for inflation to 2004 levels

© *Dr. T. Warren Center*

Fig. 9–6 Who has dental insurance?

And so, obviously, if this many patients have dental insurance and this much of revenue comes from dental insurance, a devoted concentration on the filing and follow-up of insurance is essential. Keeping up in a regular, systematic manner prevents insurance overload, loss of control, and slow cash flow from insurance.

Most of you, hopefully, are filing electronically by now. Soon you will have no choice but to file electronically—so if you are not already doing so, make effort now to convert. Carefully managed electronic filing of claims and careful follow-up will lead to an average of a 7–10 working day turnaround on all insurance claims. There should be no 30-day past-due claims. Plus, the valuable time of your team members is not going to be wrapped up in filing claims, sending radiographs and support data, and following up for hours while they wait "on hold" for the insurance company to respond.

Be aware of the fact that managing the insurance portion of your practice can dominate a great deal of a valuable team member's time and can cost a great deal of the dentist's money if your system isn't clean, efficient, and effective. You are probably not charging for the filing but, rather, are doing this as a service to your patients. Be careful about the cost of time and money.

You may wish to seriously consider collecting the full amount—either with cash, bankcard, or a healthcare financing program, then filing the claim and letting the insurance company reimburse the patient directly. If you are already doing this—please continue. If you aren't doing this, please consider. Your patients will adjust to what they find is the norm in your practice. Especially if you have built great relationships with patients and have consistently provided them with all they expect and more.

However, if you are filing insurance, you must develop a system for filing and following up on all claims. It must work and work well. The time of each team member must be managed well and your returns must be acceptable. If you do not have a 7–10 working day turnaround on all claims; if you have 30-day past-due claims; if you don't really know the status of your insurance, please consider contacting a management expert who can help you set up that system, learn to administer it effectively, and make sure that you get great results. Too much money is at stake here. (**Contact JMI, 1-877-369-5558**)

Summary

Please be insurance aware. In other words, do all you can do to help a person maximize insurance benefits. *But do not become insurance driven*, which means do not let what an insurance company will or will not cover determine the type of treatment you recommend. Remember, insurance companies are not interested in whether or not the treatment you are recommending is best for the patient. They are interested in whether or not it is a covered benefit and will pay accordingly.

Rule of 8—Insurance Musts

1. Decide if you are going to accept assignment of benefits or not and manage accordingly.

2. Practice verbal skills and learn to communicate about insurance—including handling objections.

3. Get insurance verifications as quickly as possible—before the patient arrives, if possible.

4. Move away from unnecessary insurance predeterminations.

5. Collect the patient's estimated portion at the time of the service.

6. Make sure that all people understand that they are ultimately responsible for the treatment fee—in full.

7. Develop a *foolproof* system for filing and collecting insurance claims.

8. Make sure that you are receiving insurance payments within 7–10 working days and that you have no past-due claims.

Make it easy for people to pay. Convenience is important to busy people in today's world. Insurance has been a wonderful supplement to people's dental care and to the growth of dental practices. Now more people can use insurance benefits because they have a way to finance the difference after insurance pays. Take good care of this system of your practice.

CHAPTER 10

When Patients Complain about Your Fees

Remind yourself that angry clients probably have a need that isn't being met and believe that you have the ability at least to start the problem on the way to being solved.

– **Roberta Cava**
Difficult People

"Have your fees gone up—again?" So asks the patient!

No matter where you set your fees, some people will automatically think that your fees are too high. Patients don't really know the fees for your procedures. In fact, most non-dental people can't give you an accurate description of most procedures.

With their permission, I like to ask non-dental people questions about dentistry. I assure them that there is no right or wrong answer, that I am simply doing a survey for my own research. Here are some of the questions I ask.

"In relationship to dentistry, what is a three-surface composite restoration?" No one has ever been able to answer. "What is a porcelain laminate veneer?" No one has ever been able to answer correctly. Then I ask them the following: "You go to the dentist and she diagnoses decay in four teeth in your mouth. You have four big cavities. Then the dentist recommends that the decay be removed and that those teeth be restored to health with a tooth-colored, beautiful, long-lasting restoration. Would you want to do that?"

Everyone says, "Yes."

Then I ask, "How much would that cost—to restore those teeth the way I have described?"

No one has ever really known. They have no idea.

So, I ask, "If I told you that restoring those four teeth to health again would be approximately $1,000, would that be OK with you?"

Many people balk at this fee. Being able to pay this amount would be difficult, many say. So, I ask, "If you were able to make small monthly payments, spread those payments out over a period of time, would that make it possible for you to go ahead? In fact, if all you needed to pay each month was about $30, would that work for you?"

Everyone says, "Yes."

This is not unrealistic, would you agree? I would imagine that you have patients—on a regular basis—complain about fees. However, they don't really know what they are complaining about. They don't know what is involved with the treatment. They are just complaining. In addition, they don't really know what the fee was—or what it *should be*. Again, they are just complaining.

If a fee is $400 and you increase your fees by 10%, the fee is now $440. If a patient complains about the $440—I would guess that they would have complained about the fee at $400. Just because people complain about a fee doesn't mean that they don't want to proceed. It may just mean that they are asking for help—help in finding a convenient way to pay.

Of course, there are certain procedures that a person receives on a regular basis—hygiene, for example—where people will recognize fee increases. That's OK. What business doesn't go up on fees when the costs of operation go up?

Analysis of Fees

Frequently—very frequently—we hear doctors or team members express apprehension about increasing their fees. The following are several reasons why people express a concern about increasing fees:

1. Patients will be upset.
2. Patients will complain about fees.
3. People will think you are *gouging them*.
4. People will go down the street to another practice because the other practice charges less. In other words, fear of losing patients.

We recommend that you analyze fees every six months. I didn't say go up on your fees every six months—although you may need to do just that. I said analyze them and make logical decisions about where your fees need to be placed. Why the regular analysis? To determine if any of your costs of operation and/or costs of a procedure have gone up. If your costs go up but your fees don't, profits are reduced. The one who usually gets a slash in salary is the dentist. Right?

It is dangerous and inappropriate for anyone on the team to undermine a reasonable and timely increase in fees. If costs of operation have gone up, so must your fees. Dr. Charles Blair of Charlotte, North Carolina, says that his criteria for whether to allow a year to go by without raising fees is very simple: "If no staff member requests a raise for a year, the doctor is free to allow his fee schedule to remain unchanged."

When you analyze your fees, you may find that they are just fine. However, if they need to be adjusted 3, 5, 10% or whatever, do so. Make sure that your fees are equitable and that they are *in line* for your area and that they reflect the quality of care you are offering. Remember my opening scenario of this chapter—most people will not even recognize that you have adjusted your fees. Especially if you are continually trying to update and upgrade the services you are providing.

When we first go into a practice to consult, and every time thereafter, we do a thorough analysis of the practice. We analyze each system and all of the statistical data. Before we go in—and during our first consultation—the dentist and the team members begin setting goals for each of these systems.

Once we know where they are at the moment and where they want to go, then we begin designing and integrating a plan of action to help them accomplish those goals. In order to take a practice to its full potential, a careful analysis and establishment of fees must continually take place.

The Law of Supply and Demand

In today's dental world, we often see practices *so busy* that they are stressed to the max! These practices are trying to get through each of their frantic, stress-filled days, so they can't even imagine putting in the necessary time to *clean up* their systems. The *busy-ness* of the practice and the day-to-day demands are holding them hostage. They are seeing huge numbers of patients and have a hard time seeing people expediently. New patients have to be *put off* much too long; hygiene patients cannot be seen in a timely manner; major procedures are put off too far because the appointment book is stuffed full of smaller appointments—lots of them.

Being *too busy* can begin to squeeze patient time, increase overhead, and produce stress. The dentists and team members need to orchestrate a plan to increase revenue while decreasing both cost of operation and stress. Focusing on the fulcrum of the practice—which is thorough diagnosis, careful and complete treatment planning, and well-organized and presented consultations—will lead to more comprehensive care, longer appointments, less stress for patient and provider. And certainly, if you are too busy and can't see patients expediently, then the law of supply and demand is in your favor. You could consider increasing your fees. You may lose a few patients over this fee increase, but you will be able to focus more intently on gaining higher levels of case acceptance and you will begin to get your practice in control.

Dentists must get out of the *habit* of thinking that high numbers of patients per day is the only way to be productive. It isn't. The key to productivity isn't how many patients you see but, rather, how much dentistry you are doing. We base the Jameson Method of Management on what we call the *Model of Success*. Here is an outline of this model:

1. See fewer patients each day
2. Do more dentistry per patient (when and where appropriate)
3. See those patients for fewer visits
4. Minimize the number of team members
5. Maximize their talent
6. Increase the profit
7. Share the profit
8. Decrease stress

Raising Fees — When and by How Much?

There are 3 ways to increase the profitability of your practice.

1. Increase the production

2. Decrease the costs of operation

3. Increase the fees

Let's look at the impact of increasing fees. If a practice is full of existing and new patients, increasing fees by 10% may cause a small percentage of patients to go elsewhere. However, if the overhead of the practice is 65%, the practice would have to lose 22.3% of its patient family before bottom-line profits would be negatively impacted (according to Dr. Blair). If the practice increases fees by 10% across the board without adding other additional overhead items, the *bottom-line* profits of the practice will increase more than 28.6% (for practices whose overhead is 65%). The higher the overhead, the greater the increase to profit margin realized by a fee increase.

I must tell you that we have recommended a 10% fee increase in hundreds of practices but have never had 20–25% of the patient family leave—not if the practice focuses on quality throughout and has invested in great relationships with patients.

If you want to increase profitability by increasing your fees by 10%, you must be prepared for possible negative response by your patients. You must be strong—and ready—for a *few* people to leave your practice to go to a lower fee competitor. However, I have rarely seen this happen. Everyone on the team including the dentist must agree that seeing fewer patients in a day, doing more dentistry per patient, and seeing the patients for fewer visits is a desirable goal. You must believe in the equitability of your fees.

The verbal skills of how to deal with patient objections about fees are very important. You do not want people to leave you. You do not want people to be hostile about your fees. And so, how you handle the *very normal* complaints about fees will make all the difference in the world.

Example

Patient: Haven't you guys gone up on your fees since my last visit?

Team Member: Yes, Ms. Jones, there has been a slight increase in our fees. Our costs of operation have gone up and, therefore, our fees reflect that. We refuse to compromise the quality of our care, and so, we carefully position our fees to reflect our commitment to the best.

Patient: Well, it seems like every time I come in here it costs more.

Team Member: No, not every time. But I can appreciate what you are saying. When the cost of a procedure goes up, we increase our fee in order to cover those costs. We prefer to do this rather than use cheaper materials. Cheap materials produce average dentistry, and, Ms. Jones, the last thing in the world that we want to do is put average dentistry into your mouth.

Let me say again, that all of you—every team member—must believe that the fees you are charging are equitable for the services being rendered. Dr. L.D. Pankey taught us that a fair fee is one where the patient perceives that the service she received is appropriate for the money she invested and that the doctor and team feel the fee they received was acceptable. That's a fair fee.

Insurance and Fees — Usual and Customary

There is no question that having a patient receive a letter from an insurance company inferring that the dentist's fees are above usual and customary can cause confusion on the part of the patient and is an inference that the dentist is charging too much. This is a prime indication of a third party coming between the doctor/patient relationship. There is no question that any of us would be upset if the patient developed a misconception about the legitimacy of the presented fee.

One other issue can arise. If letters from the insurance companies are sent to the patients and if the patients call or make a scene in the office, the team members can become *gun shy* real fast. They begin to think, "Hey, maybe our fees are *too* high," or "Our poor patients can't pay for that treatment if the insurance company isn't going to pay, so maybe we should drop our fees."

That kind of mindset and attitude on the part of the dentist or the team members can lead to financial suicide.

The answer to complaints about fees is not to lower the fees. Upon reevaluation of your fees, your patient flow, your cost of operation, and your desired mode of operation, more than likely your fees are just fine. For the most part, dental fees are equitable and fair, or, they may be too low.

The following steps need to be taken, however, so that you can deal professionally with the complaints that you are going to get:

1. Have the entire team practice the verbal/communication skills of handling the patients' objections.
2. Create a letter that can be sent to patients when a protest about "usual and customary" occurs (Fig. 10–1).
3. Place a letter into the practice armamentarium to send to insurance companies and to the state insurance commissioner to *protest* their intrusion into the patient/dentist relationship (Fig. 10–2).

Dear *Patient Name:*

It has come to my attention that your insurance company has sent you a letter stating that my fees are "above usual and customary." I can understand how you would be confused and upset by this letter. Therefore, I am happy to provide a response to give you some information that may shed some light on this issue. I have sent a letter to your insurance company, a copy of which is enclosed, for your review.

We appreciate dental insurance, and we believe that it is a wonderful supplement to a person's dental healthcare. However, it is not meant to be a "pay all"—only a supplement. As such, the amount paid for the premium determines the amount of available benefits. The more paid, the more received. The less paid, the less received.

Another point of confusion is about how an insurance company determines "usual and customary." Their fees do not reflect any standard of care, but rather are a median fee based on fee schedules from all doctors in a designated area, which can include several different zip codes. This "median" fee, again, does not take into consideration an individual practitioner's own costs of operation or standard of care. Therefore, the fees are arbitrary and average rather than carefully determined.

We do our very best to provide above average care to you and to all of our patients. Our fees express an equitable exchange of value — fair fee for excellent services.

Sincerely,

Fig. 10–1 Patient "usual and customary" letter.

Date

Insurance Company Name
Street
City, State Zip

Dear ______________________:

It has come to my attention that your company has taken the liberty to notify certain patients, who are insured under your health plan, that you feel my fees are above the usual and customary or normal rate for the community in which I practice.

I have verified my fees with the National Dental Advisory Service fee profile for this area and can verify my fees have proved not to be in excess of those of my peers. While I believe that you have the right to communicate to your policy holders, I further believe that you have an obligation to communicate the truth. Your company has determined in its adjudication policies that it is unwilling or unable to pay for the quality and standard of dental care that the insured has chosen.

I would like to request therefore, that you seriously consider rephrasing your communication to accurately reflect your company's ability to reimburse. Otherwise, please cease and desist with your present communications which are inaccurate and intrusive in the doctor/patient relationship.

Sincerely,

John H. Jameson, DDS

cc: Insurance Commissioner, State of ________________________________
Patient

Fig. 10–2 "Usual and customary" letter for the insurance company and insurance commssioner.

Summary

Certainly you don't want to lose patients. You don't like to have patients complain about your fees. And you may be afraid that patients will go down the street to seek lower fees. However, that will happen much less than you might imagine. Dentistry is so personal. If a person has come to trust you and your team, he will not leave you for fees if he perceives that the fee he is paying is equitable for the service he is receiving.

You may have some patients who do give you a hard time. But, do *not* "let the minority rule the majority." Don't think that because one or a handful of patients protest your fees that you are going to go *belly up*. Not raising your fees when *your* own costs of operation goes up *will* make you go *belly up*. And then, who wins? Not the patients, because you aren't in business anymore.

Put a mirror up to your practice. Are you epitomizing quality throughout? If not, make adjustments where necessary. Visualize the patient's experience with you and make sure each and every visit matches your idea of excellence. Then set your fees accordingly.

Study communication skills so that you can present fees and overcome objections. Provide care to be proud of and let your fees stand as a clear indication of your practice of excellence.

Chapter 11

Overcoming the Fear of Cost: Handling Objections

It costs 5–6 times more to win a new customer than it does to keep one.

– Michael LeBoeuf, PhD
GMP: The Greatest Management Principle in the World

"Well, Doctor, I'd like to go ahead with this treatment. I know I need it. But it just costs too much! I can't afford it right now. I'll just have to wait."

Have you heard this before? Does the response ever come at the completion of your excellent presentation of recommendations?

Do you get discouraged? Do you wonder what you can do to deal with the objection, the barrier, the fear of cost?

Let's look at a step-by-step way to handle objections, specifically the objection of cost.

1. **Validate your services and your quality to yourselves.**

Do you feel that the value of your services exceeds the fee you are asking? Before *anything* else happens, you must convince yourself of your own worth.

Exercise

List the services you provide for your patients—from the initial contact through the entire treatment. Now as a team, answer the following questions:

A. What makes your services *special*?

B. What *added-value* touches do you provide that make your practice unique?

C. What do you do that goes beyond the expected?

2. **Validate yourself to your patients.**

You must establish a relationship of trust and confidence with a patient before treatment acceptance will result. Your *ongoing* internal marketing program should have this as its foundation. In planning your marketing/educational program, ask this question, "Does this marketing tool make a statement (consciously or subconsciously) about who we are, what we do, what our purpose is about?"

If the answer is "yes," then the marketing tool is probably going to serve your purpose well. If the answer is "no," then you may need to rethink the project.

• KEY POINT •

- Your entire team must believe in the services you are providing.
- You must have a strong commitment to your work and to the patients you serve.
- Know that you, as care providers, add value to the lives of those people.
- Make sure that the treatment your patients are receiving is an equitable exchange for the fee. Thus value = value.

3. **Validate your services.**

In your efforts to validate your services to existing and potential clients, do the following:

A. Use testimonial letters from enthusiastic patients.

B. Use *before* and *after* photographs of your patients to illustrate a particular service you provide. (Be sure to obtain written permission from your patient.)

C. Provide civic presentations throughout your community using *before* and *after* photographs of treatment you have provided.

- Concentrate on one subject at a time, *i.e.*, cosmetic dentistry, nonsurgical periodontal therapy, preventive dentistry, etc.
- The program must not be self-serving—but, rather, educational.
- Leave a written piece with each participant.
- Keep the program short, 20–30 minutes.
- Use layman's language.
- Use visual aids—Microsoft PowerPoint is an excellent medium
- Be enthusiastic and energetic.

4. **Make sure that every aspect of your practice epitomizes the professional image you wish to project.**

All of these foundational efforts work to establish a *value* for the service that far outweighs the *fee*.

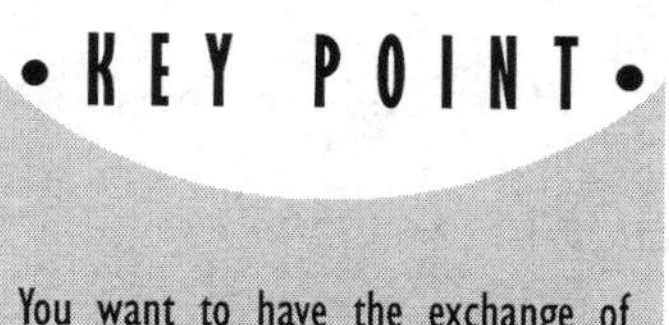

You want to have the exchange of value be equitable—but perceived to tilt in the favor of the patient.

Handling Objections

Tom Hopkins of Scottsdale, Arizona, is one of the nation's leading sales trainers. I have had the privilege of studying with Mr. Hopkins, and he has totally changed my attitude about objections. I used to dread an objection. Why?

Because I *assumed* that if a person objected—in this case to the cost of the dentistry or to our financial options—that he didn't want to have the dentistry at all. I felt terrible because I thought an objection meant that the person was upset or irritated. Avoidance of a controversial issue seemed to be a good way to get out of feeling uncomfortable.

Then, I studied with Tom Hopkins and learned that an objection—including the objection of cost—is actually a step forward in completing an agreement. If your patients do *not* pose any objections or raise any questions, they're probably not interested. In other words, I learned to look forward to an objection because that meant that the person was interested. That's what we want. Now I know that an objection is a gift.

Four insights about objections

1. You identify an objection by asking questions and listening.
2. An objection is a request for further information.
3. If a person presents an objection, that means that she is interested.
4. Objections are the steps necessary to the close.

An objection is actually an opportunity for you. It defines a specific area of concern. You will need to ask questions to isolate or identify what objections, if any, might get in the way of a person going ahead with treatment.

When an objection is posed by a patient, take the following steps:

1. **Hear out the objection.** Don't interrupt. Encourage the person to express himself. Objections often diminish when a person is allowed to talk about it. In addition, this gives you another chance to listen, to show concern, to empathize (not sympathize), and to let the person sense your understanding. Thus, you *validate* your patient.
2. **Actively listen.** Rephrase and reflect back to the person what you think you have heard him say. This gives you a chance to clarify, reinforce the patient, and move forward.
3. **Reinforce the importance of the objection.** *There's no benefit to disagreeing with or arguing with a patient.* When you listen to the concerns, reinforce those concerns, share in the development of possible solutions, you will be less likely to see that patient leave without scheduling an appointment.

Example

Patient: I don't want to lose my teeth, but I sure don't want to spend this much money if this isn't going to last.

Dentist: Keeping your teeth for a lifetime is important to you, and you want to make sure that the investment you make is going to be one that lasts for as long as possible.

Patient: Yes.

Dentist: I totally agree with you.

4. **Answer the objection.** Provide further education. Stress the end results and benefits of the treatment you are recommending. Turn the objection into a benefit. Establish value. Use the *feel-felt-found* response.

   Dentist: Mr. Jones, I understand how you *feel.* Many patients have *felt* the same concern about making an investment in comprehensive dental care, until they *found* out that an investment in quality, comprehensive care now will provide better health, last longer, look better, and save money in the long run.

5. **Confirm the answer.** Get the patient involved with you by asking questions. Then stop and wait for the response. This involvement helps a patient to feel like he is an active part of the decision-making process. And that's *exactly* what you want.

   Dentist: This type of comprehensive care provided now would answer your concern about making a stable, long-term investment, wouldn't it?

6. **Change the direction of the conversation—move forward.** Using a phrase, such as *by the way*, change the flow of focus of the conversation. Move to another area of interest that will move the conversation in a positive direction. Such as follows:

   Dentist: By the way, Mr. Patient, do you have any particular scheduling concerns that we need to be aware of?

7. **Close.** Once you have dealt with the objections, ask for a commitment—*close*. Closing an agreement means *asking*. If you don't ask for a commitment, you are giving your patient permission to procrastinate.

   Dentist: Mr. Jones, do you have any further questions about the treatment that I am recommending for you—any questions about the clinical aspects of the treatment?

   Patient: No. I can see what is wrong and what you need to do.

   Dentist: Then, when you and Jan develop a financial agreement that works for you, shall we go ahead and schedule an appointment to begin?

   Patient: I guess so. Might as well go for it.

There is the dentist's close. Now the FC will need to do the same thing. She will reconfirm the dentistry, present the total fee, the options for payment, get a commitment for one of those options (or a combination of options), and will close. Then, she will schedule that first appointment.

• KEY POINT •

If you know something is going to be brought up as an objection, you bring it up. This gives you an opportunity to turn a potential negative into a positive.

Remember that you control a conversation with questions. When a person poses an objection—don't freeze up and feel that you've hit a dead end. Not so. As you skillfully learn to handle objections you will find that these objections are progressive steps taken to *move ahead.*

Example

Dentist: Ms. Jones, before I give you the results of my analysis and before I explain the treatment I recommend for you to reach optimum oral health, first let me tell you that if you have any concerns about the financing of your treatment, we do have convenient, long-term financing right here in our office. I tell you this so that, for now, we can both concentrate on your treatment. But please know that we will discuss financial options in full. We want to make sure that you are clear and comfortable with this important part of your treatment. OK?

Examples of Closing Sequences

Dentist: And so, Ms. Jones, the financing of the dentistry seems to be a concern for you.

Patient: Yes.

Dentist: Finding a financial solution will make it possible for you to proceed? Am I right?

or

Dentist: Ms. Jones, if I understand you correctly, this is the type of dentistry you would like to receive.

Patient: Yes, it is.

Dentist: Then, once we make the financing of the dentistry comfortable for you, is there any reason why we shouldn't go ahead and schedule an appointment to begin your treatment?

or

Dentist: Now that we have agreed on the treatment that you will receive and once Jan has worked out the details of your financial agreement, we will schedule your first appointment and go ahead. How does that sound?

Learning to Handle Objections

Objections diminish when a person is allowed and encouraged to talk about them.

1. Restate the patient's wants and needs.
2. Actively listen to his concerns. Rephrase and feed back his objections.
3. Validate the person by using the feel-felt-found statement of empathy (noted in previous example).
4. Turn the patient's objections around by asking a question to establish value.
5. Encourage the patient to share with you in the development of a solution.

You can't push anyone into making a decision, but you can lead a person carefully and caringly by asking questions and listening. You can't *talk* people into going ahead but you can *listen* them into *going ahead*.

• KEY POINT •

If a person is allowed to be a part of a decision-making process, he/she will be more likely to buy into the decision.

One More Time: Examples of Verbal Skills That Identify and Overcome Objections

Example

A person says, "That's just too much."

When a person tells you the fee is too much, actively listen to make sure you're hearing them correctly.

Dentist/BA: You feel the fee is too high for the services I'm recommending for you? Or is the investment difficult for you at this time?

Patient: I'm sure the treatment is worth the fee, but I can't afford this right now.

Dentist/BA: Tell me, Mr. Jones, if we can make the financing comfortable for you with a convenient monthly payment plan, would this make it possible for you to proceed?

Patient: Probably.

Dentist/BA: How much per month could you invest?

His answer to this question would let you know if you could go ahead by offering him a bankcard or a healthcare financing program.

Example

Patient: Well, I want to do this. I hate my smile. But $3,000 is just too much!

Dentist/BA: How much too much is that, Mr. Jones?

Patient: About $1,500 too much. I saved $1,500 for this—but, wow, I had no idea it would be this much!

Dentist/BA: So, the solution we're looking for is a way to finance the $1,500 beyond your current savings, is that right?

Patient: Yes.

Now you know that the $3,000 isn't the problem, it's the $1,500 that needs attention and assistance.

Example

Patient: I'll have to think this over.

Dentist/BA: Well, I appreciate that, Ms. Jones. I know you wouldn't take the time to think this over if you weren't interested. So that I can make sure that I am clear, won't you please tell me, what is it that you need to think about? Is it whether or not this is the type of treatment that would be best for you?

Patient: Oh, no. I know that I need this.

Dentist/BA: Then do you need to think about whether or not I/Dr. Jameson would be the one to provide that treatment?

Patient: No, if I do this, I want you to do it. I don't want anyone else to stick their hands in my mouth!

Dentist/BA: Then, tell me Ms. Jones, is it the money? Do you need to think about whether or not you are able to make this investment now?

Patient: Yeah. Money is a bit tight right now.

What has happened in this example is that because of careful and caring questioning, the true problem has been identified and can now be addressed. The communication skills here make it comfortable and possible for the patient to say that she needs to find a way to pay for the treatment. Many times a patient will say that she needs to think it over, and the dental person with whom she is conversing will just say, "Oh, OK. Well, give us a call when you are ready."

At that moment, the whole issue drops in a bucket. You must identify what the problem is for the patient. You must make it comfortable for her to tell you if there is a financial issue. Some people are embarrassed or too proud to come out and tell you that they need some financial help. Let the patient know that you understand the situation, and that you have alternatives. Open doors that historically have been closed.

Example

Patient: I can't believe I need this much work! How is this possible?

Dentist/Business Manager: I can't tell you that, Mr. Jones. There are many things that affect your oral health: age, nutrition—what and how you eat—home care, stress. Have you been under stress during the last year or so?

Patient: Man, have I!

Dentist/Business Manager: Our responsibility is to evaluate your situation and make a thorough diagnosis based on a comprehensive gathering of data and a complete analysis of that data. Then, after careful study, we make recommendations that we believe will help you to get and maintain oral health for a lifetime. And that's what we have done.

You have total control in the decision making. Whether or not you proceed with the treatment that I/we are recommending is completely up to you, and the choice is yours alone. However, my/our responsibility as your dentist/dental team is to do the very best job we can to diagnose, treatment plan, and present to you a course of action that we believe would be in your best interest. Is that OK with you?

Tom Hopkins has taught me the difference between an objection and a condition. My understanding of this difference has been very helpful as I work with people—whether in the dental office or elsewhere.

An *objection* is a request for further information and shows that the person is interested in a continued discussion of the proposal.

A *condition* is a situation that is going on in a person's life that absolutely prevents her from going ahead—at least for the moment. Say that a person has just been released from the hospital and has high bills there or that a person has lost a job or has four kids in college. All of these are conditions that might prevent her from accepting treatment. However, it doesn't mean that she doesn't want it.

You are responsibile for doing the very best job you can of diagnosing, treatment planning, and presenting the dentistry. Make the financing of the dentistry as comfortable as you can, then get out of the way, and let the patient make her own decision.

As you are presenting, ask closing questions that will identify objections—or in some cases—conditions. If you identify a condition, let the patient know that you will be there when she is ready and that you will stay in touch. Knowing the difference between a condition and an objection lets you know where to go and how to get there. The communciation skills for this type of identification are critical. The very best way to identify a condition or an objection is by asking questions and listening—actively.

Here is an exercise for you. Practice will give you the necessary confidence to communicate financially.

1. List the main financial barriers or objections your patients give to you.
2. Using the skills from this chapter, formulate scripts that will help you deal with and overcome those objections.
3. Role-play using these scripts.
4. After the role-playing, answer these questions.
   A. Did I listen carefully?
   B. Did I repeat what I thought were the patient's main concerns?
   C. Did I validate the patient?
   D. Did I answer each objection with a values question?
   E. Did I go through the steps of dealing with an objection?
   F. When I overcame the objections, did I close?

Summary

Do not fear an objection, even the objection of money. Rather, look at this as an opportunity.

Know that, if you do your best and the person does not go ahead, they are rejecting the treatment proposal. They are *not* rejecting you.

Combine a strong belief in your team and the services you provide with the skills to get that message across. Then you can deal effectively with, "Gee, Doc, it costs too much!"

• CHAPTER •

12

Financing Cosmetic Dentistry

Once you decide to have cosmetic dentistry, you can work out the best method of paying for it.

– **Dr. Ron Goldstein**
Change Your Smile

One of the most fulfilling aspects of being a dental professional is being able to make a positive change in a person's smile—a change that will enhance a person's feeling of self-worth and self-confidence. The rewards of providing cosmetic dental care are many.

1. The challenge of performing highly intricate dental procedures.

2. Enhancing a person's self image.

3. Using one's artistic and clinical skills.

4. Having patients *want* to be in the chair.

5. Expressions of gratitude from patients instead of complaints.

6. Healthy revenue for the practice.

However, with few exceptions, cosmetic dental treatment will require a greater investment than $500 (there's that number again)—the place where people begin to balk at the cost of treatment. So, what are your choices?

- Don't do cosmetic dentistry.
- Only do one tooth at a time.
- Carry accounts on your own books, letting patients make small monthly payments directly to you.
- Do the dentistry for free.
- Do cosmetic dentistry only on the wealthy population.
- Design payment options that will make the financing of your dental care comfortable for the majority of your patients while keeping you out of the banking business.

Of course, the last is the answer of choice. Offering the payment options recommended in chapter 3 will give the majority of your patients an opportunity to receive cosmetic treatment while keeping you out of the banking business. You need to be doing what you do best: providing exquisite dental artistry.

Our Own Experience

John uses the services of an excellent lab in the central part of the country. The manager of that lab tells me that John sends in more prescriptions for cosmetic cases than any of their other clients. They are amazed, considering where John practices. In our small town of 2,500 people in rural Oklahoma where our patient population is predominantly low- to middle-income, hard-working, *salt of the earth folks*, the lab cannot believe how much cosmetic dental treatment we provide.

Why is this possible in our practice? The No. 1 reason is because John *decided* he wanted to provide this type of care. He wanted to add this to his treatment mix. In addition to quality restorative dental treatment, which he loves, he also enjoys and sees benefits of cosmetic dental treatment.

Once he *decided* to *make this happen*, we created a plan of action, which included advanced hands-on training, courses, and improved management and marketing strategies to move this forward. We knew that we had to open our own doors. We are very clear about one fact: *No one is going to make anything happen for us.* If we want to accomplish a goal, then we must assume the responsibility to make things happen. Our decision to expand the cosmetic aspect of our practice was Step 1. Developing a plan of action was Step 2. This plan of action included developing ways to use our healthcare financing program to assist our patients with the financing of their cosmetic dentistry. Then, Step 3 was to decide who we needed to make this happen for us—team members and resource entities. Who was going to do what? Step 4 was to determine time frames that we wanted to establish to make sure that we were moving forward on a constant basis. And Step 5 was—and is—as important as anything else—to evaluate our progress and see how we were doing. If the plan wasn't working, then we knew it was important to alter the plan. Just because a plan might not have been working right off the bat, we were not discouraged. We stepped back, solidified the things that were working, and altered the things that weren't.

Apply this same five-step goal accomplishment scenario into your practice. I have alluded to this several times throughout this book because this process is a part of execution—getting things done. No matter how much you want to do something, no matter how great your ideas, if you aren't able to execute the project—to get results—nothing will happen. Don't give up. If you want something badly enough, you will pick yourself up when you stumble or fall, and you will dust yourself off to see what is still there and what has been scraped away. What is left after the healing may be a bit tougher, but it is usually stronger and better.

Wisdom comes from the *tough* times—not from the smooth times.

Educating the Population

We know that the majority of people are not aware of the fabulous opportunities that are available in dentistry today. Thus, we developed an educational program for our community and for our patient base that would introduce people to the new developments and the new possibilities.

The following strategies are a few of the segments of our marketing program. None of these strategies are new or unique; they are just good. The key to the success of any marketing program is in *just doing it.* If you are seriously interested in developing the cosmetic aspect of your practice, stop waiting for people to come in and ask you about changing their smile. Open your own doors. Pave your own way. Get serious about educating people about what's going on in dentistry and what you are doing to make more opportunities available.

Marketing Strategies That Work

1. **Practice brochure.**

In our practice brochure, there is a section in the middle of the brochure that addresses our understanding of the value of a beautiful smile. We note that we appreciate how the smile affects a person's self-image. We invite people who are interested in exploring the possibility of a smile makeover to ask about cosmetic dentistry.

These brochures are sent to all of our new patients. They are handed out at health fairs and bridal fairs where we participate. At these fairs we take one of our intra-oral cameras and show people the results of cosmetic dental treatment with *before* and *after* stored images of completed cases. In addition, at the fairs, we show a brief patient education program. We have a portable digital player and monitor that allows us to play the program continuously.

We also give our active patients copies of our brochure to give to friends and family members who need a dental home—or who might be interested in cosmetic dentistry. We let our own patient family be our sales force. In the brochure, we let people know about our comfortable financial options (See Fig. 5–6).

2. **Patient education program**

In addition to showing the patient education program at the health and bridal fairs, we show it to new and existing patients who express an interest in cosmetic dentistry. There is no better way to answer questions or to stimulate interest than to show a person a program that demonstrates various situations and the solutions that are available.

We have a patient education program showing in our reception area. We have this on continuous play—without sound. The program is organized around the types of treatment we offer in our practice, particularly cosmetic or aesthetic restorations or smile makeovers. People who may be in the reception area who have accompanied a patient to an appointment may discover ways that they could get healthier or enhance their smile. We make sure that our reception area and our entire facility support our goal to help people obtain and maintain oral health for a lifetime and to introduce ways to access a more beautiful smile (Fig. 12–1).

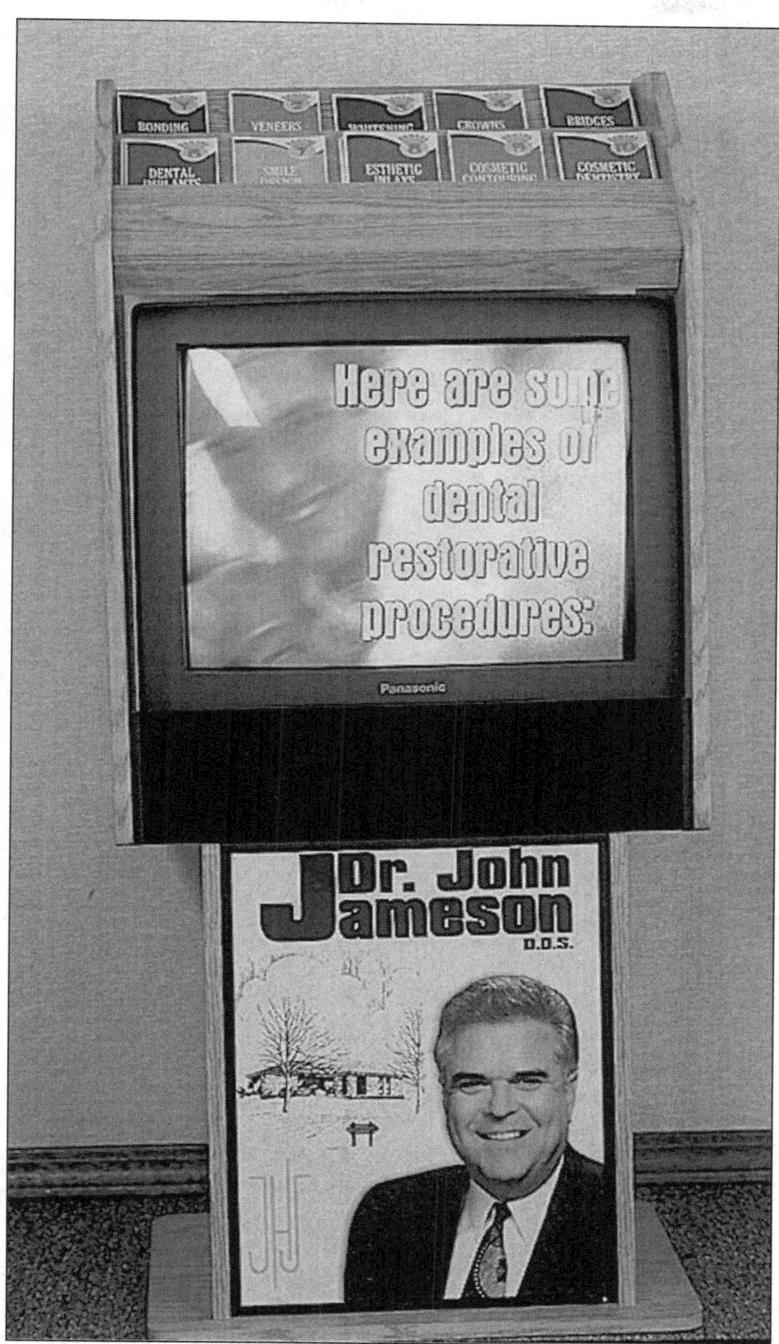

Fig. 12–1 Promote cosmetic services in your practice.

3. **Patient education newsletters.**

You have already read about my belief in patient education newsletters, and you have read about how we produce our own newsletter. We send this out once a quarter. We try to highlight one type of cosmetic situation or procedure in each edition or, certainly, in every other edition. Nothing that we write about in our newsletter stimulates more interest or initiates more telephone inquiries than our issues about cosmetic dentistry. Again, we refer to our financial options on a regular basis. We want to constantly work at clearing any barriers related to financing (see Fig. 5–2).

4. **Networking with healthcare specialists.**

These professionals—dental specialists, plastic surgeons, dermatologists, and others—are interested in not only health and well-being but also in appearance enhancement. Their patients come to them for both reasons. However, many of these marvelous and highly skilled professionals are not aware of what can be done to enhance a person's smile.

We work with many plastic surgeons—many of whom have dual degrees: DDS and MD. These extraordinary surgeons know that they cannot obtain an excellent and complete result if a person has a challenging smile or disfigured teeth. They are interested in working with talented dentists who provide a level of care that is relative to their level of care.

In interviews with me, numerous plastic surgeons have told me that they want to interact and network with dentists who focus their practices on cosmetic dentistry. However, they say that not many of the dentists contact them. Those who do, often find a productive and beneficial relationship.

Schedule a meeting or a luncheon with an interested plastic surgeon. Take beautiful examples of the cases you have completed. Make sure you take the *before* and the *after* photographs. Take your brochures. Let him know who you are, what you do, and the kinds of results that you are able to acquire.

Most plastic surgeons are familiar with patient financing programs. Most of them have these up and running in their practices. They will be pleased to know that you are involved with patient financing as well.

5. **Dental specialists.**

In addition, do not assume that the dental specialists with whom you network know what is happening in the area of cosmetic dentistry. They have much to learn to stay current with the complexities of their specialty. They will be pleased to have you bring them up-to-date on what you are doing in your practice and will be enthusiastic to work with you. In many of your cases, working with the specialists will be mandatory to access excellent results. Reciprocal referral, of course, is healthy.

If your specialists aren't involved with patient financing, you might introduce them to your program at the same time that you are introducing them to the treatments you are providing. This will be important to your patients who want and need the care but need a way to pay.

Be proactive. You make the first effort to get together. You will be well received.

6. **Networking with appearance specialists.**

Beauty salons, fitness centers, modeling agencies, clothing boutiques, etc, are more than happy to network with you. You can send people their way. Consider providing a gift certificate to patients who receive cosmetic treatment—gifts to receive care from one of your networking friends. They, in turn, may be willing to place your brochures or cards in their facility and may be willing to reciprocate by referring.

7. **Brochures and books.**

Have written information—which includes photography—available in your reception area, the treatment rooms, and in the consultation area. You will want to provide written backup support for the type of treatment you are recommending in the form of educational brochures. Let patients take this material home so that they can share the information with a spouse, a friend, or family members. This may prove to be beneficial when it comes to making a decision about going ahead. You may wish to have a professional company produce a brochure/mini-magazine about cosmetic dentistry and you (Fig. 12–2).

8. **Before and after photography.**

Be sure to include photography in every appointment. You will want to build your own set of *before* and *after* photographs to show people not only the features and benefits of recommended treatment but also the fact that you can produce the desired results.

I can't tell you how many times I have spoken with doctors who express pleasure with the results of a particular case. They will want to show me the

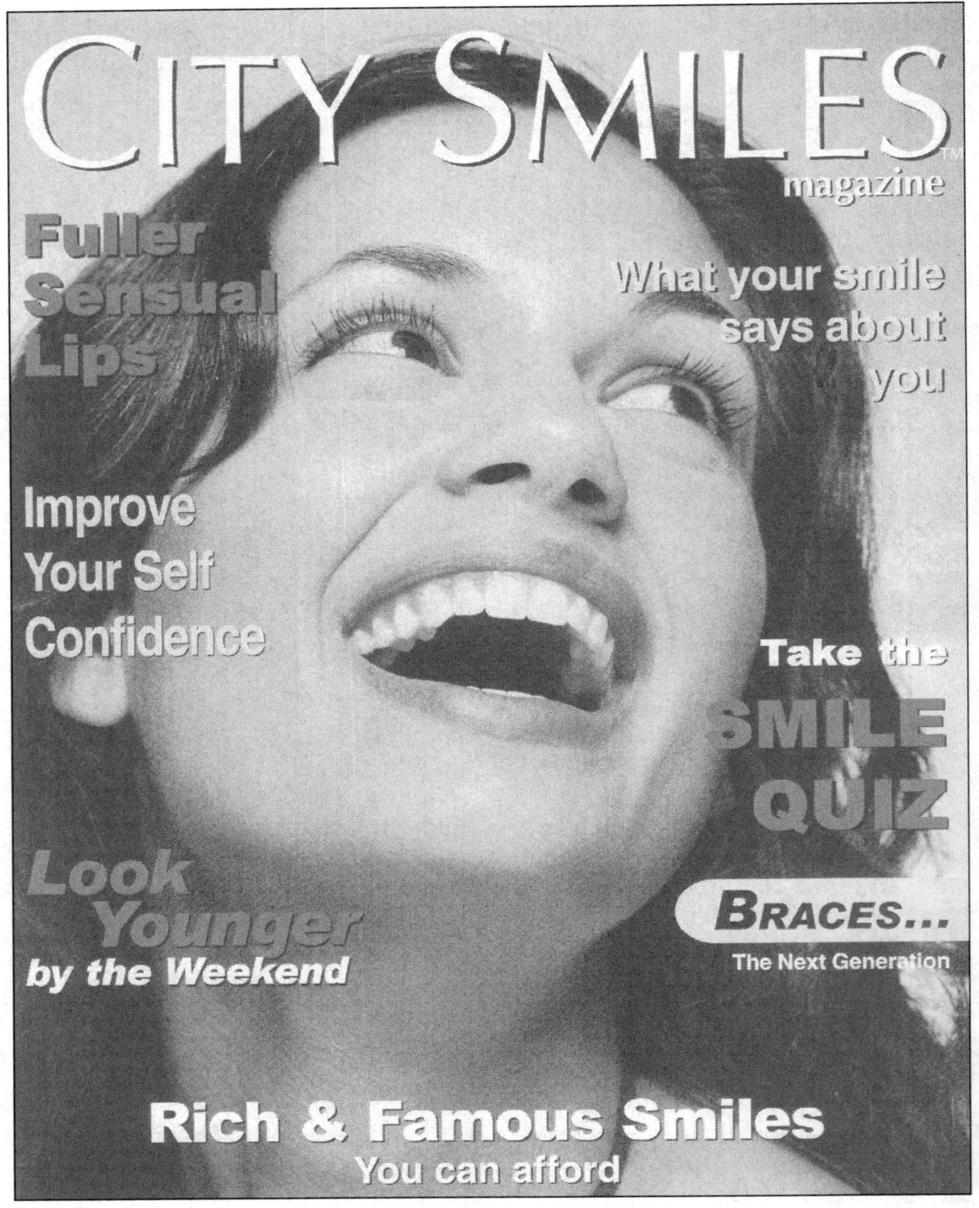

Fig. 12–2 Promote cosmetic services in your practice. Contact Dental Image Works at (214) 477-2076.

photographs of the results of their treatment. The person will look great. So, I ask to see the before photograph. A sad look comes over their face as they say, "Yeah, it would be great to have had both the *before* and the *after*—but I forgot to take the *before*." Don't let that happen to you. Make it a part of every appointment to take *before* photographs of the situation. Store these images in the patient's record. Then, take your *after* photographs so that comparisons can be made.

This is an extremely effective way to validate a patient's decision to have gone ahead with treatment and will offset buyer's remorse. These can also be very powerful when you are showing a potential patient the benfits of treatment, the results they can access, and proof that you can produce those results (Fig. 12–3).

In addition, you can send *before* and *after* photographs to the patient following treatment. Send this to their place of employment. If they don't want anyone to see, they will tuck it away. However, most people who receive cosmetic dentistry are pretty open about sharing their *before* and *after* photographs with others. Include two of your cards in your note or letter so that they can refer friends and family member or work colleagues to you.

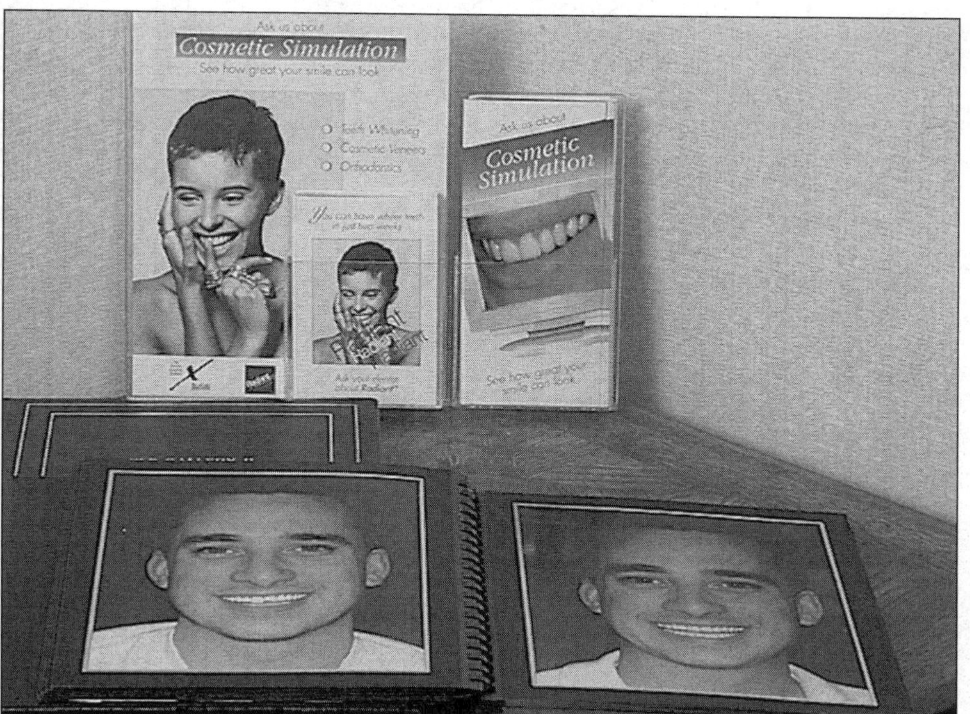

Fig. 12–3 *Before* and *after* photos.

9. **Intra-oral/digital cameras and imaging systems.**

There is nothing better than an intra-oral or digital camera to show a person *up close* and *personal* how their teeth and smile *really* look. An up close evaluation of the smile will give the patients a chance to tell you what they like most, what they like least, and what they would like to change about their smile (Fig. 12–4).

With stored *before* and *after* photographs, you will be able to show patients—on a large monitor—examples of similar situations. They will be able to identify with these situations and see the results you were able to accomplish.

Cosmetic imaging systems let you give the patient an idea of what they can do with their own smile as you use the imager to explore possibilities.

10. **Community presentations.**

About once a month, a member of our team goes to one of the civic groups in our area and makes a 20- to 30-minute presentation with visual aids. We use a powerpoint presentation to illustrate what is happening in the world of dentistry, particularly in the area of cosmetic dentistry. We have brochures about our practice and brochures about cosmetic dentistry available for handouts. There is always much surprise on the part of the attendees as to what can be accomplished. We almost always receive a new patient who is interested in a change of smile (Fig. 12–5).

11. **Newspaper articles.**

We find that most newspaper editors are very interested in positive, informative articles regarding modern dentistry. We provide these articles plus photographs to the editors and tackle the subject of cosmetic dentistry as often as possible.

Also, any time a member of our team receives an award or does something special in the community, we try to get this in the newspapers. This has proven to be a tremendous source of new patients.

If you and your team attend a course on cosmetic dentistry presented by one of the top clinicians in the country—or in the world—try to have a photograph taken with the clinician. Then, write an article—very reader-friendly—about the course, your attendance, and include a note about the person with whom you have studied. This is newsworthy.

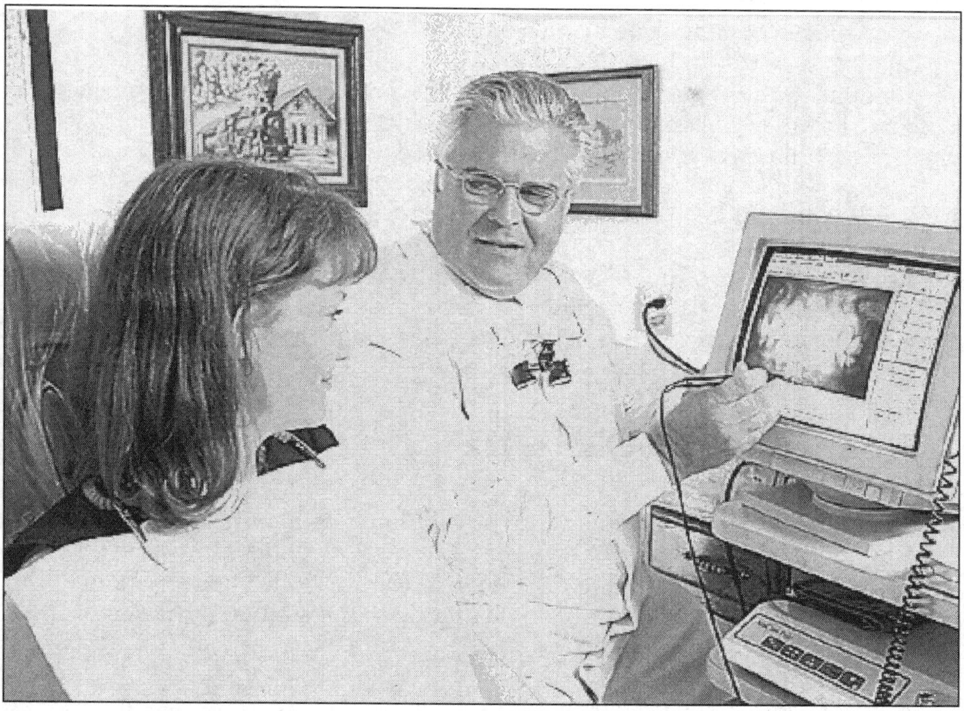

Fig. 12–4 Intra-oral camera photography.

Fig. 12–5 Dr. Jameson providing a presentation at a civic group meeting

11. **Newspaper or magazine advertising.**

Regular, well-prepared advertising in the press can prove to be beneficial for you. Professional guidance on the development of your ads and on the placement will prove to be valuable (Fig. 12–6).

12. **Television and Radio.**

Professionally produced spots addressing cosmetic dentistry in the practice can be extremely effective. These must be produced professionally or they come across as cheap and are offensive rather than stimulating.

Now Just Do It

These are but a few of the many ideas that can be effective to stimulate interest in the cosmetic aspect of your practice. Once again, however, I must stress the fact that nothing is better than referrals from happy patients who recommend you because they are so pleased with the results of their own smile makeover.

In each one of our marketing strategies, we include a pleasant message about the fact that we do have comfortable financing available. We do not want to stimulate the interest in cosmetic dentistry only to have it squelched because of the fear of cost.

Overcome this potential negative before the fact. Address the issue of cost. Let people know that there are options available for payment that will make it possible for them to receive a change of smile without having to worry about how they will pay for it.

Handling the Objection of Cost as it Relates to Cosmetic Dentistry

When you are presenting your treatment recommendations, you will close your presentation by finding out if there are further questions. If not, you will ask if the patient is ready to go ahead and schedule that first appointment. Remember from our previous discussion about objections that you are serving a couple of purposes by closing: You are asking for a commitment, and you are trying to identify any objections or any barriers to treatment acceptance.

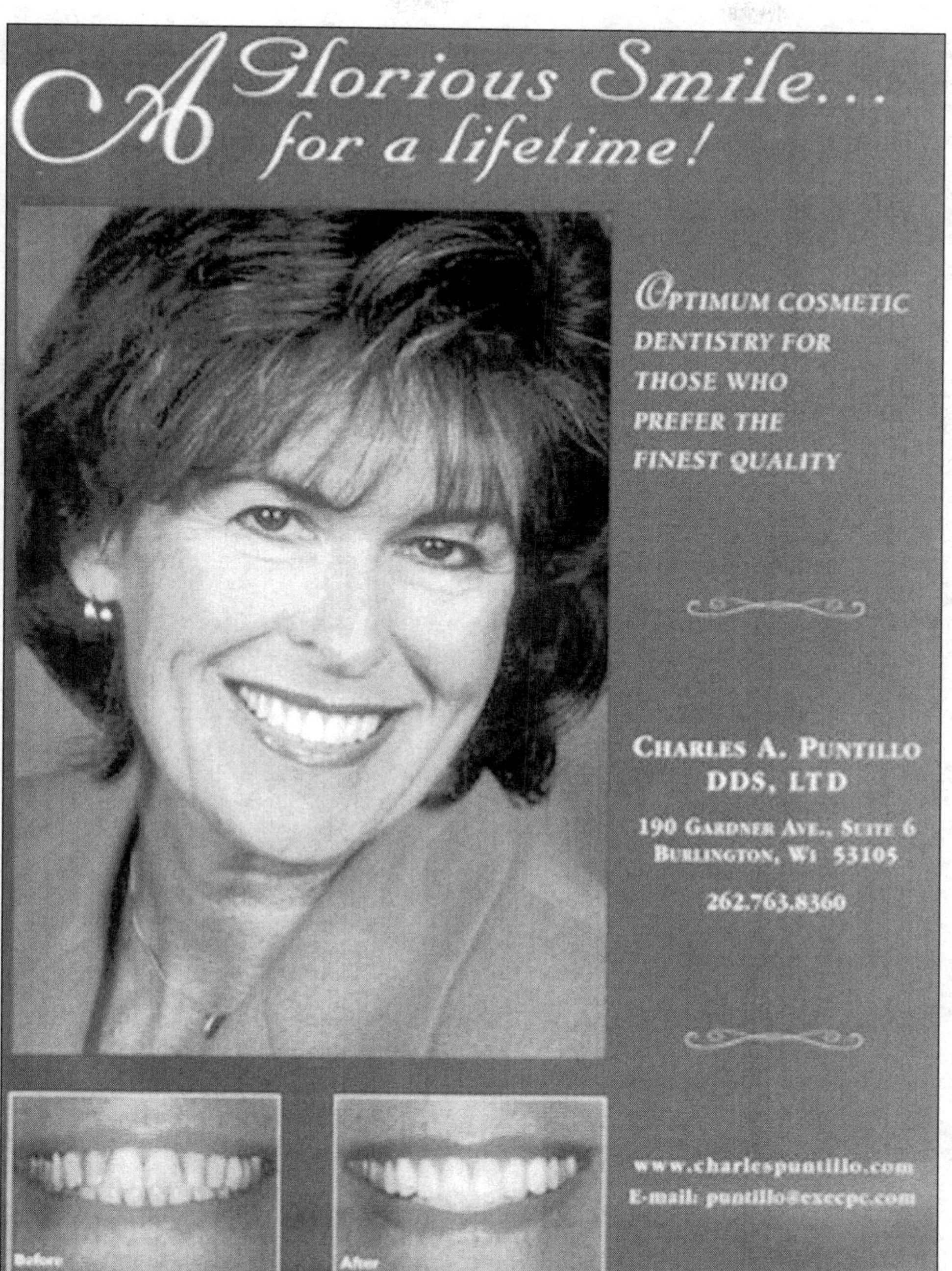

Fig. 12–6 Magazine ad from our client Dr. Chuck Puntillo.

You must identify these objections before you can do anything to eliminate them. Identifying a problem is the first step in the solving of that problem.

When you have completed your presentation and are asking for the commitment, the objection of cost may emerge. That's OK. You want and need to know if this is the type of treatment a person wants, and if so, what it will take to make it possible to go ahead. If the patient says that they do want this change of smile but need a way to pay it out, you now have a way of offering this type of financing without doing it yourself.

Example

FC: Ms. Jones, the fee for the smile makeover that Dr. Jameson has recommended is $6,400. How would you like to take care of that?

Ms. Jones: Oh, I have insurance that will take care of most of it, so I'll let you find out how much they will pay, then I'll pay the difference.

FC: Ms. Jones, since the treatment you will be receiving is cosmetic in nature, the insurance companies do not cover this.

Ms. Jones: What? I can't believe I pay this much for my insurance, and it doesn't help me when I need it!

FC: I can appreciate your disappointment. However, since insurance is not a factor here, let's talk about other avenues for payment. What works for you?

Ms. Jones: Well, I can pay for a part of this, but not all of it. Can we do this treatment a little bit at a time?

FC: That would not be in your best interest. Dr. Jameson is going to be providing eight veneers across the front teeth in the upper part of your mouth. You want to do these all at once so that the length, the color, and the fit are just right. You are interested in getting a beautiful smile, and so are we. The veneers need to be done all at one time.

How much of an initial investment would you be able to make?

Ms. Jones: Oh, I guess I could give you $3,000 at the start. But that would deplete my savings, and I'd have to pay out the rest.

FC: OK. That would work. If you were to make an initial investment of $3,000, then how much would you be comfortable paying per month?

Ms. Jones: Oh, about $100 per month.

FC: We will contact our financial partner to see about accessing a line of credit for you. Once they have established that line of credit, you can provide us with the initial investment of $3,000. Then we can finance the other $3,400. Then, you would only be required to pay about $100 per month. Would that work for you?

Ms. Jones: Yes. It would. That would be fine.

FC: Great. Let's complete the application right now.

The Financing Program as a Vehicle

John is a great dentist. So are you. John's team is fabulous. So is yours. He goes to courses continually to upgrade his skill level. I'm sure you do the same. So, what makes the difference?

We think that one of the reasons he is able to provide so much quality restorative and cosmetic dentistry is that we can finance that dentistry through our healthcare financing program. Since cosmetic dentistry is not covered by dental insurance, for the most part, the patient must come up with the entire fee.

By offering the options that I have addressed, we make it possible for most anyone who wants and needs cosmetic dentistry to receive it. We do not have high-level executives in our practice who want a new smile. We have salt-of-the-earth people who want the best. They just need a way to pay for it—a way that fits into their particular financial situation.

Extended Payment Plans

During the past few years, most of the healthcare or patient financing programs have added an extended payment plan. I described this in chapter 3, "Workable Financial Options." This option came because both doctors and patients were seeking treatment that exceeded most of the lines of credit that had been established with the traditional financing plans. Treatment for implants, comprehensive restorative, and cosmetic cases are big-ticket items. So, the financing companies responded.

These programs—where a person can access a line of credit of $500–25,000 or more—make it possible for people to receive the treatment but still keep a reasonable monthly payment structure. The length of time that a person takes to pay off the account depends on how much he can pay per month.

These programs have, I believe, been one of the major vehicles for the advancement for cosmetic dentistry. There are many other factors—but this is, surely, one of them. No matter how much someone wants a beautiful smile, he can't proceed if he can't afford it.

Lessons from the Plastic Surgeons

We work with several plastic surgeons and many dentists who concentrate their practices in the area of cosmetic treatment. They want a patient to pay for the services up-front. They tell me that if a patient owes them money, that somewhere down the road the person seems to find aspects about their cosmetic change that she doesn't like. Perhaps this is true. If a person owes you money, he may find and express fault with the treatment as an attempt to get out of paying the remaining balance. (This could be true with any treatment, wouldn't you agree?)

If a person owes you money or wants to have a balance excused, he will try to blame you *for something* so that you look like the bad guy and he looks like the good guy. A patient may—subconsciously—be embarrassed about poor money management. He may try to transfer a feeling of personal guilt to a feeling of blame to you. Practice preventive management. Use the financial options I have recommended and prevent problems related to money. Then both you and the patient can rejoice in the new smile.

Summary

If you follow the recommended financial protocol, no one will owe you money. No one will have an outstanding balance with you. Payment will be complete by the time the treatment is complete. If a patient owes money, it will be to a separate entity, not you. This will lead to pleasant relationships, ones that are based on mutual benefit. You win—the patient wins. Stress is reduced for both parties. That is one more way to kindle or rekindle the joy of dentistry.

• CHAPTER •

13

Devising a Collection System for Past-due Accounts

Realize the importance of getting the money in. Do not be sentimental about this; you are in business, you deserve to be paid for the service you give, and you should be.

– Peter Glazenbrook

Happiness and Fulfillment in Dentistry

If you follow the advice given in the preceding chapters, then you will *get out of the banking business.* I am sure that you have realized that I would encourage you to remove yourself from carrying any accounts receivable except for a very short turnaround on insurance payments, if you are taking assignment of benefits. No private-pay accounts receivable. What a stress relief!

However, you may presently have some past-due accounts that have been there before you changed your way of financing. And no matter how astute you are in managing your new financial system, some accounts *may slip through the cracks* from time to time. Hopefully this will not happen now, but you need to be prepared and educated for how to handle these past-due situations. Therefore, a careful, sequential collection program for the recapturing of these accounts must be put into place and followed with persistence.

Think of past-due accounts as a major **C.O.S.T.** Key essentials of your collection system so that you minimize costs while maximizing efforts are as follows:

1. Consistency
2. Organization
3. Swiftness
4. Tenacity

C.O.S.T.!

Develop a Collection System That Gets Results

Consistency

Devise a foolproof system for discovering immediately when an account is overdue. Do this with consistency. Any system within your practice must be established, well-managed, and performed with consistency. Consistency will ensure your success. Remember: the success of your practice will be in direct proportion to the success of your systems. In addition, one reminder that an account is past-due without a second reminder (should the account remain unpaid) makes the first letter or notice ineffective. Your patients will need to be reminded in a regular, timely, and professional way that their accounts are past-due and that, as a professional organization, you can be counted upon to follow up and follow through with your responsibilities, and you are asking them to do the same thing.

The purpose of developing a system is to make sure that you access great results. If you develop a system but do not honor each step of the system, you are making a decision to have that system fail—or not work nearly as well. You are choosing not to gain excellent results. Why would you do that? If something is worth doing, its worth doing well. Consistency is a requirement of a results-oriented system.

Organization

The organization of your collection system must be structured very carefully. Spend time developing your system. Get coaching from people who know how to handle accounts receivable and collections to help you. Make sure that your patients are treated equally and that your financial protocols are administered consistently. You will have different situations that will require different skills. This will be included in your plan of action.

Here are recommendations for establishing your collection system.

- Run an aged accounts receivable list each month
- Evaluate each account carefully to see the amount past due, the date of the last payment, and the amount of the last payment
- Double-check any formal financial/written agreement to see if the patient is abiding by the agreement

Establish a fair time schedule to determine the speed with which requests for payment should be made. Once you establish the time schedule, follow it with *consistency*. (There's that word again!) With a 30-day payment requirement, a bill becomes past due on the 31st day. If bills/statements are sent monthly and a 30-day billing cycle is in place, 45–60 days may pass before payment is received. A 15-day cycle may need to be instituted.

When an account becomes delinquent, based on the decided length of time, a rebilling charge should be filed. However, notice of intent should be made in advance of such a charge. Notice of this intent should always be acknowledged as a part of the system when the original agreement is made. It is always best to inform a patient of expectation before the fact. This notice can be a printed message on statements, stickers, or letters.

Every evening, before the day is finished, the BA needs to review the patients who are coming into the practice the next day. She will identify any persons who either need to make a payment that day or who have a past-due account that needs to be collected.

At the morning meeting or at the beginning of your day, the BA needs to make sure that the appointment coordinator knows who will be paying that day and how much is required. In addition, she will identify those past-due patients that need to be escorted into the BA's office for a private discussion of the past-due account. Obviously, the goal is to get a written agreement on how the account will be settled. Negotiate a settlement of the account while you have that patient face to face with you.

Example

Let's say that Ms. Patient owes $248 and that the account is 60 days past due. She is coming into the office today for an emergency appointment. The BA has identified this fact. When Ms. Patient arrives, the appointment coordinator or whoever is greeting the patient says the following to Ms. Patient: "Ms. Patient, Jan, our business administrator, has some paperwork that she needs for you to complete. We have a few minutes before the doctor sees you. Let me show you into Jan's office." Or before the patient leaves the office that day, make sure that she is escorted into the business office so that the BA has a chance to negotiate that settlement.

In establishing your financial system, firmness is essential. Offer the appropriate flexibility to meet the financial needs of your patients but be firm in adhering to your system. Firmness and fairness to both parties are critical to successful collections.

Swiftness

The sooner you contact a person about the past-due status of his account, the more likely you will be to get those monies collected. Nothing will be more harmful to your collection efforts than tardiness or inconsistency.

Experts in the field of professional collection offer many helpful strategies to accomplish the greatest results in your collection efforts. They know how long and how hard you sometimes have to work to get an account collected. Therefore, they recommend a specific time line for successful collections to take place.

The following is the best time line as suggested by professional collection agencies. You are not a professional collection agency, but it would make sense to follow the guidelines of the people who do this for a living and who are only paid if they collect your account. They have to find ways to accomplish results or they are out of work.

Even though I will be referring to various methods of collection efforts, remember that the best way to collect is face to face, the second best way to collect is over the phone, and the third best way to collect is through the written word.

The following is the ideal collection time line.

At 31 Days Past Due: Collection procedure should begin at 31 days past due via telephone and letter. The thrust of these messages—both verbal and written—should be that the account is past due and that payment is necessary and expected.

At 45 Days Past Due: A second letter and telephone call needs to be sent and made. This message should be a request for payment within 15 days.

At 60 Days Past Due: A third letter and telephone call should be made. This message is a firmer one. The message is direct and states that payment is required and expected immediately.

At 75 Days Past Due: A fourth letter and telephone call is made—one that is firmer yet. This is an either/or confrontation; either the bill is paid or you will be forced to turn the account over for legal action.

At 90 Days Past Due: Three months of collection efforts have occurred—120 days have passed since the service has been rendered. A fifth letter is sent, no telephone call. This letter tells the debtor about the action that is going to be taken—legal action, collection agency, small claims court, etc. When the letter is sent saying that action will be taken—do so. Otherwise your efforts are wasted, and your credibility is lost.

Collection experts say that if an account is 120 days past due and the patient has made no effort to pay, this account is uncollectible! Be aware of this.

Tenacity

Management of an effective collection system takes careful planning as well as consistency and *tenacity* in administration. Stick to it. Don't let the patients think—or realize— that just because you sent a notification of a past-due status that they don't need to worry because they won't hear from you again, you won't remember, or time will pass before you notify them again. Be serious about this. Once you start a collection procedure—follow it through to the end.

The following criteria underlie successful collection:

- Be prompt and regular with your contacts.
- Increase firmness as the account delinquency increases.
- Have appropriate messages in letters or notices.
- Establish a method for follow up and refer to it daily
- Move quickly on all past-due accounts. Do not let too much time pass between contacts. Let people know you are serious.
- Be aware of individual differences and needs. Flex to meet individual needs but do not let emotion get the best of you.
- Have a knowledge of the legal requirements of collecting.
- In creating collection letters or making collection calls, messages must be clear but courteous; firm but fair; positive rather than negative; tenacious but not offensive; solid but not rigid.

Monitoring Your Collection System and Financial Arrangements

Establish a tickler file for your financial arrangements. Do this either on your computer or in a physical tickler file. Do everything you can do on the computer. Don't waste your time doing something twice. However, if you find that the physical form of monitoring—through a manual tickler file—works better for you, then this is fine. Whatever it takes. Establish the system and then work the system.

After an agreement for payment of a past-due account has been determined, make note of this agreement. Organize these agreements so that you will know when you can expect payment. Place it in the appropriate place in the tickler file or computer. This file will ensure accurate tracking of each account. Monitor this carefully to immediately discover if someone is late with an agreed-upon payment

When you place a card in the manual or computerized tickler file, give the patient a five-day grace period before you make a telephone call about the past-due account. In other words, if a payment is due on the 20th of the month, place a financial card in your tickler file on the 25th. Then, if a payment has not been received by the 25th, make your call. *Review your tickler file every day.* If a payment has been made, make note on the card of the date of the payment and the amount received.

If a payment is not received on the assigned day (remember, you have given the patient a five-day grace period), call the patient and ask for payment and/or arrange for a new due date. Record the new date. File the card or computer entry on the new date due. If you do not receive payment on the new date, make a second telephone call.

Example

> Mr. Jones, this is Cathy with Dr. Jameson's dental office. Mr. Jones, during our conversation last Friday, you indicated that you would be placing a check in the mail that day. We have no record of receiving that payment, and I was concerned.

If the patient makes a partial payment, call them. Thank them for the payment that they did make. Then ask for the balance of the payment.

Example.

> Thank you, Ms. Jones, for your $50 payment. We appreciate this. However, our agreement was for $100 this month, and I was calling to see when we could expect the balance of your payment.

Let the person know that the agreement was for a different amount, and that you need to get a commitment for the balance. This is critical, because otherwise, the patient will think it is OK to send the smaller amount. Then your arrangement will stretch on forever.

Figures 13–1, 13–2, and 13–3 are examples of tracking devices that are workable. In addition, computerized analysis and tracking of account information and agreements works quite well. Choose one that works best for you—and use it *consistently*.

FINANCIAL ARRANGEMENTS CARD

Patient: ______________________ Date: ______________

Guarantor: ______________ Address: ______________________

Phone: (Home) ______________ (Business) ______________

Total: ______________ Financial Agreement: ______________________

Date Due	Amt. Due	Amt. Paid	Date Paid	Date Contacted	Comments

Fig. 13–1 Financial arrangements card.

Guarantor's Name: ______________________
Phone: **(Home)** ______________ **(Business)** ______________
Total Balance: __________ **Financial Arrangements:** __________

1st Call:	**2nd Call:**
Date: ______	Date: ______
Payment Due: ______	Payment Due: ______
Date Due: ______	Date Due: ______
Last Payment Due: ______	Last Payment Due: ______
Amount Paid: ______	Amount Paid: ______
Notes: ______	Notes: ______
3rd Call:	**4th Call:**
Date: ______	Date: ______
Payment Due: ______	Payment Due: ______
Date Due: ______	Date Due: ______
Last Payment Due: ______	Last Payment Due: ______
Amount Paid: ______	Amount Paid: ______
Notes: ______	Notes: ______

Fig. 13–2 Call form.

Payment Agreements

Date Due	Name	Telephone	Amount Due

Fig. 13–3 Payment agreements form.

Summary

Establish a protocol for collection and stick with it. The professional management of past-due accounts is mandatory to control your **C.O.S.T.** Your collection system must be handled with the following:

1. Consistency
2. Organization
3. Swiftness
4. Tenacity

C.O.S.T.!

• CHAPTER •

14

Collecting Past-due Accounts: Written Communications

You cannot save money with what you produce, only with what you collect.

– Darrell Cain, CPA, President of Cain, Watters, and Assoc. PC

Written communication with your patients who have a past-due account is a very important step in receiving payments and in controlling your accounts receivable. It may be the only communication you will have with some accounts. In this chapter, I give step-by-step instructions on how to administer the written part of collections. Written communication—just like all systems in your practice—needs to be properly and carefully established, administered with consistency, and must obtain desired results.

There are four phases of collection. Your written and verbal contacts with your patients will follow and fit into the following four phases:

- Notification of the past-due account
- Reminder of the past-due account
- Negotiation on how to settle the account
- Action to be taken if compliance is not obtained

The Notification Phase

When an account becomes 31 days past due, the patient's statement needs to notify him of the delinquency. Be brief and to the point with your message. A stamped or computerized notice on the statement is appropriate (Fig. 14–1). Make sure that a due date is included on every statement.

PAST DUE

PLEASE SEND PAYMENT

BY RETURN MAIL

Fig. 14–1 Stamped notification.

An alternative to the stamped notice on a statement would be a straightforward handwritten message on the statement indicating the past-due status. There's something pretty effective about the fact that you take the time to write a personal note on the statement. The patient will realize that you aren't just sending your statements off the computer without ever looking at them. Use a bright color of ink for your handwritten note so that it will stand out when the patient reads the statement

Or, of course, you could send a separate individual letter to the patient at this early—but important—part of your collection effort. This letter can be sent under special cover or can be included with the statement (Fig. 14–2).

Dear Mr. Patient:

Your bill of $248 was due on July 6. Our records show that your account is now more than thirty days past due. We appreciate your attention to this matter and will look forward to receiving your payment by return mail.

Thank you,

Business Manager

Fig. 14–2 Notification letter.

Note: Each time during a collection letter series when you contact a patient, inform the patient of the amount due, the date the payment was due, and the length of time payment has been past due.

If you do not receive payment after this initial notification, move into the second phase of collection—*the reminder phase.* Fifteen days should be the time allowed between your first notification of the past-due account and your second notice—*the initial reminder.*

The Reminder Phase

The reminder phase of the collection process begins when notification has obtained no results. A series of notices and letters making a request for payment needs to be sent in a systematic manner.

During this *soft* phase of collection, your message should *assume* that the patient intends to pay but has simply overlooked the bill. The following series of notices can include several types of correspondences:

1. form letters
2. stamped notices on statements
3. preprinted notices
4. personal letters

Following are some examples of each.

Form letters

A form letter is an impersonal way to remind the patient of the debt. This form can be a preprinted, computerized, or a copied form. The patient owing you will see this as an impersonal, standardized process but may be stimulated to take action (Fig. 14–3).

Stamped notices

Stamped notices on the statements can encourage action. These will have a stronger effect if they are in a different color—i.e., *red* (Figs. 14–4 and 14–5).

Dear Mr. Patient:

Our records indicate that your account is past due. A balance of ________ is _______ days past due.

We would appreciate your attention to this matter.

Sincerely,

Business Manager

Fig. 14–3 Form letter.

PAST DUE

PLEASE SEND PAYMENT

BY RETURN MAIL

Fig. 14–4 Stamped notice A.

REMINDER:

Your account is

PAST DUE

We look forward to

receiving your check

TODAY!

Fig. 14–5 Stamped notice B.

Preprinted notice

Preprinted stickers can be attached to the statement or preprinted inserts can be produced that will deliver different messages. Use of several different bright colors of paper can bring attention to the notice (Fig. 14–6).

Your account is past due **PLEASE REMIT!**

Fig. 14–6 Preprinted stickers.

Personal letters

Of the four types of notices, the personal letter is most widely used and is the most effective. *The other forms are to be used only once.* After that, they become ineffective.

However, the personal form letter can be a series of letters reminding a patient of the status of the account. These letters should become more urgent and stronger as the account ages. All personal reminder letters need to be courteous, but they do become more specific and more intense as time passes. Make sure that these are straight and to the point.

Personal reminder letters—a suggested series

The personal letter should be nonthreatening, informal, and congenial. The following is an example of a series of personal letters that can be used to deal with a delinquent account (Figs. 14–7, 14–8, 14–9, 14–10, and 14–11).

In this phase of the collection process, present the problem, the amount due, and the amount of time it has been past due. *Then request that action be taken.* This phase does not make any specific appeal other than a request for payment. Compromise is not offered. Continue to assume in your correspondence that the patient intends to pay but has inadvertently overlooked the bill. You want to keep the patient on your side. You do not want to antagonize the patient. If the patient becomes irritated, the chances of being paid are reduced.

Dear Mr. Patient:

In reviewing our records, we find that you have an outstanding balance of $248 for services provided on ____________________________.

You may have overlooked your previous statement. Therefore, we wanted to bring the status of your account to your attention.

We would greatly appreciate your attention to this past due account and will look forward to receiving your check so that we can keep your record clear.

If your payment and this letter have crossed in the mail, please accept our thanks for your payment.

Sincerely,

Business Manager

Fig. 14–7 Reminder letter A.

Dear Mr. Patient:

Perhaps you have overlooked your bill for $248 for the services we provided for you on ____________________________________.

We would appreciate your attention to this past due account and will look forward to receiving your payment.

Thank you,

Business Manager

Fig. 14–8 Reminder letter B.

Dear Mr. Patient:

We have not heard from you regarding your $248 past due account. Perhaps you have overlooked or misplaced our previous notices. Therefore, because we are sure you want to take care of this account, we are sending this letter reminding you of your past due balance.

We appreciate your business and will appreciate your attention to this past due account. We look forward to receiving your payment in the next few days.

Thank you,

Business Manager

Fig. 14–9 Reminder letter C.

Dear Mr. Patient:

Your account of $248 is now 60 days past due. We have reminded you of the status of this account several times in the past two months.

Once again, we remind you that your account is past due and request your immediate attention to it.

If there is a problem, please know that we are here to help. Your telephone call will be appreciated.

Thank you,

Business Manager

Fig. 14–10 Reminder letter D.

Dear Mr. Patient:

We, again, call your attention to your now seriously past due account of $248. You account is now ___________ days delinquent.

Notices as well as detailed statements have been mailed to you several times.

We need to have this matter brought to a close. We will appreciate your payment.

Thank you,

Business Manager

Fig. 14–11 Reminder letter E.

If notification and reminders do nothing to move a patient to action, then move your collection efforts to a stronger phase. Dr. Carl Caplan states in his *Encyclopedia of Dental Practice Management* that "the dental practice should not falter in its enforcement of a collection policy. It is not unfair to expect patients to meet their financial obligation. The dentist does not want to develop a *soft touch* reputation."

The Negotiation Phase

No Payment? What do you do now? Negotiation for the settlement of the account can *and should* take place.

Your initial efforts to collect an account *assumed* that the patient *would* pay. You *just knew* that the statements had been misplaced or that there had been some confusion. You have tried to give the patient the *benefit of the doubt*. However, no payment has been received and no effort has been made to settle the account. In a stronger effort to settle the account, you need to find out the reason for the nonpayment and negotiate a payment agreement that is comfortable for the both of you.

You must move into a stronger mode of operation in your collection efforts. Each correspondence in this aspect of the collection sequence must be carefully planned and must be a part of an intensifying sequence of letters. Even though your efforts are getting firmer, you still want to *try* to maintain a good relationship with the patient. This will give you a better chance of settling the account. This is a tough balancing act—getting firmer while still maintaining a good relationship.

Your goal is to arrange a discussion with the patient regarding the resolution of the account. Each account must be treated individually. The purpose of this series of letters is to schedule a discussion appointment and come to terms with a payment agreement.

The Psychology of Collection

In his book, *Past Due: How to Collect Money*, Norman King suggests that an understanding of the psychology of collection is critical to the success of such efforts. A variety of emotional appeals can be used during this portion of the process. Mr. King suggests that some common emotional appeals might be "sympathy, pride, justice, self-interest, cooperation/discussion, and fear."

Sympathy

Collection letters that appeal to the patient's sympathy try to make the patient aware of the fact that the dentist and the practice have provided a service both in treatment rendered and in the extension of credit. Now, because of the patient's inability or unwillingness to take care of the account, the practice is in a difficult position.

The effect of such an appeal letter is to draw on the person's *sympathy*. If this is a person with an *understanding heart*, this type of appeal will be effective for you.

Be cautious with this type of an appeal. If the appeal is not handled with expertise, the letter might appear *whiny* and the effect will be less than favorable. But if your letter is carefully constructed and can petition a person's sincere interest in your situation, payment could result (Fig. 14–12).

> Dear Mr. Patient:
>
> In order to maintain comfortable fees for our patients and in order to continue to provide the best possible dental care, we must constantly work at controlling our costs of operation. When you send your payment for your outstanding balance of $248, we will no longer need to invest in statements, reminders, and postage. We will then be able to pass those savings on to you and to our other valued patients in the form of affordable, quality care.
>
> Working with us on the resolution of your past due account will help all of us control the rising costs of health care.
>
> We look forward to receiving your payment. Thank you for your cooperation.
>
> Thank you,
>
> Business Manager

Fig. 14–12 Sympathy letter.

Pride

Collection letters that appeal to a patient's sense of *pride* conjure a sense of guilt for having avoided or *pushed aside* a legitimate debt. The majority of your patients will have a sense of pride and a sense of responsibility about their debts. They will be—for the most part—men/women of their word.

Therein lies the power of the appeal to people's pride. You have *assumed* that their integrity is in tact, and that circumstances have made it difficult to meet responsibilities. Most certainly, they do not *intend* to default on this balance.

Make note of how faithful with payment the patient has been in the past and how much you respect their attention to their account. The appeal to pride is effective with many people (Fig. 14–13).

> Dear Mr. Patient:
>
> We have been so grateful for your continued loyalty and for your consistently prompt payments in the past. Please know that we have appreciated this.
>
> Currently, we find that your balance of $248 is ________________ days past due. We have made several attempts to inform you of the delinquency of this account. We value and respect you. Therefore, we are requesting an appointment to discuss a solution to bring the account to a current status. Please call our office today to schedule an appointment with me to negotiate a comfortable settlement of your account.
>
> I will look forward to your call.
>
> Thank you for your immediate attention to our request.
>
> Business Manager

Fig. 14–13 Pride letter.

Justice

Collection letters that appeal to a patient's sense of *justice* try to make the person owing the money feel the creditor is not being treated justly because of his/her action or by a failure to act. The main impetus of such a letter is to emphasize that a valuable service has been rendered in a timely fashion and that you, as the creditor, believe and encourage *aboveboard* business relationships (Fig. 14–14).

> Dear Mr. Patient:
>
> In our recent letter to you, we asked for payment of your delinquent account in the amount of $248. We fully believed that we would receive the payment.
>
> Knowing that you are a person of your word, we were surprised when the payment did not arrive on the date upon which we both agreed. As we discussed during our financial consultation, we do not carry long term accounts on our own books. By not abiding by our agreement, you have placed us in a very difficult position.
>
> I am sure we can look forward to your attention to this past due account.
>
> We would appreciate your prompt payment.
>
> Business Manager

Fig. 14–4 Justice letter.

Self-interest

Collection letters that appeal to *self-interest* have a strong impact on most people. This type of collection letter would be used best at the end of a collection letter sequence. It is a more intense letter than previous efforts.

The self-interest letter combines an appeal to both the emotion and to the logic. Tom Hopkins of Scottsdale, Arizona, whom I referred to earlier, believes that you have a stronger impact if you *sell an idea to the emotion and back it up with logic.* Therefore, combine these two appeals in your self-interest correspondence. The debtor must realize the benefits of taking care of the account and that their credit standing might be damaged otherwise. At this point, do not be specific about the action you will take if the account is not rectified (Fig. 14–15)

Dear Mr. Patient:

On several occasions, we have contacted you regarding your delinquent account of $248. We have not heard from you and are wondering why.

We placed trust in you by financing your dentistry in our own office. We are disappointed that this trust has not been upheld.

You are aware, I am sure, that mishandling of credit makes it difficult, if not impossible, to maintain those privileges in the future. In addition, poor credit ratings can negatively affect you for a long time to come.

We are sure that you will want to take care of your debt so that your good credit will be restored. This, of course, will benefit both of us. We want to reestablish that trust we once placed so confidently. Please immediately resolve this issue.

We appreciate your prompt attention to this matter.

Business Manager

Fig. 14–15 Self-interest letter.

Cooperation/discussion

What you are trying to obtain through your consistent, carefully planned collection effort is an opportunity to discuss the situation so that a resolution can be developed. You want to work this out. You are asking for cooperation from the patient and are willing to give the same.

Collection letters that appeal to or request a discussion come at the end of your collection letter series. It is, simply, an offer to sit down, one on one, with the patient to plan a settlement.

This type of an appeal is straightforward, mature, and will bring positive results in many cases. The letter simply opens the door for the discussion. Arrangements for settlement will be made during the discussion (Fig. 14–16).

> Dear Mr. Patient:
>
> Maintaining good oral health is critical to a family's overall health. We congratulate you for having realized that fact and for providing this care for yourself and for your family. Maintaining a good credit rating with our practice gives you the assurance that this type of care can continue.
>
> You can certainly understand our position. In order to reestablish good credit with our practice, it will be necessary for you to honor the agreement we originally made. We have, on numerous occasions, sent you statements and reminders about the status of your account. These notices were very clear in their message that payment was due and payable on the date given.
>
> May we ask that you mail us a check for the overdue amount? If, for any reason, this can not be provided, won't you, please, extend us the courtesy of phoning our office so that we can discuss a comfortable resolution? Let's develop a plan of action that is a win/win for each of us.
>
> We look forward to your call. We want to work with you.
>
> (302) 321-4355
>
> Business Manager

Fig. 14–16 Cooperation/discussion letter.

Your previous letters of increasing intensity have led you to this point—the point where a discussion is encouraged. (Discussion of "fear" letters continues later in this chapter.) Once the discussion is arranged, plans for resolution of the account are made. You have moved out of the mode of notifying, reminding, appealing. Now you are ready to negotiate.

Options for Settlement

There are several options available for negotiation of delinquent accounts.

Note: Cash, check, or bankcards are all acceptable methods of payment. Ask for them. Get those credit cards over the phone. You can get the patient's information, the credit card number, the expiration date, and sign the voucher as an *over-the-phone* transaction. Get the information to the credit card company and send a receipt to the patient.

Immediate payment. This is the ideal solution. It indicates that the account will be paid in full—immediately. This is the ideal. But, at this point in the patient's payment history, the likelihood of this settlement is rare.

Extended payment. Be careful with this offer. Remember the length of time and the effort you have already put forth to resolve the issue of the late payment. If the patient does not have an excellent explanation for the delinquency of the account or if proof of willingness to pay cannot be presented, be wary of this offer. If you do make such an offer, extend the account for 30 days only.

Postdated checks or pre-signed or authorized bankcard vouchers. Postdated checks can be collected. This offer comes when the patient expects funding at a specific time. You must be able to establish if the expected income is real or imaginary. This is, of course, difficult if not impossible to do.

The benefit of the postdated check is that you have the payment in hand. The downside of the postdated check is that should the postdated check bounce, you are back to your original problem. However, collection experts say, "Get those postdated checks!" They say that 95–98% of postdated checks clear the bank. Owners of collection agencies encourage their collection professionals to get postdated checks, because the results are so positive when they can get that check in hand.

When you receive a postdated check, this creates a different relationship than does a *regular* check. This does not represent that funds are currently available to cover the check. A postdated check changes a check from a demand instrument to a time instrument and the check is not payable until that specified date.

The Fair Debt Collection Practice Act, or Public law 95–109, September 20, 1977, Section 808 clearly states that credit grantors can ask for postdated checks. To check on the legality in your state, contact your state banking officials.

Collection experts say that a person who writes a postdated check is responsible for notifying the bank of the postdated check. The check is to be dated for the date when the transaction is to take place.

Also, pre-authorization of bankcard payment is an acceptable and recommended method of payment by the major creditcard companies. *Call Visa at 1-800-VISA-311* for further information and for their support materials and you can access this support material from the other bankcard companies, as well. Plus, you can use your own personally developed pre-authorization form. Complete this form. Keep a copy for your records and send a copy to the patient (see Fig. 9–4).

Scheduled Payments. This is probably the most common method of settlement. With this option, a schedule of payments is established that will fit into the patient's monthly budget and will satisfy the practice. Ultimately, of course, a total resolution of the account results.

Try to collect at least half of the balance immediately, then split the remaining balance over a couple of months.

This would be for people who do not have a bankcard—or have a bankcard but it is maxed out.

EFT. Consider this option during the negotiation phase of collection. If you are receiving little or no cooperation from the debtor and if you want to find out who they bank with, send them a small refund check. If they deposit this into their account, you will have the banking information.

Example

A patient owes $800. You negotiate a series of payments whereby the patient pays $400 immediately and $200 on the 15th of the next two consecutive months.

Notice that an exact amount and an exact date have been established. This is critical. Write down the agreement on a financial agreement card (refer to Fig. 9–2) and place in the tickler file. Keep a copy and give or send a copy to the patient. Then, if you have not received the scheduled payment, pick up the phone and make a call to the patient stating that you have not received the scheduled payment and are concerned.

The recording of this type of information and your conscientious follow-up are critical to the success of the agreement. Use that tickler file.

The following recommendations for tracking your collection efforts are made by Skylar Financial Control Corporation of San Francisco, California:

1. Record all your collection conversations.

   A. Without a record, you cannot remember the status of an account when you call again (see Fig. 13–2).

   B. Your version of a conversation will be valid in court when you can show your regularly recorded conversations in writing.

2. Use the calendar or tickler file for any follow-ups.

   A. If payment is promised on a certain date, mark your calendar or tickler file for that date and call if payment is not received.

   B. Similarly, note any action that is supposed to occur in the future, such as *patient is due to get a job in a month and start paying* (See Figs. 13–1 and 13–3).

Fear

You have appealed to a host of emotions. You have encouraged patients to respond to your notices, reminders, and efforts to *work with them* on the resolution of the delinquent account. Most people will have responded to one or the other of your appeals.

However, with about 1 person in 100, a willingness to pay does not occur. Some people really will not have the ability to pay. Others will refuse to pay or to honor their responsibility to you.

Up to now, you have approached the person with an *assumption* that he/she is going to pay. Now, you must *assume* that they are not going to do so. You should still try to persuade the person to take care of the debt, but it is now appropriate that you notify them that stronger measures *are* going to be pursued. This is your most intense appeal—the appeal to the sense of *fear*. It is a letter that demands action.

This letter is the final letter in your series of correspondences with the patient. It is, also, the first step in more forceful action. In this letter, you let the person know that you are serious, and that you have taken this as far as you are going to take it within your own office.

The demand letter

Notice that this appeal to fear is firm, direct, and serious. However, the door is not completely closed for settlement outside of the law (Fig. 14–17).

Dear Mr. Patient:

Our records indicate that your balance of $248 is now 120 days past due. Our efforts to contact you and to negotiate a comfortable settlement of this account have produced no results.

Therefore, unless we receive a payment for the total amount of your delinquent balance within 10 days from the postmark of this letter, we will be forced to turn your account over for legal action.

Avoidance of this legal action is in your favor. We encourage you to contact our office immediately. Otherwise, we have no choice but to proceed with alternate measures.

Business Manager

Fig. 14–17 Demand letter.

This final appeal includes the following three specific steps:

1. A synopsis of previous efforts to collect
2. Your decision to turn the account over to professionals
3. A last opportunity to settle the account

Companies Who Can Help You

Turning to help from the professionals can start here. There are companies today who will pick up at the demand letter phase. These companies—professional collection agencies—will send a letter, on their letterhead stationery, to the past-due patient and inform them that if the account is not settled within the specified length of time that there will be a blemish placed on their credit report. This blemish will appear on the credit report for up to seven years.

Martin Ferrell, President and CEO of American Credit Bureau, says that many people will pay these accounts immediately. Or, if they do not pay, the first time they try to access a loan and can't because of this blemish, they may pay off the account. There are minimal fees to the dentist for this service—not a percentage of the collected fee. The fees are only charged if the account is reconciled.

Certainly, if this demand letter doesn't work, further and more proactive collection efforts can be applied.

Some Further Guidelines

Always control emotions when you are involved with collection procedures. Control your anger, your hostility, and your resentment. There is a fine line between solid and acceptable collection procedures and defamation. Make sure of the following:

- All of your information is valid.
- Do not make derogatory remarks and do not accuse the patient.
- Do not use profanity. Do not profess anger.
- Address the letters specifically to the debtor, personally.
- Include an *out* in each letter.

Summary

Collection is tough. It is not *usually* one of the *favorite* responsibilities in a dental practice. However, (1) if you have a firm financial protocol in place; (2) if financial arrangements are carefully made and written down; (3) if you have a collection system in place, the efforts will be more palatable and more successful. Remember, the key to success in collection is consistency, organization, swiftness, and tenacity—*C.O.S.T.*

• CHAPTER •

15

The Telephone: Its Role in Effective Communications

The telephone is, in many instances, the most effective form of account collection.

– Dr. Charles Blair
Marketing for the Dental Practice

If the guidelines in the initial chapters of this book are followed, you will have very few, if any, accounts receivable and very few past-due accounts. But, when you begin to *change your financial life*, you will probably have some past-due accounts that will need your attention.

Essential information for good collection to take place includes getting a very solid handle on who owes the practice, how much they owe, the length of time that the account is past due, and the date of the last payment. Discussing the account with the patient face-to-face is the best way to collect those past-dues. The next best way is through the effective use of telephone collection calls. The least effective way is through the written communication. A combination of all three is usually necessary to reach the people and to establish the mode of payment that will work best for that particular person.

It is not always possible to converse with a patient face-to-face, and so making collection telephone calls is critical. The manner in which you handle those calls and the verbal skills used make the difference.

The goal of your collection calls should be to maintain a good relationship with your patients while letting them know that you expect payment from them. You want to keep lines of communication open, and you want to get to a point where negotiation of an acceptable settlement is reached. Ultimately, both the team member and the patient should feel good about the call and the resulting negotiation. The end result of an effective collection system is accounts receivable control.

What to Do

Take the time to get ready for your calls. Know that you are doing a service to the doctor and to the practice as a whole. In a way, you are helping to support job security for you and the other members of the team. You have provided a great service. A patient made an agreement with you but he is defaulting on the agreement. It does not do anyone any good—including the patient—not to address this unacceptable behavior.

Organize

1. Keep a copy of the agreement for your record and mail the patient a copy
2. Keep your records updated each time you correspond with the debtor.
3. Follow up on any action you have said you would take.
4. Stay calm. Losing your temper, becoming angry, or getting defensive will only cause the debtor to do the same thing.
5. Stay in control of the conversation by asking questions and by keeping the person involved in the conversation.
6. When you ask a question, stop and let the person make a response Do not feel like you have to fill voids in the conversation. Pausing at appropriate times keeps you in control

7. Speak slowly, calmly, and clearly.

8. Make sure that a firm agreement has been reached before the conversation ends

9. Make sure that you keep an accurate record of all transactions and all conversations, then follow up on any agreements. Do what you say you will do

10. Maintain a positive attitude. It is okay to expect patients/debtors to abide by their agreements. You respect them. You can expect respect in return

11. Persevere

When making collection telephone calls, remember the following:

- Identify yourself.
- Immediately state the purpose of your call.
- Make a statement about the status of the outstanding account (amount past due, days past due, and the date of last payment).
- Ask questions to discover the problem.
- Review the original payment arrangement.
- Use active listening to determine objections.
- Work out or negotiate a settlement for the problem.
- Summarize the agreement. Record the conversation and the agreement.
- Send the patient a copy of the agreement and keep a copy for your files.
- Thank the person for his/her cooperation.

Collection telephone scripts

Here are some guidelines that will help you get ready for the challenge of making telephone collection calls. The better you are prepared, the greater your success. The greater your success, the stronger your confidence.

Preplan your call. Be completely prepared. Have all necessary data in front of you. Have the chart in front of you. Get your financial agreement form or card so that you will know what was—or was not—agreed upon. On this card will be the results of past collection efforts so that you will know exactly what has been done, what was said, and the results of previous conversations.

Review the patient's history—clinical and financial—before you pick up the telephone. If you need to have a discussion with people in the clinical or business area who have dealt with this person or this situation, do so in advance of the telephone call. Your success and your confidence will be in direct proportion to your preparedness. Don't get hung out there because you were not prepared and did not know the appropriate information.

Be sure not to put the patient on the defensive. Great communication skills will be vital. You must be an excellent listener. You must know the strategies of negotiation. You do not want the person to become defensive because if a patient does become defensive, he will become angry. The patient will not be as interested in working out an agreement with you. In addition, you risk losing the patient and having him bad-mouth you all over the town.

(I know. You are saying, "Well, if this person owes me money and if he gets rough, I don't want him in my practice anyway." I know. However, we are going to approach this collection situation in a positive way with the goal of a quality negotiation of settlement and of a continued relationship with the patient in mind.)

Focus the conversation on taking care of the patient. Let the person know that you are interested in him and that you want to work out an agreement that is good for both of you.

Key principles in a negotiation process are as follows:

1. Discover what the person's needs are at this time.
2. Listen as the person shares concerns and needs. Listen without judgment.

3. Define your own needs—what you are and are not willing and able to do.

4. Make it clear that you are interested in making this agreement beneficial to the patient. (People need to know, "What's in this for me?")

5. Do not settle for an agreement that is not good for both parties. A win/win resolution is a must.

Sample Script for Collection Calls

Hello, Ms. Jones? This is ______________, from Dr. ___________'s office. Ms. Jones, in reviewing our records, we find that your balance of $__________ is ___________ days past due. We have not received a payment since ______________. Is there a problem?

Listen to her answer. Repeat back to the person what you think you have heard her say. Express a sincere concern for the problem. Empathize, but do not sympathize. Understand the situation but don't feel sorry and back off from expecting payment.

So, you have had some unexpected expenses that have made it difficult to fulfill your responsibility to our office. I understand how that sort of thing can happen, and I am sorry you have had these difficulties. However, our agreement called for a payment of $______ due on the ______________. In order for our accountant to maintain his records, I must be able to tell him when we can expect your payment of $_______.

If the patient becomes angry or defensive, stay calm. Don't get upset. Don't hang up. Do everything possible to make sure the conversation stays on an even keel. Make sure you end the conversation in a positive, peaceful, settled manner.

If the patient becomes defensive, or if the patient does not show an inclination to be cooperative, use an *I* message to express your problem. An I message expresses your problem in terms of how it is affecting you in a negative way. It is not a put-down message that places the person on the defensive. You also want the patient to know that you are interested in creating a situation where both of you benefit.

Ms. Jones, I felt concerned when we did not receive the payment you agreed to make to our practice, because late payments mean late penalties for you. This will add to the total amount due, which I am sure you would like to avoid. Plus, not being paid for our services in a timley manner puts stress on our business. Therefore, let's work together to come to an agreement that is comfortable for both of us.

Always thank the person for an agreement. Repeat the agreement to make sure that you have a common understanding of that agreement. Inform the patient that you are recording the agreement and that you will be sending her a copy of that agreement.

Thank you, Ms. Jones, for you cooperation. Let me review our agreement to make sure we both have the same understanding. We can expect to receive a payment by check of $83 on the 15th of January, on the 15th of February and on the 15th of March. The March payment will clear your account with us. Is that your understanding? Are you comfortable with that agreement? I will make a note of this for our files, and I will send you a copy of this agreement.

Make sure to record the information, then make a copy and send it to the patient. Include a self-addressed envelope for the payment . Place a note in your tickler file so that you will be alerted as to when you are to expect that patient's payment.

During Telephone Collection Calls

While the telephone has proven to be very effective for collection, it must be used carefully and professionally. Be cognizant of the Telephone Harassment Laws and abide by those regulations. Violation of the regulations can lead to loss of telephone service, fines, and/or criminal action.

The following need to be avoided:

1. Calls, anonymous or otherwise, made in a frightening, abusive, or harassing manner.

2. Calls that interfere with the use of the telephone by other customers.

3. Calls for purposes that are against the law.

4. Calling at unreasonable hours of the day or night. (Do not call before 8 A.M. or after 9 P.M.).

5. Making one call after another to the same person.

6. Calls to people other than the debtor to discuss the past-due account.

7. Calls that make threats.

8. Calls making false accusations about damaging a person's credit rating.

9. Calls stating that legal action is going to take place if, in fact, it is not.

10. Calls demanding payments for a debt that is not actually owed.

11. Calls that give inaccurate information about the original agreement.

Summary

Your efforts to collect via the telephone will be effective. Practice the skills outlined in this chapter. Gain confidence as a result of your study and practice.

Written communication is vital, but not as effective as face-to-face or telephone communcation. This is a significant part of effective collection—the telephone.

• CHAPTER • 16

When All Else Fails

The reason many patients don't pay a healthcare bill is they know there are no consequences.

— Martin Ferrell, President and CEO, American Credit Bureau

You have pursued a past-due account with consistency, organization, swiftness and tenacity. Nothing happens. No response. No payment. Now what?

You, as the creditor must now choose between four stronger efforts to collect your money:

1. demand letter from a professional credit bureau

2. pursuit of the debt by a collection agency

3. small claims court

4. an attorney

Let's analyze these methods of collection. What are they? How do they work? When is each of these processes appropriate? What can you expect?

Demand Letter

I referred to this letter at the close of chapter 14. If you have consistently pursued an account and a patient has been unwilling to work with you on a settlement or you have not been able to reach them, consider accessing the help of a professional.

At this early stage of work with certain credit bureaus or collection agencies, they would send a letter to your patients—from the company itself—identifying the problem account and calling for payment. They will inform the patient of their intention to place a *blemish* on the patient's credit report. The patient may respond to this initial letter. However, if the patient doesn't, a second letter is sent indicating that the *blemish* has, in fact, been placed on the record. This **blemish** will appear for up to seven years on that report. One of the major *red flags* that could keep a person from getting any kind of financing or from getting a loan in the future is having *uncollectibles* show up on that credit report. If a patient doesn't respond to these notices, then, with your permission, further collection efforts are initiated.

The response from patients from this kind of professional notice lets that patient know you are serious and that you intend to be paid. You deserve to be paid. Plus, in my opinion, by placing this *blemish* on a patient's report, this might prevent the patient from going to the office of one of your colleagues and doing the same thing. This, of course, infers that doctors will do a credit check before committing to any kind of financing!

Please note this chapter's opening quotation by Mr. Ferrell, "The reason many patients do not pay a healthcare bill is that they know there are no consequences." Don't put yourself in this kind of jeopardy.

A Collection Agency

If none of your efforts prove to be fruitful, consider the employment of a collection agency. This, of course, would occur only after you have done everything you could possibly do to collect the account through your own efforts.

Once you make the decision to turn an account over to the agency, you are out of it. You should stay out of the way and should not do anything else to try to collect the account. This action—turning the account over for collection—

will probably end your relationship with the patient. But, at this point, you have probably decided to do this anyway. Do everything you can to settle the account, but if your efforts fail and you turn the account over to a collection agency, step out of the way and let them do their work. By his/her actions, the patient has chosen this action.

You may find that the professional collector has a stronger effect on the debtor and that the collector can get more done. In other words, because there is no personal relationship between the collector and the debtor, more pressure can be applied, which will result in positive action.

Many of the same steps of collection that you have used will be followed by the professional collector: telephone calls, a sequence of specific letters, and so on. However, in most cases, the pressure placed by the professional will be taken more seriously.

Which Agency

How do you decide which agency to employ? There are more than 5,000 collection agencies across the country. Make sure that the agency you choose has an office in the location of the debtor. Check references and make sure that the agency has a good reputation. You do not want to employ an agency that has developed a reputation of improper handling of debtors. In other words, the agency must be professional—not overly aggressive. Be sure that the agency does not misrepresent itself with words such as "United States," "Federal," "National," etc.

The agency you choose should operate a free demand service. This would indicate that the creditor—you, the dentist—would prepare a triplicate form, one for the debtor, one for the agency, and one for the practice. This form states that if payment isn't received, that the collection agency will take any and all necessary steps to collect the money.

A set amount of time is given—usually 10 days—and the form would state that if payment isn't received within that 10 days, that action will be taken. If, by some chance, you receive payment within that 10-day period of time, you must let the agency know so that action is not taken. Thus, it is called *free-demand service*. You would pay nothing to the collection agency if the patient pays within the assigned time frame. This is similar to the demand letter, as indicated previously.

If, however, you feel that the debtor will not settle the account within 10 days, the account should be placed as a regular collection service, and action will begin immediately. The fees charged by collection agencies vary from state to state and from agency to agency. Be absolutely sure that you check out the fee schedule before you turn any account over to an agency. Their fee schedule should be provided at your initial contact with them. Ask for it.

If the agency must access the skills of an attorney to complete a collection transaction, the fees—obviously—will go up. If this action must be taken, you will be informed of the action, as well as the additional fee.

You Need To Know

The collection agency, after having spent some time pursuing an account, may recommend that you accept a partial settlement. This is, always, your decision. If this recommendation is made to you, bear in mind that the debtor wins out. He/she hasn't paid you anything. Now, you are being asked to settle for less than the owed amount. In addition to the reduction in debt, you will be paying a fee to the collection agency.

Example

Say a person owes you $1,000. The debtor agrees to pay 50% or $500. In addition to this lowered amount, let's say that you are paying 30% to the collection agency. You will be paying $150 to them for their services. Thus, on the $1,000 amount you are owed, you would receive $350. The debtor wins. But, in some cases, this is better than nothing at all. Having at least pursued the account through a professional means, you gain some satisfaction as to the principle of the matter. This person should not receive services in your practice from that point forward.

The negative information about this person's collection status will be placed on his/her credit record and will inhibit future loans for a period of time—usually seven years.

Small Claims Court

Small claims court is a vehicle for the small business owner—the dental professional—to use when (1) an account is past due, (2) efforts to collect privately have failed, and (3) the amount owed is under $1,000. (Check with your state for this maximum amount. It differs from state to state.)

Small claims court is used only when all of your own pursuits have been ignored. Be sure to do a credit check on a delinquent patient to see if there is any money that can be collected and if they have the ability to make monthly payments. Otherwise, you may want to think twice about putting the time, effort, and money into small claims court.

With small claims court, you need not hire an attorney. You may appear in court yourself or a designated member of your team may appear to represent the practice. There are fees for this service, but they are much less than attorney fees.

The court appearance will take time out of work. However, if there are enough accounts, or if there is a high enough past-due amount, the time spent could prove to be very cost effective. Many debtors are encouraged to pay when they realize that you are serious about the matter.

In most states, small claims court will handle cases of less than $1,000. In some states, cases can be pursued only if the disputed amount is above $1,000. In other states, there is no such thing as small claims court but rather magistrates court. In addition, certain states will not allow a team member to appear in court for the dentist if he/she is incorporated. In that case, the dentist or an officer of the corporation would be required to appear.

Call your local authorities at your city hall to find out which court will handle cases of your type and spend a bit of time investigating the protocols of your particular state. Being prepared will save you time and money in the long run.

One of the benefits of this type of court is that the time spent in court is minimal. The actual presentation of the case takes but a few minutes. A supervisory judge will either rule on the case himself or will assign the case to an attorney or an arbitrator. Most of the cases today are decided by an arbitrator. This person in most instances will make a decision based on the specific instance and will apply fairness and objectivity.

In most states, the creditor (the dentist) would file the suit. In other words, you or your practice can do this without the assistance of any third party. In fact, many states will not allow a third party, such as a collection agency, to file suit in small claims court. Again, check into your state regulations.

A statute of limitations is enforced in most states—usually four years. Hopefully, you would have filed suit long before the four-year statute of limitations. Why?

1. The sooner you begin and the more persistent you are with your collection efforts, the better your results will be.

2. Judges in small claims court are more likely to rule in your favor if you prove that you have made careful, consistent efforts to collect. Showing that you are on top of your business will be to your advantage.

3. If the debtor goes under, you will be more likely to receive at least some payment if you are one of the first to file a suit.

How does small claims court work?

There are five steps to take to participate in small claims court. They are as follows:

1. Pay a fee to file the suit.

2. File your statement.

3. Serve the debtor with papers.

4. Present your records of proof.

5. Arrange a date for the hearing.

Pay a fee to file the suit. There will be nominal fee required for this entire process to go forward. There may be some other fees that you will be responsible to pay. These fees can be added to the amount owed by the debtor.

File your statement. Each court system will require different types of paperwork. The dentist, who is now the creditor, will become the *plaintiff*, in legal terms. The dentist (or the office) will fill out a statement which will give information, such as your name, the debtor's name, the past-due amount, the date you provided the services, and the history of your collection efforts.

Your statement will be handed to the court clerk, who will type the statement. This will then become the claim of the plaintiff. You will sign one copy of this statement, one copy will be given to the judge, and one copy will be given to the debtor, who will now become the *defendant*.

Serve the debtor with papers. The claim of the plaintiff is served to the defendant. If this person cannot be found, he must be sought through more extensive methods, such as tracking services provided by individuals or certified or registered mail.

The tracking services are provided by people such as a sheriff, a marshal, or another law enforcement person. This would be a person who has no involvement with the case in any way. The papers must be served to the defendant in person. The papers cannot be left with another person or in the mailbox. If the server does find the person or makes an effort to give this person the papers, but the debtor refuses to take them, then the server puts the papers down and leaves. Obviously, stronger methods are not appropriate.

Present your records of proof. Certified or registered mail can be used in most states as a method to serve the defendant with papers. The court clerk usually does this. The defendant must sign for the mailed papers. If this person is accustomed to collection methods, she may not sign for the document. It will be up to you to contact the court clerk to find out if the defendant has received the papers. You must do this before your day in court.

Arrange a date for the hearing. You set your court date when you file your statement. You need to leave enough time between your filing and the court date for the defendant to have been served. It is not always necessary, but it is wise to have all of your records of service and of collection efforts with you when you appear in court. Gather this information and be able to present it in an organized fashion.

Small claims court is not as highly structured nor is it as highly intense as regular court. The fact that the debtor has been brought to court over this past-due account makes him more likely to pay. You, the defendant, and the arbitrator may all sit down together to discuss the issue. No one else will be involved.

If the debtor, or defendant, does not show up for this day in court, what happens? If this happens, then you will be awarded a default judgment. You think, "Well, I'm back to square one." Actually, you are better off because you have the power of the court behind you. You have a judge's decision and because this debt is now on record, you can do things that you couldn't do before.

Collecting payment once a judgment is acquired

Once you receive a judgment, several ways in which the money can be collected from the defendant are the following:

- Wages
- Bank account
- Automobiles and other vehicles
- Property (except residence)

Before wages or other property can be accessed, or levied, you must have a court order. This is called a *writ of execution.* You receive this writ from the court clerk following the passing of the judgment. You will then send this writ to the sheriff or marshal or another law enforcement person in the debtor's county. You will pay a fee to this law person and you will give instruction as to where the debtor or the property can be found and what is supposed to be seized or collected.

To levy on a bank account, you will need the following: (1) the original and one copy of the writ of execution and (2) a letter of instruction about what to do, such as, "levy this person's bank account," or "levy this person's wages," etc.

If the debtor has no job or no bank account, then levying vehicles or property is the next option. Obviously, this is difficult and takes a great deal more time and effort.

If you are going to pursue a levy on a person's wages, here are a few things to note. This is known as a garnishment.. The employer is known as the *garnishee.* Limits may apply as to how much money can be withdrawn from each paycheck. Most states do not allow an employer to dismiss an employee because of garnishment.

The employer, although an innocent third party, does become the legal trustee or custodian of the debt owed by his employee. The court action is a restraint on him, not allowing him to pay full wages to the employee but rather transferring a part of the moneys to the said creditor.

In many states, once a writ of execution is obtained for levying of wages, the court orders the garnishee (debtor's employer) to appear in court to discuss the issue of the owed monies. This does not usually go over very well with the employer, as you might imagine. If the employer fails or refuses to appear in court, then the court pursues the garnishee—or the employer—a formerly innocent bystander. This is an acceptable and workable method of collection but use it as a last resort.

Levying a person's bank account or personal property is called attachment. Limits are usually set as to how much can be attached. Attachment is a legal provision that allows the creditor to access a person's banked funds or available properties. The purpose of this legal action—the attachment—is to prevent people who do have available funds and/or properties from ignoring their responsibilities and spending their money on themselves or on other things besides the debt.

The requirements for attachment vary from state to state, but most states do make this collection apparatus available. The process of acquiring an attachment is similar to garnishment. All procedures flow through the court itself once a judgment is received.

Why would you consider attachment?

- The debtor is hiding in an effort to avoid the creditor or legal action.
- The debtor has left your state to avoid legal action.
- The debtor makes an effort to remove or sell property to avoid legal acquisition of those properties.

Benefits of small claims court

The advantages of small claims court are that the process is quick and simple. There are costs involved, but those costs are much less significant than either a collection agency or an attorney. With the power of the court behind you, much greater leverage is in your favor. With this leverage, you can do just about as much as a collection agency or an attorney.

Tips on small claims court

- Allow for at least two weeks for your court date.
- Be on time in court, if need be.
- Be able to spend time in court, if need be.
- Be on time for your case—even if you have to wait once you get there.
- Be prepared. Bring all your documents with you to court.
- Be concise. Give a precise, accurate, short description of your information.
- Don't become angry. Don't lose your cool.
- Do not slander your defendant.

The Attorney

You, as the creditor, have the right to go to court to force a debtor to settle a past-due account. When you work through an attorney, you usually can exert more pressure than if you were to handle this by yourself.

Just like you, the attorney goes through a specific series of collection letters. If the attorney receives no response from the debtor, then stronger measures are taken. The attorney notifies the debtor that the attorney will take the debtor to court. If no action is taken at that point, then court it is.

It will be expensive for you to have an attorney take one of your debtors to court. You need to discuss those fees and costs before the fact.

Gather your documentation—the clinical records, all records of collection efforts, information about the debtor—including information about the debtor's property, bank accounts, employment, income, etc. For you to be able to attach or to garnish, you must know if the debtor owns property valued at least in the amount of the debt plus the expenses of the suit. You can usually gather this information from the attorney or the collection agency. A credit check needs to be done by you or by your professional agents in order to see what is available—if anything. This will help you make a decision about your actions. If there is not enough said property, then it really does not pay to pursue the account through the courts.

The use of an attorney and the court system is complicated. Three specific stages of pursuit are as follows:

1. pleading the case
2. trying the case
3. executing the settlement of the account

In the first stage, the pleading of the case, the creditor—or the dentist—is represented by the attorney. The dentist becomes the plaintiff. All information is gathered, a petition is filed, and a summons is issued. The debtor can file an answer to this summons and set up his/her own defense. If there is no response or answer to the summons, a default judgment results.

In the second stage, trying the case, the trial takes place. Information is shared and a judgment is ruled. If the judge rules in favor of the plaintiff, the court determines how much is to be paid. In some states, an automatic lien on property is established.

In the third stage, the execution of the settlement, the court instructs a law enforcement person to collect the amount—often from the person's property. This property is seized and is put up for sale by public auction. The proceeds from the auction are turned over to the court, court fees are withdrawn, and the creditor receives the balance. If no property is available, the judgment is docketed for the future when property is available.

As was pointed out earlier, if the amount due is less than $1,000, you are better off to go through the small claims court. There is less time and money involved and less headache.

The fees for the services of an attorney are high. Most attorneys will not work on your smaller debts. However, on those larger debts, this is a very acceptable method of collection. As was discussed earlier, attachment and garnishment can result from the attorney's efforts.

Bankruptcy

You receive a bankruptcy notice on one of your patients. Now what? Bankruptcy used to be a bad word. Now, it's commonplace. For the debtor, bankruptcy is the final chapter in trying to spell relief from indebtedness. It is a voluntary or an involuntary move on the part of the debtor to declare insolvency to the courts. When bankruptcy is declared, the creditors line up to divide assets, sell properties, receive pro rata percentages of payment relative to the size of each claim.

You might get a portion of your balance from the sale of the debtor's assets. But, if you do receive any payment at all, it will probably be only a portion of the overdue amount. Historically, 10–15% receipt of the claim is the norm.

For the person declaring bankruptcy, getting out of debt and getting a fresh start are the advantages. Even the best business person may be caught in an unsolvable situation that makes it impossible to satisfy debts. Bankruptcy allows this person the opportunity to continue working to pay off debts. In addition, this gives the creditor some hope of payment or solution.

Personal bankruptcy

Two types of bankruptcy deal with individuals—Chapter VII and Chapter XIII.

The Bankruptcy Reform Act of 1978 made it pretty easy for an individual to declare personal bankruptcy. Once bankruptcy has been declared and court proceedings begin, all creditors must back off and wait for results to be determined. Since the Reform Act, multitudes of personal bankruptcies have been declared.

Key points about Chapter VII

Chapter VII bankruptcy is the voluntary declaration of bankruptcy by an individual. The person, the debtor, files bankruptcy with the court. The court then reviews the situation and decides yes or no on the declaration. If the court says yes, it begins the process of selling the debtor's assets and distributing the proceeds of the sale to creditors. Chapter VII allows the debtor to retain enough assets to live—some home equity, car, and personal items. Under this type of personal bankruptcy, the debtor cannot refile for bankruptcy again for six years.

Key points about Chapter XIII

Chapter XIII bankruptcy involves people whose "principal income is derived from wages, salaries, or commissions." When the debtor declares himself insolvent and unable to service debts, bankruptcy is declared. This petition by the debtor, states that the debtor wishes to resolve all debts by reorganization, consolidation, or extension of those debts. This will be done out of future earnings.

The following steps are taken following the declaration of Chapter XIII bankruptcy:

1. A list of assets and liabilities is determined.
2. A referee is acquired and the fee is established.
3. The case goes before a judge or the referee.
4. All creditors meet. (A 10-day notice of the meeting is given.)
5. The debtor is examined.
6. Witnesses testify.
7. A plan of action is determined.
8. The plan is accepted or rejected.
9. If accepted, the debtor continues to work to service debts.
10. Some payment adjustment may be made as to amount owed and amount actually paid.

11. The amount owed is paid to the court, who then makes equitable distribution.

For the creditor, this type of bankruptcy is better than most. The rate of payment is higher than most bankruptcies. In some reports, indications say that 92% of debts will be serviced.

For the creditor

Without question, the Bankruptcy Reform Act of 1978 has made it easier to declare, and get by with, not servicing debts. For you, the dentist, the creditor—the act has made it more difficult to access receipt of debt.

We all know that if pushed too hard, a debtor will simply declare bankruptcy and walk away from indebtedness or at least, put off payment of debts for long periods of time.

Ultimately, pursuing debts in the early stages and doing this consistently and effectively as outlined is the best way to collect the monies owed to you for services rendered.

Summary

You have made a financial arrangement. You have provided the service. You deserve to receive payment for treatment rendered. Being too timid about your collection procedures is not the answer.

It is not your fault if a person has financial difficulties, but it is your responsibility to pursue the account. Remember, the sooner you begin your tracking of and pursing of a past-due account, the better chance you have of collecting it.

Review all steps of collections as previously outlined. Put these steps into an action plan that will work for you. Be firm, yet fair; be tough, yet equitable; be persistent. Be prepared. These principles are the key to successful collections.

CHAPTER 17

Getting the Most Out of Your Collection System

You never hear, "that's not my job" on a high performing team.

— **Dr. Ken Blanchard**
The One-Minute Manager Builds High Performing Teams

Your collection system. Complex, isn't it? Making sure that this system is healthy is a benefit to the entire team. I have heard clinical team members say, "I don't need to learn about collections. That's not my job!" If anyone thinks that or says that, then you can take the word team out of the sentence—because you don't have a team. There is not one system in the practice that can function comprehensively if all the systems are not in place. As I have said previously, there are 25 different management systems in your practice. If 24 of those are working well but one of them is *out of whack* or not working well, that dysfunctional system will have a negative impact on all the other 24. The systems are too closely related to separate them. Let's look at the following example:

Example

If you do a great job of presenting your recommendations and a person really wants to go ahead with treatment, but he feels that he can not afford the dentistry, you will not be able to do the dentistry. If a financial agreement is not worked out, a patient will not proceed. If people do not say yes to treatment, it does not matter how well you present your cases, how well you schedule, how well you maintain the restorations in hygiene—you will not be able to do any of those things. If people do not say yes to treatment because they can not find a way to pay for it, no one gets to work.

So, as a clinical team member—no matter what your role, dentist, assistant, or hygienist—if the financing system is not in place, you do not get to do the kind of dentistry you want and need to do. If you do not get to do the dentistry you want and need to do, no one has a job. No one gets paid. It is the dentistry circle of life! One thing impacts the next. All things and people are interrelated. One person's job interacts and influences every other person's job. None of us works alone.

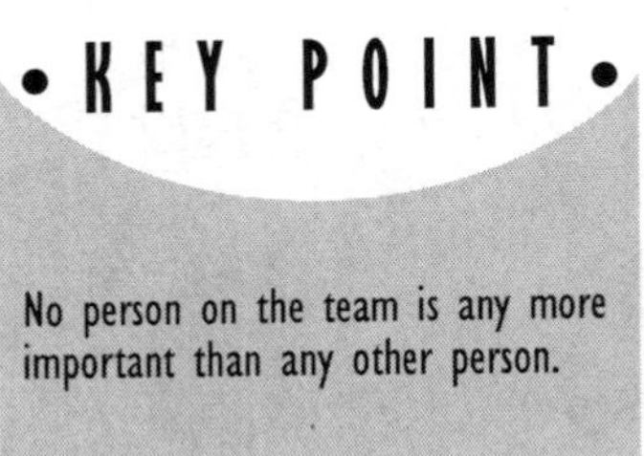

• KEY POINT •
No person on the team is any more important than any other person.

And no one particular job or responsibility is any more important than any other. And so on.

See the connectedness? All systems intertwine in one way or another.

So, establishing, supporting, and administering a healthy financial system—which includes many subsystems—is good for everyone and is everyone's responsibility. In this manner, everyone wins. If monies are in the bank and if collection percentages are healthy and if the practice is profitable, then job security is established, everyone (including the doctor!) gets paid and raises can be considered. If raises are given but there has been no increase in profit margin, the raises come right out of the doctor's pocket. That does not make for happy dentists! And as we all agree—we want our doctors to be happy. A happy doctor makes for a happy team, right?

I'm sure that you agree with me by now that collecting what you produce makes good sense. Having the revenues from completed dentistry sit on your books losing value is stressful as well as costly. Therefore, having a collection/financial system in place that works, and works well, is good business and makes for happier dentists and happier dental teams.

In summary of our study, let's review some of the musts attached to establishing and administering an effective collection system. The 25 critical factors that will let you get the most out of your collection system are as follows:

1. As a team, study the psychology of money. Develop insights into this very intimate part of a person's life—money. The more you empathize with your patients, the more bonded you will become with them. Your rapport with them will translate into trust and confidence—the key elements of gaining high levels of case acceptance.

2. Have a written financial protocol that everyone in the practice knows and understands. Make sure that your protocol is good for the patients and good for the practice.

3. Offer payment options that will meet the needs of the vast majority of your patients. However, make sure that you are not setting up a banking business within your practice. Offer options that will make the financing of your dentistry comfortable for your patients and will not put you in a position of loaning money. You can not afford to loan money and run a financing business in your practice. In addition, you are dental professionals not banking professionals.

4. Make sure that everyone on the team enthusiastically supports the financial system and options. The team's enthusiasm will be reflected in the patient's enthusiasm and acceptance.

5. Get involved with and promote a healthcare financing program. Make it easy for people to pay you. Have solutions available for the vast majority of your patient's financial situations.

These financial programs let the practice receive its money up-front while letting patients have a chance to spread small monthly payments out over a long period of time. Thus, the patients will not be financially stressed by having to come up with large sums of money at one time.

For most people, the decision to go ahead with the dentistry does not come down to "How much is the total investment?" Rather, saying yes to treatment often depends on "How much do I have to pay per month?"

6. Maximize your healthcare financing program by using the six strategies as outlined and detailed. From your initial contact with a patient, let her know your commitment to quality dental care and to convenient financing.

Let your patients know that you do not want the financing of the dentistry to get in the way of them receiving the very best care possible. Years of statistical data by JMI on the implementation of these six steps have shown that production increases from 4–38%.

7. Make financial arrangements with all patients prior to service. Prepare a written financial agreement that outlines not only the services to be rendered but also the financial responsibility and the method of payment chosen. Then and only then will the person in the business office—or anyone else—know how much to collect at each appointment. In addition, she will know the method of payment selected so that he can be prepared for the collection sequence at each appointment.

With careful and precise financial agreements written and placed carefully in the patient's record, the BA will be able to collect professionally and will not be scrambling at the last minute to ask questions of the clinical team, such as, "What did you do today? How much did you charge? How is the patient going to pay? What are you going to do next time? How much is that going to be? How will the patient pay for that?" She will, also, never have to say to the patient, "Would you like to pay today?" or "How much would you like to pay today?" or "Oh, don't worry about that today. I'll send you a statement."

8. Maintain an accounts receivable balance of no more than half your average monthly production. When you follow the recommendations within this book, your only outstanding balances will be insurance balances (if you are accepting assignment of benefits). Do not let your past-due accounts get out of hand. Run aged accounts receivable reports every month—separating your reports into 30, 60, 90, 120 days past due. Be aware of the status of each account at all times.

Dentists and BAs need to stay in touch with one another about these accounts. Putting your head in the sand in relation to your past-due accounts is poor business and does nothing to accomplish the goal of collecting what you produce.

9. If you are accepting assignment of benefits from insurance companies, collect the expected private pay portion of a patient's fee at the time of the service. Do not wait to collect the patient's portion or co-pay after insurance has paid. This is financial suicide. Depending on how long you are waiting for insurance, you risk not being at the top of a patient's priority list of "Who is going to get paid this month?" Do not put yourself into this potentially detrimental situation.

10. Set a goal to have a 7–10 working day turnaround on all insurance claims. File electronically and track your paid claims and any past-due claims daily. There should be no 31 days past-due claims.

Approximately 50% of the revenue of the average dental office comes in the form of an insurance check. Therefore, as difficult as it may be to manage insurance, this crucial system within your practice deserves special attention.

Make sure your system of filing and tracking insurance claims is without flaw. File each claim daily and make sure that if a claim becomes past due that you are in contact with the insurance company exploring the problem.

If you are not doing electronic processing of claims, do so immediately.

11. If there is a balance after insurance has paid, send a statement the day the insurance check is received. Better yet, have a pre-authorization form from your bankcards or from your healthcare financing program. This pre-authorization will allow you to charge an insurance balance the day it presents itself.

Remember, you can produce your own pre-authorization form. Use the professionally produced ones or produce your own, it does not matter. Get these completed and on file for all of your patients. It is good for them and for you (Fig. 17–1).

12. If you have any patients with an outstanding balance, send statements each month to those people—even people whose balance reflects an insurance balance.

When you are making a financial arrangement with a patient, let each one know that you will be filing the insurance as a service—but that if for any reason insurance has not paid within 45 days, he/she will be receiving a statement. Tell the patients that you want them to know the status of their account at all times.

From the beginning, let people know that you file insurance as a service to them. Let them know that they are responsible for their balances. If you wait to send statements after all insurance has paid—and if the person has a balance—too much time has passed, and the patient may be less motivated to pay you. Keep them accurately informed as to the status of their account.

Convenient Pay Consent Form

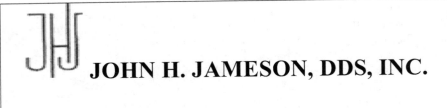

I understand that my insurance may not cover the entire estimated portion for my dental needs, therefore, I am authorizing Dr. John H. Jameson, DDS, to charge any remaining balance to:

☐ Visa ☐ Mastercard ☐ American Express ☐ Discover

CC#____

Exp. date____________

Signature:____

This card will be kept on record in my file for future use. If I desire to change this card I will contact the office with the new information.

Signature:____

101 JAMESON DRIVE, P.O. BOX 459, WYNNEWOOD, OK 73098, (405) 665-2041

Fig. 17–1 Example of pre-authorization form

13. Place messages on your statements to notify the patient of any past-due status, but do not kid yourself and think that this will be enough. A telephone call made at the 31-day past- due point will accomplish much better results. The quicker you contact a person regarding the past-due status of an account, the better your chances of collecting. Collection experts will tell you that the longer an account goes unattended, the weaker your chances of getting paid.

14. Using the letters included in this book, establish a clear, consistent sequence of collection letters. Remember to increase the intensity of the letters according to the past-due status of the account.

    These letters must be sent out like clockwork in order to access good results. The letters are not offensive. They are professional letters that follow the four stages of collection that must be adhered to if you are, indeed, going to collect those delinquent accounts. Remember the following four phases:

    A. Notification phase

    B. Reminder phase

    C. Negotiation phase

    D. If all else fails phase

Remember, C.O.S.T

- Consistency
- Organization
- Swiftness
- Tenacity

15. Itemize your walkout statements and your mailed statements (if you have any). Let people know how much service is really provided at each and every appointment.

16. Make it easy for the patients to pay you. On your statements, let people know that they can pay with a bankcard. If your computer will not let you program your statements to say this, get a stamp. Also, VISA has stickers for

statements that make it possible to pay in this manner. Or produce inserts for your statements (Fig. 17–2).

17. Place a due date on all statements. (Notice on your own bills at home that there is always a due date.) You will expedite payment by placing a due date on your statements. The due date should be within 15 days of the billing date.

18. At the end of every month, divide the amount of money collected by the amount of dollars produced. This will give you the collection percentage for the month. Keep a running tabulation of this throughout the year. Maintain at least a 98% collection ratio. Set the goal—98% collection (or more).

19. Have a person on the team responsible for accounts receivable control. Make sure that this person is analyzing your accounts receivable throughout each month—all accounts. Better yet—analyze your accounts every week. Remember, the sooner you begin working with a past-due account, the more likely you will collect it.

20. The person in charge of accounts receivable control needs specific time to make collection calls—time that is without interruption or distraction. These calls are not easy and need special attention. She will get more done in less time if she can earmark a certain number of hours—non-patient hours—for accounts receivable control.

    This critical part of the practice must have attention. It is hard to pay the bills if the dollars are not in the bank. But it is hard to collect those dollars if the time is not scheduled for working on the accounts. Time well invested? I would say so.

21. Analyze your fees every six months and increase those fees at least once per year or when procedures or costs go up. You may also have your fees professionally analyzed.

22. Make sure to practice good communication skills so that each interaction with a patient will go as well as possible. Of all the communication skills, listening may be the most important while at the same time may be the most difficult. Do not let the busyness of your days get in the way of being able to listen to your patients. Listen your way to success.

23. Study the intricate and important skills of telephone communication. Here is your most important marketing tool and your initial contact with a patient. You represent the practice each and every time you are on the phone. Handle with care!

For Your Convenience We Accept Visa, MasterCard, Discover, and Healthcare Financing Program

Please Complete the Following:
Visa ______ MasterCard ______ Discover ______Amex ______
Healthcare Financing Program ________

Amount ______________________ Card Number ____________________________
Expiration Date ________________
Signature ____

For Your Convenience We Accept Visa, MasterCard, Discover, and Healthcare Financing Program

Please Complete the Following:
Visa ______ MasterCard ______ Discover ______ Amex ______
Healthcare Financing Program ________

Amount ______________________ Card Number ____________________________
Expiration Date ________________
Signature ____

For Your Convenience We Accept Visa, MasterCard, Discover, and Healthcare Financing Program

Please Complete the Following:
Visa ______ MasterCard ______ Discover ______Amex ______
Healthcare Financing Program ________

Amount ______________________ Card Number ____________________________
Expiration Date ________________
Signature ____

For Your Convenience We Accept Visa, MasterCard, Discover, and Healthcare Financing Program

Please Complete the Following:
Visa ______ MasterCard ______ Discover ________Amex ______
Healthcare Financing Program ________

Amount ______________________ Card Number ____________________________
Expiration Date ________________
Signature ____

Fig. 17–2 Statement insert.

24. Identify the major objections you receive from patients when they are discussing their financial responsibility. Study the scripts in this book and learn them. Do *practice exercises*—or role-play—so that you get comfortable with these verbal skills. In addition, outline any objections that you may have that I have not covered. Develop your own verbal skills based on the communicative skills that I have outlined.

25. Access training in the area of collection. Do not assume that just because someone is good in business administration that she will automatically be good at collection. There are specific skills that go along with the making and administering of financial arrangements. There are, certainly, specific skills related to the collection of past-due accounts.

Let the talented person on your team who is responsible for this very important and very intricate system in your practice have the necessary armamentarium to carry out those responsibilities successfully.

Access books—such as this one, tapes, courses, and special consultation in the financial area of practice management. The dollars that you invest in your team, in your financial system, and in your practice will come back to you multifold.

At JMI, we hold specific symposiums on business administration, where the skills of managing a dental office are intricately taught. Included in this study are the skills of financing. We believe that these skills are absolutely important to the healthy running of a business

Summary

Approach collection efforts with a positive attitude—a productive attitude. Know that it is OK to collect what you produce. Know that you have provided a service. There was an agreement for payment of the service. You are, simply, asking people to maintain their part of the agreement. If you expect to get paid, you will be. You never know what you will get unless you ask.

Know that the very best way to collect an account is face-to-face. The second best way to collect an account is over the telephone. The third most effective way to collect is by the written word. All of these methods are a part of an effective collection system, but face-to-face is best. Therefore, getting and maintaining an excellent collection system within the practice is essential. Collect at the time of the service. Preventive management will save time and money in the long run.

CHAPTER 18

And Finally

Change is the law of life.

And those who only look to the past and present are certain to miss the future.

– John F. Kennedy

Congratulations for purchasing this book and for getting to this, the last chapter. By doing so you are obviously interested in improving the business systems in your practice. You are aware of—but not afraid of—the financial challenges that face both you and your patients. Implementing the skills and strategies outlined in this book will help you to deal with these challenges in a positive and beneficial way.

Know that your practice is a conglomeration of systems—25 systems. (See Appendix B for your own evaluation). Each of those systems must be carefully and caringly developed. You must commit time and money to the development of your people. This is the very best investment the owner of a business can make. As a leader and as a CEO, do not shortchange your people, yourself, or your business by not making this crucial investment.

Once your systems are established and training has been provided, then members of the team must be *committed* to administering the systems consistently. Even though there are times when you must *flex*, do not let flexing become the norm. If you do so, your systems will weaken and will fall apart. If 1 of the 25 systems is not working well, that will have a negative effect on all of the other systems.

For example, if you are *not* collecting what you are producing, you cannot continue to improve the clinical efficiency in your practice, because you will not be able to afford new and better equipment and instrumentation. If you are not collecting what you are producing, you cannot afford to hire and pay qualified employees so that your team is strengthened. And so on. I continue to stress the interrelatedness of your systems because this truism cannot be denied if your ideal practice is to be realized.

You have been given a path for developing a financial system in your practice. A good, workable financial protocol has been suggested. Healthcare financing programs were explained, and you were encouraged to get involved with these programs. I suggested six ways to build your practice using a healthcare financing program and verbal skills—lots of them—were outlined for the presentation of these programs.

If you are interested in developing the cosmetic aspect of your practice, a review of the financing of cosmetic dentistry was suggested. A discussion of how to overcome and handle the objection of cost—including some suggestions of how to handle your patient's complaints about your fees—was outlined.

Devising a collection system in your practice is critical for the reduction of accounts receivable and for the continued *cleanliness* of your collection system. You may need to spend some time cleaning up old accounts, but once you do, you will never have to be in the accounts receivable business again, once you follow the instructions within this book.

The area of financing and collection need not be a dreaded, feared, or ignored part of the management of your practice. You are providing a fabulous service to your patients. You are a healthcare business, and, as such, must run your business astutely. Getting and keeping control of your collection system is good for you and for your patients.

Remember, if you do not run a profitable business, you cannot afford to stay in business. Then, everyone loses; you and the patients alike. They need you and the services you are offering. *Collect What You Produce!* That makes it possible for you to continue to serve, and it makes dentistry much more fun.

Finally, stress will be controlled for all parties if the strategies of this book are implemented and followed. Stress can be controlled in the dental environment through excellent management and excellent communication.

At JMI, we believe that our success is built on your success. Our mission is to increase productivity, profitability, and to control stress through effective communication, management, clinical, and technological skill development. The Jameson Method of system development is the core of our work and helps us to fulfill our mission.

The Jameson Method focuses on just that: METHODS — *the essentials for elevating personal and professional productivity.*

Move proactively, purposefully, intentionally

Evaluate expected results from the very beginning

Trust prioritization for maximum energy

Honor relationships and personal interaction

Optimize team development and synergy

Develop yourself and your team

Systemize your practice for profitability, productivity, and stress control

Please, give yourself permission to establish clarity on what you consider your ideal practice—the practice of your dreams. Then do what is necessary to make that dream become a reality. There is no reason to settle for anything less. Life is too short to accept anything less than your ideal—whatever that means to you. While life is short—it is, also precious. The gifts, joys, and blessings available to each and every one of us are abundant. You are worthy of that abundance. Open yourself to the possibilities.

Thank you for studying with me. You honor me with your trust and your confidence. Call us. Ask your questions. Share your challenges and your successes with us. We are only a phone call away. 1-877-369-5558. My very best to you—now and always.

Cathy

APPENDIX A

Healthcare Financing Programs and Financial Resources

3Dee Treatment Funding
Brosnan House
179 Darkes Lane
Potters Bar, Hertfordshire
EN6 1BW, UK
01701 653260 (tel)
01707 644521 (fax)
team@ft-associates.com
www.ft-associates.com

American Credit Bureau
1200 N. Federal Highway, Suite 200
Boca Raton, FL 33432
800.750.9422 (tel)
800.361.3888 (fax)
info@americancreditbureau.com
www.americancreditbureau.com

Cain, Watters & Associates
Comprehensive Financial Services
5580 Peterson Lane Suite 250
Dallas, TX 75240
972.233.3323 (tel)
972.663.3799 (fax)
cwainfo@cainwatters.com
www.cainwatters.com

Care Credit
2995 Red Hill, Suite 100
Post Office Box 1710
Costa Mesa, CA 92626
800.300.3046, ext. 4519 (tel)
714.491.7005 (fax)
info@carecredit.com
www.carecredit.com

CitiHealth Card
5726 Marlin Road, Suite 101
Chattanooga, TN 37411
877.354.8337 (tel)
423.296.8133 (fax)
citiproviders@elitedr.com
www.healthcard.citicards.com

Dental Care Finance
27 Applecroft
Park Street
St. Albans, Hertfordshire
AL2 2AP, UK
01727 875459 (tel)
01727 874899 (fax)
briancarter@btinternet.com
steveryounguk@yahoo.co.uk

Dental Fee Plan

225 Turnpike Road
Southborough, MA 01772
877.377.7526 (tel)
877.417.9935 (fax)
dfp@feeplan.com
www.feeplan.com

Enhance Patient Loans

Denplan Court
Victoria Road
Winchester, Hampshire
S023 7RG, UK
0800 3283223 (tel)
01962 840846 (fax)
www.enhanceloans.co.uk

Healthcare Creditline

Post Office Box 271710
Tampa, FL 33688
800.334.6749 (tel)
813.961.7868 (fax)
info@healthcarecreditline.com
www.healthcarecreditline.com

VISA

800.VISA.311

Enhance Patient Financing

5620 Paseo del Norte, #127-537
Carlsbad, CA 92008
877.4ENHANCE (877.436.4262)
760.941.6689 (fax)
info@enhancepatientfinance.com
www.enhancepatientfinance.com

The Helpcard

Post Office Box 829
Springdale, AR 72765
800.945.4357, ext. 316 (tel)
800.245.7491 (fax)
info@helpcard.com
www.helpcard.com

Unicorn Financial Services

1701 Hermitage Boulevard, Suite C
Tallahassee, FL 32308
888.388.633 (tel)
877.758.7633 (fax)
sales@unicornfinancial.com
www. unicornfinancial.com

Norwest Financial

(Consult Your Local Directory)

American General Finance

(Consult Your Local Directory)

Wells Fargo

(Consult Your Local Directory)

• APPENDIX • B

25 Management Systems

The success of your practice is in direct proportion to the success of your systems.

— **Cathy Jameson, PhD**

		☹ ☺
1.	Teamwork	1 2 3 4 5 6 7 8 9 10
2.	Effective Communication	1 2 3 4 5 6 7 8 9 10
3.	Mission Statement / Vision / Goals — Strategic Planning	1 2 3 4 5 6 7 8 9 10
4.	Personnel Management	1 2 3 4 5 6 7 8 9 10
5.	Organizational Meetings	1 2 3 4 5 6 7 8 9 10
6.	Financing	1 2 3 4 5 6 7 8 9 10
7.	Insurance Management	1 2 3 4 5 6 7 8 9 10
8.	Collections	1 2 3 4 5 6 7 8 9 10

	☹ ... ☺
9. Scheduling	1 2 3 4 5 6 7 8 9 10
10. Overhead Control / Fee Analysis	1 2 3 4 5 6 7 8 9 10
11. Monitors	1 2 3 4 5 6 7 8 9 10
12. New Patient Experience	1 2 3 4 5 6 7 8 9 10
13. Diagnosis / Treatment Planning / Consultation	1 2 3 4 5 6 7 8 9 10
14. Treatment Coordination and Acceptance	1 2 3 4 5 6 7 8 9 10
15. Full Use of Technology and Equipment	1 2 3 4 5 6 7 8 9 10
16. Patient Education	1 2 3 4 5 6 7 8 9 10
17. Clinical Efficiency / Ergonomics	1 2 3 4 5 6 7 8 9 10
18. Documentation	1 2 3 4 5 6 7 8 9 10
19. Advanced Hygiene Program	1 2 3 4 5 6 7 8 9 10
20. Hygiene Retention	1 2 3 4 5 6 7 8 9 10
21. Sterlization / Infection Control	1 2 3 4 5 6 7 8 9 10
22. Marketing / Practice Building	1 2 3 4 5 6 7 8 9 10
23. Sales Dynamics in the Dental Practice	1 2 3 4 5 6 7 8 9 10
24. Building the Cosmetic Aspect of the Practice	1 2 3 4 5 6 7 8 9 10
25. Leadership	1 2 3 4 5 6 7 8 9 10

• BIBLIOGRAPHY •

Blair, Dr. W. Charles and John K. McGill, J.D. *The Blair/McGill Advisory.* Charlotte, North Carolina. Blair, McGill & Company.

Blanchard, Dr. Kenneth, Donald Carew, and Eunice Parisi-Carew. *The One Minute Manager Builds High Performing Teams.* New York, New York. Harper Collins, 2000.

Caplan, Dr. Carl Michael. *Dental Practice Management Encyclopedia.* Tulsa, Oklahoma. PennWell Publishing, 1985.

Center, Dr. T. Warren. *Dentistry Today.* Montclair, New Jersey. Dentistry Today, Inc., 1990.

Gordon, Dr. Thomas and W. Sterling Edwards, M.D. *Making the Patient Your Partner: Communication Skills for Doctors and Other Caregivers.* Westport, Connecticut. Auburn House, 1995.

Hopkins, Tom. *The Official Guide to Success.* Scottsdale, Arizona. Tom Hopkins International, Inc., 1982.

Jameson, Cathy, PhD. *Great Communication = Great Production.* Tulsa, Oklahoma. PennWell Publishing, 2002.

Jameson, Cathy, PhD. *The Cosmetic Workbook.* White Plains, NY. J.F Jelenko, 1990.

Jameson, Cathy, PhD. *Dental Practice Success Newsletter.* Ardmore, Oklahoma. Sprekelmeyer Printers, Volume 2, Number 1.

Jameson, Cathy, PhD and W. Paul Woody. *How to Work with General Dentists.* Oklahoma City, Oklahoma. General Business Services, 1996.

Kelsay, J.D., Ed. *Collecting Medical Accounts.*

King, Norman. *Past Due: How To Collect Money.* Facts on File, Inc., 1983.

McCormack, Mark H. *What They Don't Teach You at Harvard Business School.* New York, New York. Bantam Books, Inc., 1984.

LeBoeuf, Dr. Michael. *GMP: Greatest Management Principle in the World.* New York, New York. Penguin Group, 1985.

Murphy, Kevin J. *Effective Listening: Hearing What People Say and Making it Work for You.* New York, New York. Bantam Books, Inc., 1987.

Oakes, Dr. Woody. *The Profitable Dentist.* New Albany, Indiana. Excellence in Dentistry.

Peterson, Bob and Bonnie. *Dental Practice Success Newsletter.* Ardmore, Oklahoma. Sprekelmeyer Printers, Volume 2, Number 2.

Visa. *Tools for Patient Payment.* San Francisco, California. Visa U.S.A., Inc. 2001.

Woolery, Michael F., PhD, *Creative Communicators.* Glendora, California. Royal Publishing, Inc. 1990.

• INDEX •

C

D

E

F

G

H

I

J

K

L

M

N

O

P

Q

R

S

T

U

V

W–Z